THE THIRD GOSPEL FOR THE THIRD WORLD

The Third Gospel *for the* Third World

VOLUME ONE:
PREFACE AND INFANCY NARRATIVE
(Luke 1:1–2:52)

Herman Hendrickx, cicm

A Michael Glazier Book
THE LITURGICAL PRESS
Collegeville, Minnesota

THE THIRD GOSPEL FOR THE THIRD WORLD

Copyright © 1996 by **Claretian Publications**
A division of Claretian Communications, Inc.
U.P. P.O. Box 4, Quezon City 1101, Philippines
TE 921-3984 • Fax (632) 921-7429 • E-mail: claret@cnl.net

Claretian Publications is a pastoral endeavor of the Claretian Missionaries in the Philippines. It aims to promote a renewed spirituality rooted in the process of total liberation and solidarity in response to the needs, challenges and pastoral demands of the Church today.

Published in North America
by **The Liturgical Press**,
Collegeville, Minnesota, USA

Library of Congress Cataloging-in-Publication Data

Hendrickx, Herman.
    The Third Gospel for the Third World / Herman Hendrickx.
        p.   cm.
    "A Michael Glazier book."
    Includes bibliographical references.
    Contents: v.   1. Preface and infancy narrative (Luke 1:1-2:52).
    ISBN 0-8146-5870-9
    1. Bible.   N.T.   Luke—Commentaries.   I.   Title.
BS2595.3.H46   1996
226.4' 07—dc20   96-34651
                                                                 CIP

ISBN 0-8146-5870-9

TABLE OF CONTENTS

General Foreword vii
General Introduction ix
Foreword to Volume I xiii

The Prologue (Lk 1:1-4) 1

Introduction 1
Prologue 5
Conclusion 20

The Infancy Narrative (Lk 1:5-2:52) 24

Introduction 24
Annunciation of the Birth of John (Lk 1:5-25) 29
Annunciation of the Birth of Jesus (Lk 1:26-38) 68
The Visitation (Lk 1:39-56) 104
 The Visitation (Lk 1:39-45) 105
 The Magnificat (Lk 1:46-55) 113
The Birth of John (Lk 1:57-80) 136
 The Birth of John (Lk 1:57-66) 137
 The Benedictus (Lk 1:67-79) 146
The Birth of Jesus (Lk 2:1-20, 21) 164
The Presentation in the Temple (Lk 2:22-40) 211
The Finding of Jesus in the Temple (Lk 2:41-52) 243

Bibliography 268

GENERAL FOREWORD

This book is the first volume of a commentary on the Gospel of Luke under the general title *The Third Gospel for the Third World*. The entire commentary, which may take ten years to complete, will most probably consist in five volumes of unequal length: The Prologue and Infancy Narrative (Lk 1:1–2:52); The Ministry in Galilee (Lk 3:1–9:50); The Travel Narrative – I (Lk 9:51–14:35); The Travel Narrative – II (Lk 15:1–19:44); Jerusalem Ministry – Passion – Resurrection (Lk 19:45–24:53).

This commentary intends to pay special, though not exclusive attention to whatever may be of particular interest to third world readers. We plan to dwell on questions raised by the sociological approach to the Gospels, anthropological and cultural features like matters of family, clan, and tribe, matters of honor and shame, the conditions of peasant life, etc. We will also take into account some findings of recent literary criticism. The commentary will especially try to make available to a wider reading public what the author considers to have pastoral implications first and foremost in a third world setting. But it goes almost without saying that many of these features will also be of importance to committed first world Christians.

Since this commentary tries to bring together findings of various fields of research, several of which are rather new, it is obvious that this commentary is very much indebted to scholars in these various fields. We trust that the textnotes and the bibliography of books and periodical articles which were used will sufficiently account for the extent of this indebtedness.

This book is no easy reading, although the author has tried to avoid becoming too technical; but the disciplines mentioned above and which lead to interesting pastoral implications are not exactly easy. So the reader will have to invest time and effort in order to discover and assimilate the riches of the Third Gospel presented in this commentary. We wish that you may have the courage and the stamina to bring this to a good end.

GENERAL INTRODUCTION

Although we do not intend to discuss in any detail the questions that are usually treated in commentaries, a few observations concerning our general understanding of Luke (-Acts) are in order. Some of these will be further developed in the commentary itself when we discuss verses or episodes for whose interpretation they are useful or even necessary.

We will use the name Luke, which is traditionally connected with the Third Gospel, although we believe that, just like the other three Gospels, the Third was originally an anonymous writing. It was only at the time that the four Gospels were collected that the need arose to distinguish them and for that purpose names were attached to them. We believe that the author of the Third Gospel was a Gentile-Christian, but in view of his (her?) rather extensive knowledge of the Scriptures we believe that before he (she?) became a Christian the author was either a proselyte, that is, a Gentile who adopted the whole of the Jewish religion, or a Godfearer, that is, a Gentile who adopted Judaism, except for circumcision and some dietary laws. The author wrote for a predominantly Gentile-Christian community situated somewhere in a city of the eastern Mediterranean that was composed of both well-to-do and poor Christians. That means that when Luke speaks of the poor he thinks in the first place of urban poor.

The issue of anti-Judaism in early Christian documents in general and in Luke-Acts in particular is one of the most vigorously debated topics in New Testament studies today. Jacob Jervell (1972) and Jack T. Sanders (1987) seem to be standing at opposite poles from one another and establish the limits within which other scholars work. The former defends Luke's positive attitude towards the Jews whereas the latter defends that Luke-Acts is an anti-Jewish writing, although he himself in no way approves of anti-Jewish views. At first glance, one may well wonder if Jervell and Sanders are reading the same books. After a closer look, however, we are forced to recognize that both offer plausible interpretations. There are sections in Luke-Acts in which a positive attitude toward Jewish religion is apparent. The infancy narrative (Lk 1–2) shows pious and hopeful Jews in glowing terms. But there are also large sections in which people who are called Jews are shown to act in ways that would presumably be unacceptable to Luke and his audience. No wonder, then, that some have stated that Luke-Acts is one of the most pro-Jewish and one of the most anti-Jewish writings in the New Testament (Gaston, 1986: 153). A major difficulty in both approaches lies in the failure to specify the character of the one perceived to be the reader of Luke-Acts (Tyson, 1995: 19-23).

Considering the implied reader's knowledge of locations, persons, languages, events, measurements and money, religious practices, and literature, one has developed a certain profile which can be summarized as follows:

1. Our reader is a generally well-educated person with a rudimentary knowledge of eastern Mediterranean geography and a familiarity with the larger and more significant Roman provinces.
2. The implied reader is familiar with some public figures, especially Roman emperors. He/she has limited knowledge about the primitive Christian community and its leaders.
3. The implied reader is not expected to know any language other than Greek but is comfortable with some foreign terms and names.
4. The implied reader is knowledgeable about public affairs, especially those that are of concern to eastern Mediterranean and Jewish communities.
5. The implied reader has a working knowledge of common Greek and Roman measurements and coinage.
6. The implied reader has a limited knowledge of both pagan

and Jewish religions, an aversion to some pagan practices, and an attraction to Jewish religious life. But he is probably not Jewish and is not well informed about certain significant aspects of Jewish religious life.

7. The implied reader is familiar with the Hebrew Scriptures in their Greek translation and acknowledges their authoritative status but is not familiar with those methods of interpretation that find the fulfillment of the scriptures in Jesus.

These considerations lead to the conclusion that, in many respects, the implied reader in our texts is similar to those characters in Acts that are called "Godfearers" (Kraabel, 1981: 113-126). For the most part, Godfearers are described as devout Gentiles who are attracted to Jewish religious life. In Acts they are often grouped with Jews. In some cases they probably should be perceived as proselytes, who nevertheless are not the same as Jews. They may be found either in Palestine or in the Diaspora, but they are always connected with Jews in some way. The principle that operates in Luke-Acts seems to be enunciated in Acts 10:35: "Among all Gentiles, the person who fears him [God] and adheres to justice is worthy of him." Although the centurion in Lk 7:1-10 is not explicitly named a Godfearer, he, along with the centurion Cornelius in Acts 10–11, stands as an intratextual representation of this implied reader. Both are described as righteous Gentiles who are acquainted with and attracted to Judaism. They are generous to the Jewish people, and they pray to the Jewish God, but they continue to live as Gentiles. These considerations would allow us also to include Theophilus (Lk 1:3; Acts 1:1), as "lover of God," among the intratextual representations of the implied reader. As a lover of God, he should be understood as a Gentile who is favorably disposed toward Jewish religious life. In addition, Theophilus must know something about Christianity, as Lk 1:4 shows. We may thus tackle Luke's address to Theophilus quite seriously without finally being able to say anything specific about Theophilus' social or political position or his existence outside the text (Tyson, 1995: 24-26).

Luke-Acts may, therefore, be approached as an evangelistic text addressed to Godfearers. The treatment of Jewish religion and people forms part of the rhetorical strategy used by the implied author in addressing the implied reader. [The concepts of implied author and implied reader, instead of trying to determine the actual author of the narrative, ask what kind of author with what point of view is implied by the intentionality of the text itself (and what aspect of himself or herself the actual author chooses to reveal) and what the text's assorted perspectives can indicate about the kind of readers for whom the narrative was envisaged – Kurz, 1993: 9]. Positive images of Judaism are consistent with the assumed attitudes of a Godfearer as he is first addressed. But negative images, which show the inferiority of Judaism to Christianity and help to explain Jewish rejection of the Christian message, urge the Godfearer to abandon the philo-Judaism with which he began. He is shown that the purpose of Torah and the prophets is to point to Jesus, that Jews are now to be defined as those who rejected Jesus, and that only token adherence to Torah is necessary (Tyson, 1995: 38).

However, recently it has been pointed out that three aspects of the Godfearers need further investigation and clarification. First, the Godfearers in Lk 7 and Acts 10 are both centurions. What is the significance of this? Second, the Godfearers in Luke-Acts are often people, especially women, of considerable social standing. What is the significance of this for the understanding of the Godfearers in Luke-Acts and the setting of the book? Third, those identified as "Greeks" (*Hellēnes*) in Acts often seem to be Godfearers. If Luke uses the term *ethnē* to designate pagan Gentiles (Sanders), is it possible that *Hellēnes* is another technical (or quasi-technical) term for God-fearing/ God-worshipping Gentiles in Acts? (McRay). And what would that tell us about them and about Luke-Acts? (De Boer, 1995: 68-69).

FOREWORD TO VOLUME I

In 1975 I published a first commentary on the infancy narratives of Matthew and Luke at the East Asian Pastoral Institute. In 1984 a revised edition of this book was published by Geoffrey Chapman in London. In the nearly ten years between the first and the second edition a number of important studies on the infancy narratives were published, among which I would like to mention George M. Soares Prabhu's *The Formula Quotations in the Infancy Narrative of Matthew* (1976), Raymond Brown's *The Birth of the Messiah* (1977), Lucien Legrand's *L'Annonce à Marie* (1981), and Joseph A. Fitzmyer's *The Gospel According to Luke I-IX* (1981). The revised edition benefited very much from these and other publications. Since 1984 a number of important studies on the infancy narratives have again seen the light. However, the present volume is not a revision of the Lukan half of our 1984 publication but an altogether new book which constitutes the first volume in a multi-volume commentary on the Gospel of Luke. Among the books published since 1984 – and running the risk to overlook some equally important publications we would like to mention Stephen Farris' *The Hymns of the Lukan Infancy Narratives* (1985), Paul Bemile's *The Magnificat within the Context and Framework of Lukan Theology* (1986), Richard A. Horsley's *The Liberation of Christmas* (1989), Thomas Kaut's *Befreier und befreites Volk* (1990), Bruce Malina – Richard Rohrbaugh's *Social-Science Commentary on the Synoptic Gospels* (1992), Mark Coleridge's *The Birth of the Lukan Narrative* (1993), and Joel B. Green's *The Theology of the Gospel of Luke* (1995). In the same period a wealth of commentaries on the Gospel of Luke and monograph studies on various aspects and themes in Luke or Luke-Acts were also published. For the prologue we would like to mention especially Loveday Alexander's *The Preface of Luke's Gospel* (1993). We tried to integrate as many as possible of these insights in the present commentary to make them available to people who may have no access to the books and periodical articles in which they are found and/or cannot afford to buy them.

THE PROLOGUE (LK 1:1-4)

Introduction

For many years it has been widely held that Luke's preface marked his work as belonging, at least in aspiration, to the Greek literary world, more precisely to the literary tradition of Greek historiography. This approach found its apogee in the work of H.J. Cadbury; and although there have always been difficulties in this "received opinion," it is only in comparatively recent times that there have been serious attempts to question this view (Alexander, 1986: 48-50; 1993: 102). It is improbable that Luke would have set out consciously to write "Greek history" or to present an apology for the early Christian movement to Roman authority. And in literary terms Luke's preface, while looking "rhetorical" compared with, for example, the opening verses of Mark or Matthew, is not actually very successful rhetoric. Formally too, there are many differences perhaps ignored because they are so obvious. Thus Luke's preface is one sentence long where Thucydides', a prominent Greek historian, consists of twenty-three chapters, each at least four times the length of Lk 1:1-4. Besides, Luke does not contain any of the moral reflections which are a characteristic of the Hellenistic historians; the Greek historians by convention speak of themselves in the third person rather than in the first as Luke does; and they never open with a second-person address (Ibidem).

A new, full appraisal of the literary evidence should take in as wide a range of Greek prefaces as possible, from the fourth century B.C., by which time the classic forms were already established, down to the second century A.D., the latest possible date for the composition of Luke-Acts (Alexander, 1993: 11). It should also make use of the recent advances in the study of

1

Hellenistic style. A checklist of the characteristics of Luke's preface as far as form, syntactical structure, topics and style are concerned (Alexander, 1986: 53; 1993: 12-14), leads to the characterization of Lk 1:1-4 as a "short, detachable passage in which the author stands briefly aside from his own narrative to explain who he is, what he is doing, why and for whom. At its simplest, we might describe it as a *label* with an *address*" (Alexander, 1986: 54).

Classical literature is reluctant to step outside the bounds of a given literary form to add the kind of explanatory label which we find in Lk 1:1-4. Evidence of this phenomenon is found in the long and multiform tradition of *technical* or *professional* prose, which has been called the "scientific tradition," in which "scientific" is not used in its modern sense to exclude "arts" subjects, but in a sense closer to "academic," "technical," "specialist" and professional (Alexander, 1993: 20-21). This tradition contains a group of texts which do have the kind of "label + address" preface we find also in Luke, that is, they have brief personal prefaces in which the author speaks of himself in the first person and frequently addresses a second person by name. These prefaces are by no means uniform, but they do reveal a discernible pattern. The topics most common in the prefaces may be summarized under seven heads:

(1) the author's decision to write;
(2) the subject and contents of the book, with explanation where necessary of particular aspects of the presentation (e.g. illustrations);
(3) dedication: the second-person address, and topics related to the dedicatee;
(4) the nature of the subject matter;
(5) others who have written on the subject or have opinions on it, whether predecessors or rivals;
(6) the author's qualifications;
(7) general remarks and methodology (Alexander, 1993: 69).

By way of illustration we cite here Hero of Alexandria, *Pneumatica* I, lines 1-17; (1st century A.D.? on engineering):

Since the subject of air has been considered worthy of attention by ancient philosophers and engineers, the former expounding its power theoretically and the latter by reference to its observable effects, I have myself thought it necessary to write an orderly presentation of the traditions of the ancients, and also to introduce my own discoveries; for in this way those wishing subsequently to engage in the science will be assisted. And judging it to follow on from the properties of water-clocks, which I have already treated in four books, I am writing about this also, as I have said, for it to be a continuation. For it is through the combination of air, fire, water and earth, and of the three or rather four elements, that a variety of conditions is brought about, some of which answer to the most important needs of life, while others display marvels of a striking kind.

A comparison of these explanatory prefaces in scientific texts with Luke's preface allows us to find parallels in this scientific tradition for virtually every feature in Lk 1:1-4. Luke's work, therefore, belongs to this category of "scientific literature" or "technical prose." Thereby we do not want to suggest that Luke might deliberately have chosen "a scientific preface-style" as some kind of signal to his readers about the kind of book his gospel was going to be. Indeed, linguistics and socio-linguistics have taught us that the choice of style can operate at a much deeper level of a writer's consciousness. Faced with the formidable task of composing a formal opening to mark the presentation of his book to Theophilus, Luke drew on the only style he knew which was at all appropriate to the occasion. If we suppose that his experience of non-biblical literature was limited to the technical writings of a trade or profession, this preface-style would seem to him simply the "correct" style to use for an opening paragraph, the appropriate "linguistic manners" for the occasion.

Beginning a book is the most difficult point in its composition, especially for the inexperienced author; what more natu-

ral than to fall instinctively into the style used for such open-
ings in the books he knows best? While telling us something
about the author and his world, this observation presumably
also tells us something about his readership – at least about his
primary and named reader, Theophilus. Both Luke and Theophilus
must have been familiar with the scientific, professional literature of their time.

Can the influence of scientific writing be traced any further
on in Luke-Acts itself, or does it cease with the abrupt change
of style at Lk 1:5? In fact, that change may itself be regarded as
a characteristic feature of scientific writing (Alexander, 1986:
67). At the end of the preface, the normal style is resumed. It
has been argued convincingly that the biographical content of
the Gospel and Acts is by no means an insuperable obstacle to
viewing Luke as a writer set firmly within the context of the
scientific tradition. The scientific tradition is the matrix within
which we can explore both the social and literary aspects of
Luke's work, both the author himself and the nature of his writings
(Alexander, 1986: 70).

Concluding, we may say that Luke, far from trying, and
failing, to compose a "historical" preface, was actually composing within a different literary tradition, which had its own preface-conventions, and that this tradition, which we have called
the "scientific," provides significantly better parallels to Luke's
preface, both in general and detail, than the conventions of
Greek historiography. Such details of the preface as those that
are not paralleled in the scientific tradition are no better accounted for by the "historical" parallel; rather, they belong to
no Greek literary tradition as such but are idiosyncrasies reflecting Christian or biblical modes of speech (Alexander, 1993: 103).

What does it mean to say that Lk 1:1-4 is a "scientific preface"? Potentially this conclusion is one of great significance. If
we can firmly say that Luke's work "belongs" to this category of
"scientific literature" or "technical prose," then we have an
immediate link to a large and neglected area of "middlebrow"
literature of the first century A.D., written in a language iden-

tical neither with the vernacular *Koine* of the papyri (probably as near as one can get to the spoken *Koine* of the streets and market-places of the Eastern Empire), nor with the classicizing prose of the *literati*. It is literate but not literary, written language designed primarily for conveying factual information; and it is chiefly preserved in the technical treatises of the scientific writers. This opens new vistas for a socio-historical investigation which will ask questions like: What are the social dynamics implied in the relationship between the author and his readership? What are the social functions of the writings inside their own communities? How do these writings interact with the world at large? What kind of people produced writings like these, and for whom? (Alexander, 1986: 60-62).

Prologue

1. Since many have undertaken
   to set down an orderly account
   of the events that have been fulfilled among us,
2. just as they were handed on to us
   by those who from the beginning
   were eyewitnesses and servants of the word,
3. I too decided,
   after investigating everything carefully from the very first, to
   write an orderly account for you, most excellent Theophilus,
4. so that you may know the truth concerning the things about
   which you have been instructed.

The prologue, four verses but only one sentence, consists of three parts. The first, Lk 1:1-2, is an explanatory clause in which Luke informs Theophilus – and his other readers – of his predecessors in the history of the gospel tradition. The second, Lk 1:3, is the main clause of the prologue in which Luke gives his "credentials" for writing his gospel. And the third, Lk 1:4, is a purpose clause in which Luke informs Theophilus of his purpose in writing the gospel. Since Luke-Acts is quite generally understood as a single work in two parts, rather than two separate but related works, it is probable that the Lukan prologue refers also to the Acts of the Apostles. For some scholars, however, Lk 1:1-4 is the prologue/proemium to the gospel alone and the evangelist did not have Acts in mind at this point (Schürmann, 1969: 1-3). In light of verses 1-2, some scholars are inclined to accept that the prologue has primarily the Gospel of Luke in mind (Stein, 1991: 36). But the more prevalent opinion is that these verses introduce the whole of Luke-Acts (O'Fearghail, 1991:96-97). It should, however, be noted that scholars do not agree about the precise nature of the unity of the work in terms of its composition and literary genre (Pervo, 1989: 309-316).

Verse 1: Since many have undertaken to set down an orderly account of the events that have been fulfilled among us,

In the opening words of the prologue Luke speaks of those who have written on the subject before him. In fact, this is the only book in the New Testamnent to begin with a concessive clause referring to other documents (Tiede, 1988: 35). From the first century A.D. onwards "predecessors" become regularly the topic of the opening clause in the scientific tradition. Does the word "many" (*polloi*) suggest that "dozens" of people had written before Luke, or can "many" be limited to a couple of sources such as "Mark" and "Q" as the two-source hypothesis holds, or to "Mark," "Q," and "L"? (Dillon: 1981: 207). Maybe it is best to understand it as meaning "others" (Stein, 1992: 63).

The term *polloi* and its related expressions appear frequently in rhetorical prefaces, but the cliché is by no means limited to rhetorical and literary writers (Alexander, 1993: 109). This conventional usage of the term is found in the New Testament (Acts 24:2,10; Heb 1:1; Jn 20:30; 21:25), Josephus (*Jewish War* 1.17) and secular Greek literature. It functioned as a *topos* (characteristic feature) and we should, therefore, beware of placing too great an emphasis on this word. But, on the other hand, the presence of convention in a literary preface does not in itself imply that none of its claims can be taken seriously (Kurz,

1993: 39). It has been suggested that three would have been sufficient for Luke to use "many," but recently it has been argued that "many" does not allow us to limit the number to two or three (Baum, 1993: 105). Scientific writers certainly show a propensity to describe their predecessors as "many." In some cases, the word is substantiated by a long list of names; in others, we simply do not know whether there were really "many." But ancient writers were probably no more inclined than their modern counterparts to write unnecessary falsehoods: convention was served by finding something to say within the accepted range, rather than by conforming to a rigid pattern. There was no convention which could *compel* Luke to mention "many" predecessors unless he wanted to do so. It is simplest, then, to conclude, short of positive indications to the contrary, that Luke meant what he said. If this causes problems for our views on gospel sources or chronology, perhaps we need to look more closely at those views and their assumptions. Part of the problem is probably the tendency of critics to think exclusively in terms of the documents we know (Alexander, 1993: 114-115). It seems better at this point to admit that we cannot be certain as to how many predecessors are to be included in the "many" of the Lukan prologue (Stein, 1991: 37). The scientific prefaces also tell us that in terms of rhetorical function, making a statement about the author's predecessors is probably the least important aspect of an opening clause of this type. Essentially these "predecessors" are only there to reassure the reader that the subject is worth spending time on. The attention of the "many" underlines the importance of the events while at the same time establishing a precedent for Luke (Nolland, 1989: 6). Ancient writers loved to show that what they were doing had precedents (Bock, 1994: 54). It is possible that the informational value of the clause lies much more in the apparently incidental opportunity it gives the author to identify his subject-matter (Alexander, 1993: 116).

Starting with Origen, many have taken the term "undertaken" (*epecheirēsan*; literally: "put their hands to") to imply that

Luke sees these former attempts as having been more or less unsuccessful. This view is supported by the fact that in the only two other instances in which Luke uses the term, Acts 9:29 and 19:13, he describes unsuccessful attempts, and it has been maintained that the verb is here "used with a thin cutting edge" (Sterling, 1992: 344). But it has also been noted that the negative connotation appears *from the context*, and that the absolute use of *epicheirein* has neutral character (Glöckner, 1975: 11-12). Most scholars today, then, reject a negative interpretation of the term and interpret it either positively or at least in a neutral way (Dillon, 1981: 207). Firstly, it is a conventional term used in literary introductions, and as such it was frequently used in a positive or neutral sense. Secondly, Luke associates his work with that of his predecessors by the expression "I too" (*kamoi*) in Lk 1:3. Thirdly, if Luke did make use of some of these other attempts, for instance Mark or Q, then a pejorative interpretation of the verb must be rejected. Fourthly and finally, Luke's positive attitude towards the "eyewitnesses and servants of the word" elsewhere (Acts 1:8,22; 2:32; 3:15; 26:16) indicates that Lk 1:2 must be understood positively, and this in turn means that Lk 1:1 must be understood positively (Stein, 1991: 37-38; Alexander, 1993: 115).

"Setting one's hand" to tell a story might well suggest written accounts here, except that other terms in the context suggest organized oral reports. So Luke's remark suggests the presence of written materials, but need not be limited to such sources (Bock, 1994: 55). Luke's predecessors have undertaken "to compile a narrative" (RSV) or "to set down an orderly account" (NRSV; *anataxasthai diēgēsin*). They did not just collect loose sayings of Jesus but presented downright narratives about Jesus, different from the tradition referred to in verse 2, which mainly consisted in pericopes or independent, self-contained units of tradition. Some scholars have suggested that whereas Mark is a gospel of proclamation and, therefore, "kerygmatic," Luke is a gospel of narration or "salvation history." Such an interpretation, however, ignores the fact that the verbs "to narrate" (*diēgeomai*) and "to preach" (*kērussō*) are used interchangeably by Luke, as is evident in Lk 8:39, where the Gerasene demoniac is told to "narrate" what God has done for him and goes out "preaching" how Jesus has healed him (Stein, 1991: 38). *Kērussō* which is parallel to *diēgeomai* clearly means a proclamation borne by faith and the same meaning should be attributed to the latter verb and, therefore, to the noun *diēgēsis*. *Diēgēsis* means proclamation of faith in the form of an account (Glöckner, 1975: 13-14).

The "events" narrated by his predecessors are more closely qualified as "the events that have been fulfilled among us" (NRSV; RSV: "the things that have been accomplished among us"). The word *pragmata*, "events, things," can be used in a religious context (e.g., 2 Macc 1:33,34), but is essentially a neutral word. The "events" referred to in this clause can be interpreted as a reference to the Old Testament prophecies fulfilled in the "life" of Jesus recorded in the Gospel and to the events in the life of the church to which Acts refers. The expression "have been fulfilled," then, should be prefered to "have been accomplished." "The events that have been fulfilled among us" may be understood in reference to "all that Jesus did and taught from the beginning" (Acts 1:1). But the phrase should not necessarily be confined to the story of the earthly life of Jesus but can very well be extended to include what had happened in the early days of the church; this view of the phrase gives a better sense to "among us" than confining the reference to the earthly life of Jesus (Marshall, 1991: 278-279). The thought is of events brought to completion, namely the events leading to salvation. The passive form of the verb suggests that these are divine acts which God himself promised and has now fully brought to pass; and the use of the perfect tense may indicate that these events are seen as a finished series in the past (Marshall, 1978: 41; Baum, 1993: 113). The factualness of these events is proved beyond doubt by the unexceptionable tradition going back to the eyewitnesses (Flender, 1967: 65).

The first plural noun in "among us" is not simply editorial;

nor is it to be identified with the "us" of verse 2, "just as they were handed on to us." The phraseology of verses 1 and 2 clearly implies two groups of people, those among whom the events were "fulfilled" and those to whom the tradition was handed down, and the same pronoun is used for both. It denotes the people who are now affected by saving history. The expression "among us" shows Luke writing as a member of an identifiable group and presumes that Theophilus and the reader will know who "us" refers to here. It may also indicate that the preface is to Luke-Acts as a whole, as "the events that have been fulfilled among us" could refer as well, perhaps even better, to the events recorded in Acts as to those recorded in the Gospel (C.F. Evans, 1990: 124). "Us" refers to those whose lives are determined by the events that have transpired: the community formed around these events (Nolland, 1989: 7). The events Luke relates extend to the time of his readers: all of them are in fulfillment of God's promises (Johnson, 1991: 27). The words "among us" emphasize the writer's conviction that his community is the center for the understanding of these events (Danker, 1988: 23).

Verse 2: just as they were handed on to us by those who from the
beginning were eyewitnesses and servants of the word,

This additional clause, subjoined to the opening clause, gives a further description of the work of Luke's predecessors: it is based on tradition handed down by a group called "the original eyewitnesses and servants of the word." The expansion of the basic period by the insertion of extra clauses is typical of the later stages of the scientific tradition; it is also very common in these prefaces to find an important new topic introduced in this unemphatic and allusive fashion. The loose position of the clause, grammatically dependent on verse 1 but inevitably read in conjunction with verse 3, reinforces the impression that it is Luke's own contact with the tradition, not that of his predecessors, which he really wants us to appreciate (Alexander, 1993: 116-117).

The conjunction "just as" (*kathōs*) introduces a statement

of the reliability of the earlier accounts, which is important for Luke, even though he is inclined to present the matter in a better way (Schürmann, 1969: 8).

The events have been "handed on" as tradition. The verb *paradidōmi*, "to hand on," "to hand down," is a technical term for the handing down of material, whether orally or in writing, as authoritative teaching (Mk 7:13; Acts 6:14; 1 Cor 11:2,23; 15:3; Stein, 1992: 64). Thus the Christian writings Luke referred to rested upon oral tradition which by its nature of separate units required compilation into a sequence. Appeal to tradition is found in historians, but even more in writers on science of some kind, where knowledge was often handed down through a succession of teachers (C.F. Evans, 1990: 125). In scientific prefaces, a common form of guarantee for the author or his material is the assertion that he has been in personal contact with authentic tradition (Alexander, 1993: 118-119). This tradition was handed on "to us," the Christians, as they came to be called by the outside world (Acts 11:26). It is not clear here whether Theophilus is addressed as belonging, or as not belonging, to "us." Luke ranges himself alongside his predecessors as a recipient of authentic tradition (Alexander, 1993:119).

The tradition has been handed on by "those who from the beginning were eyewitnesses and ministers of the word." Here is a clear allusion to the original oral level of the tradition (Bock, 1994: 58). By the use of this phrase Luke differentiates himself from the class of early witnesses and places himself in the second or a subsequent generation of believers (Marshall, 1970: 41). The fact that in the Greek text the article (not translated in English) is not repeated before "servants," and that the parallel pair of names in Acts 26:16, "minister/servant and witness," are both applied to Paul, suggests that we are dealing here with a single group acting in a dual capacity (Baum, 1993: 115-116). The group is described in terms of two roles: they are "ministers of the word," that is, they have a special responsibility for passing on the tradition; and they have "first-hand experience" of the facts they report (Alexander, 1993: 123).

Those who handed the tradition down had been acquainted with the events "from the beginning." Does this qualify both "eyewitnesses" and "servants," and if so, does it refer to a different "beginning" in each case? This depends partly on the sense we give to *autoptai*, "witnesses," but Luke's own usage of the concept of "beginning" (*archē*) is also to be taken into account. Acts 1:22, "beginning from the baptism of John," and 10:37, "beginning in Galilee after the baptism that John announced" suggest that Luke regarded John's baptism as the proper "beginning" of the apostolic proclamation, but in Acts 21:16, "to the house of Mnason of Cyprus, an early disciple (*archaios*), with whom we were to stay," Luke is not likely to refer to a disciple during Jesus' lifetime, and it must be simply a vague term of approbation. The apostolic preaching in Acts gives us no precedent for the inclusion of the infancy narratives; are these also part of the "eyewitnesses" tradition that both Luke and his predecessors were drawing on?

It is important here to realize that, whatever its Christian significance, the notion of *archē* had its own significance in the secular world. Reference to the "ancients" (*hoi archaioi*) is common in scientific prefaces: in the Hellenistic period such reference can be neutral or even derogatory, but in later centuries reverence for the ancients becomes more normal, and the word acquires commendatory overtones. This is particularly evident in reference to one's authorities: *archaios* is used to emphasize valuable links with authentic tradition. A series of rather vague uses suggests that the force of the phrase is emotive rather than precisely descriptive, and should warn us against trying too hard to find a precise temporal reference in Luke's phrase here (Alexander, 1993: 119-120).

The people Luke refers to are understood to be "eyewitnesses" who could not but speak of what they had heard and seen (Acts 4:20). "Eyewitnesses" is the neatest and most obvious equivalent for *autoptai*, but it has misleading associations for modern readers. For us, the word has forensic links: an eyewitness is characteristically a witness who was present at the time when an incident or crime took place, very often a passer-by whose connection with the incident is accidental. The Greek word is hardly ever used in this way, and a better translation may be, "those with personal/first-hand experience: those who know the facts at first hand" (Alexander, 1993: 120).

They became the "servants (*hupēretai*) of the word," a remarkable expression conveying the thought of the centrality of the gospel message and of the way in which people are its servants. The use of "servants" (cf. Acts 26:16, "... to appoint you to serve and testify to the things in which you have seen me"; Acts 6:4, "... we will devote ourselves to prayer and to serving the word") emphasizes that they were not propagandists for their own views of what happened with Jesus but had put unreservedly their persons and work in the service of Jesus' cause. This group cannot be limited to the Twelve alone, for Luke sees the group of eyewitnesses as more inclusive than that, as is evident from Lk 6:12-13, "... he called his disciples and chose twelve of them, whom he also called apostles..." According to Acts 1:21 there are many witnesses who are not apostles, and there is no reason to doubt that for Luke also witnesses who were not apostles could yet be servants of the word.

Even though "the word" may be intended here as a "general term applicable to the story of Christian origins" (Cadbury), the use which the absolute term *ho logos* acquires in Acts (8:4; 10:36; 11:19; 14:25) gives it the significant overtone of "the word of God" (Fitzmyer, 1981: 295; Glöckner, 1975: 21-22). In Acts 1:1, Luke refers to his gospel as "the first book" (*prōtos logos*, literally "first word"). In Lk 22:61, Peter remembers the word of the Lord, and in Lk 24:44, the risen Christ reminds his disciples of his words. Some scholars believe that by *ho logos* here Luke means the Christian movement, "the matter," an equivalent to "the events which have been fulfilled among us" (Lk 1:1). If so, "eyewitnesses" could go with it, and the whole phrase could denote not eyewitnesses of the gospel events and ministers of Christian preaching, but eyewitnesses and assistants to the Christian movement (C.F. Evans, 1990: 128). The term *logos* may also point to the beginning of the narrative proper in Lk 5:1, where the first use of the expression *ho logos tou theou* is found (O'Fearghail, 1991: 95). Occurrences of the term in the Gospel (Lk 8:12,13,15; cf 8:11,21) and in Acts (4:4; 6:4; 8:4; 10:36,44; 11:19; 14:25; 16:6; 17:11; 18:5) make clear that it is equivalent to *ho logos tou theou/kuriou* and signifies above all the Christian message.

Verse 3: I too decided, after investigating everything carefully from the very first, to write an orderly account for you, most ex-cellent Theophilus,

With verse 3, Luke begins the second and main clause of the prologue. An announcement of the "decision to write" is central to almost all scientific prefaces (Alexander, 1993: 70-71,125). As the main verb in the sentence, "I decided" (literally, "it seemed good to me") ought to carry weight, but, as it follows after the introductory clause, "Since many... I too decided," its force is weakened. Luke joins himself to the "many" of Lk 1:1 to record what had happened in view of his own qualifications to do so. Most agree that Luke wishes to add to this tradition of writing because he feels he has something to contribute (Schneider, 1977: 39; Fitzmyer, 1981: 296). Any interpretation that Luke is contrasting himself to his predecessors does not honor the presence of *kai* ("and"; NRSV: "too").

He has decided this "after investigating everything carefully" (NRSV) or "after having followed all things closely" (RSV). The meaning of the perfect active participle *parēkolouthēkoti* by which Luke describes his own activity preparatory to drawing up his account of what had happened, is quite disputed. Although it was opposed by Cadbury (O'Fearghail, 1991: 85) and we have to concede that to keep informed about contemporary events or participating in them is the common meaning of the term (Maddox, 1981: 4-5), "to investigate" seems the best meaning here (Marshall, 1978: 42; Fitzmyer, 1981: 297; Nolland, 1989: 42). But perhaps the scope of the verb here can be widened so that it includes both those events in the past which Luke had investigated by examining the relevant evidence, both written and oral, and also those more recent events in which he himself had personally participated (Marshall, 1991: 279; O'Fearghail, 1991: 85-89).

It is not fully clear to what "everything" (*pasin*) refers and what is its context. The adjective *pasin* may be masculine or neuter, referring to the eyewitnesses and ministers of the word, in the former case, to the *pragmata* of Lk 1:1, in the latter (O'Fearghail, 1991: 93). It seems to be related to what in verses 1-2 Luke has presented as presupposition for his own writing. He has investigated everything that has been fulfilled and handed on. The Greek verb *akoloutheō* and its compounds have a range of literal and metaphorical uses very similar to those of the English "follow." The best-attested use of the compound in Greek sources, which fits naturally with "carefully" (*akribōs*) with which it is often combined, is that of "following" as a mental activity: "being thoroughly familiar with the whole affair" (Alexander, 1993: 128).

Luke's investigation has been done "carefully" (*akribōs*). The root meaning of the word is "exact," "accurate." Thus "accurately" seems preferable to "closely" (RSV) or "carefully" (NRSV). The claim to accuracy was almost a cliché in prefaces and passages where an author was referring to his sources or methods of presentation, not only in historians, but also in scientific works (Alexander, 1993: 128).

The above discussion is related to the question of how to interpret the word *anōthen* (O'Fearghail, 1991: 89-93). Should it be translated "for some time past" (RSV) or "from the very first" (NRSV) which is equivalent to "from the beginning" (Fitzmyer, 1981: 298)? Is the purpose of Luke in his prologue to show the duration or length of his research, that is, he investigated for a long time, or to show the extent or scope of his research, that is, he investigated from the beginning? Scholarship is divided on this issue. To the present author the context suggests that Luke is primarily concerned in the prologue not so much with telling Theophilus how long he has researched this material, but rather with having covered the entire scope of the subject (C.F. Evans, 1990: 131).

Luke decided "to write an orderly account to you," literally, "to write for you in order" (*kathexēs*; found only in Luke-Acts in the New Testament), that is, using an ordering principle that sets the parts in logical relation to a coherently understood whole, an ordering according to the sense of the whole (Acts 11:4). The adverb *kathexēs* does express a succession of order. But what kind of order? Although Luke can use it in a primarily chronological order (Lk 8:1), it is unlikely to have that meaning in Lk 1:3 (Tiede, 1988: 37; C.F. Evans, 1990: 131), although that meaning has still been defended extensively in a recent study (Baum, 1993: 135-142). We would rather think of literary order. *Kathexēs* in Acts 11:4 appears neither to be primarily chronological or geographical (the latter being the case in Acts 18:32) in its "ordering" sense. Rather it suggests an ordering or sequencing of Peter's account in which the "logic" of the Cornelius encounter is illuminated for the larger narrative development or story. How are the readers, as well as the Jerusalem believers, to understand Peter's visit to Caesarea in light of the much larger story of "the word of God" (Acts 11:1) in the narrative that has been unfolding? Peter explains the significance *kathexēs* – the "narratological" sense – in light of the whole understanding of Israel's messianic salvation (Moessner, 1992: 1515-1517).

"Orderliness" may be first of all a claim to "coherence" or meaning. It seems best to interpret "orderly" here as a synonym for "organized" or "logical" (Stein, 1991: 44). Luke says that he is going to write for Theophiulus, in a systematic presentation involving the phases of salvation history in the Lukan account and the motif of promise and fulfillment, which may include a veiled reference to the Period of Israel, the Period of Jesus, and the Period of the Church (Fitzmyer, 1981: 299). To read *kathexēs* is "to get the record straight" by following Luke's narrative in sequence from the top (*anōthen*).

Only by understanding the relation of the parts to each

other and to the whole narrative can one begin to follow or appreciate Luke's distinctive contribution among the "many." He is not fully satisfied with the many others' narrative accounts though he is fully appreciative of their eyewitness sources. His way of con-figuring the fulfilled events of the "way of the Lord" (cf. Acts 24:22; 26:4-5) will lend a greater "certainty" or "firmer grasp" (*asphaleia*) to the true significance of the movement which he himself has investigated with accuracy (*akribōs*) from the top (*anōthen*; Moessner, 1992: 1527-1528).

The convention of dedication was familiar in the Greco-Roman world. It was rare in historians, but was standard in prose works of a non-literary and technical kind. The name of Luke's addressee, Theophilus, is not a Roman one; it was very commonly, though not exclusively, used by Hellenized Jews (Alexander, 1993: 133). "Most excellent" is used simply as a polite form of address, such as might be used in addressing some highly placed person (Acts 23:26; 24:3; 26:25). But nothing can be deduced from it for sure as to Theophilus' precise standing. Nevertheles, his position as Luke's literary patron, who would perhaps assist in the "publication" of the Gospel (Hauck, 1934: 17) may indicate his superior social situation. Despite the symbolical possibilities of Theophilus, the name meaning "lover of God," it remains probable that it is the name of a real, but unknown, person (Marshall, 1978: 43; Fitzmyer, 1981: 299; C.A. Evans, 1990: 20; Alexander, 1993: 199ff.). It is almost impossible to answer the question of whether Theophilus was a Christian, an influential non-Christian, or a God-fearer, that is, a Gentile who was strongly attracted to Judaism and adopted its beliefs and practices but, unlike the proselytes, rejected circumcision and most dietary laws.

It has been pointed out that, in any event, Luke's form of address, given its placement in the preface, can by no means adequately be accounted for as a phrase of dedication. Luke seems to indicate repeatedly in verses 3-4 that he is writing *for* Theophilus. As such he would present a type of reader (Giblin, 1985: 13-14). But others have remarked that Theophilus may or may not have been typical of the reading public for whom the work was intended; its real readers may well have been different (Esler, 1987: 24).

Verse 4: so that you may know the truth
        concerning the things about which you have been instructed.

In the third and final section of the prologue, Luke states the purpose for writing his Gospel. Scientific writers regularly use this way of relating the subject of the book to the dedicatee (Alexander, 1993: 136). If the "orderly" nature of Luke's account refers to a logical rather than chronological precision, it is likely that Luke is seeking to "convince" Theophilus of the truthfullness of the data concerning the life of Jesus, and this may not always involve chronological exactness. In other words, as suggested above, some material may be arranged in Luke on a basis other than chronological (Stein, 1991: 44).

The word usually translated here by "truth" is *asphaleia*, which does not mean "truth" as opposed to "falsehood," as though Luke's predecessors had their facts wrong. It refers rather to a mental state of certainty or security. Luke's narrative intended to have a "convincing" quality (Johnson, 1991: 28). *Asphaleia* means "solidity," "security," and in a figurative sense "assurance" or "reassurance," which one may obtain in what one has learned (Bovon, 1991: 42). In Greek the word is intentionally placed in evidence at the very end of the sentence (Schürmann, 1969: 14; Glöckner, 1985: 3-4; Fitzmyer, 1981: 300). Over against seven disparate occurrences of the root *asphal-* in the rest of the New Testament (Mt 27:64ff.; Mk 14:44; Phil 3:1; 1 Thes 5:3; Heb 6:19) we find eight instances in Luke-Acts: *asphaleia* (Lk 1:4; Acts 5:23); *asphalēs* ("sure, definite," Acts 21:34; 22:30; 25:26); *asphalōs* ("safely, for certain, beyond doubt," Acts 2:36; 16:23); *asphalizō* ("to secure," Acts 16:24). The term is, therefore, characteristic of Luke. It is used in connection with the security of a prison (Acts 5:32; 16:23,24), in the context of establishing the truth in a courtcase (Acts 22:30; 25:26; compare Acts 21:34). In Acts 2:36 the "knowing with certainty" is related to a faith formula. In light of the above, and taking into account the specific context of Lk 1:1-4, it seems that in Lk 1:4, Luke deals with the certainty that his readers and he himself can and should obtain with regards to the origin and the history of their faith (Glöckner, 1975: 3-11). Luke's understanding of the term is best paralleled by the adverbial form that Peter uses in addressing the Jews at Pentecost: "Therefore let the entire house of Israel know with certainty" (*asphalōs*; Acts 2:23 NRSV) or "let all the house of Israel therefore know assuredly" (RSV). Luke appears in his preface to make a strong claim about the "certainty" of the account to follow, but this must not be read as an attempt to drive a wedge between "history" and "interpretation." For Luke, the narrative is not an historical or other basis for proclamation; rather, narration *is* proclamation. Luke's terminology suggests the convincing nature of his presentation or "the certainty of these things" (see Acts 2:36; 25:26). So, while the Christian message is inseparably tied to the historical events related to its origins and progression, and Luke must therefore necessarily be concerned with "what happened," the question of interpretation is vital for him. Increasingly we have learned not to pose the historian's task with questions such as, how can the past be objectively captured? or what methods will allow the recovery of "what actually happened"? Historiography imposes significance on the past already by its choice of events to record and to order as well as by its inherent efforts to postulate for those events an end and/or origin. The emphasis thus shifts from validation to signification. The issue is, how is the past being presented? Luke's concern with truth, then, resides above all in his interpretation of the past (Green, 1995: 19-20).

It is unclear whether "you have been instructed" means getting information or being instructed as a Christian (Craddock, 1990: 16). The term *katechēsthai* does not seem to have carried at this early date the technical connotation of formal, elementary instruction in the faith, that is, "catechesis," though it moved in that direction (Giblin, 1985: 15). It later became a technical term for the pre-baptismal catechesis of new converts. This later meaning, however, should not be read into the present context (Stein, 1992: 66). Certainly it makes sense to regard Theophilus as having already received some instruction in the gospel (not of course in the later technical sense); but the plural "the words" (*logoi*, literally; NRSV: "the things") is not quite the same as "the Word," and the more neutral "the *things* about which you were instructed" is equally possible.

If Luke wishes to refer to Christian instruction, he avoids the most obvious ways of doing so; perhaps the language is deliberately colorless. Nevertheless it is perfectly possible to use the plural *logoi* of Christian teaching (e.g., 1 Tim 4:6; 2 Tim 2:13), and semantically there is no reason why it should not be used here. More generally, *logoi* is used for "stories/reports" with the stress more on the events reported than on the report itself (Alexander, 1993: 139-140).

Conclusion

The prologue has been classified as belonging to a category of narrative asides indicating the self-conscious nature of the narrator. Self-conscious narration may be divided into sub-categories which are defined by three relationships: those between the narrator and the story, between the narrator and the reader, and between the reader and the story. From the above analysis it appears that Lk 1:1-4 encompasses all three of these types of self-conscious narration.

The first evidence of self-conscious narration is to be found in Lk 1:3 in which the narrator clarifies his relationship with the story he is about to narrate. The narrative was undertaken because "I too decided... to write an orderly account." The thrust of the clause is to show the reader that the narrative has begun with a sense of necessity and order in the mind of the narrator.

A second relationship is underlined in the address to Theophilus. The narrator is writing not only out of a sense of necessity; he is writing *to someone*. The relationship between narrator and reader, which all of the asides in Luke-Acts will endeavor to strengthen and guide, is established in the first address to the reader. Not only has the narrator established such a relationship, he has made it a personal one through the vocative address, "most excellent Theophilus."

Thirdly the preface focuses on the relationship between the story and the reader. The reader has been challenged to allow the narrative to inform and strengthen his or her faith. In one sense the reader's role is passive, as the narrative will work upon the reader. In another sense, however, the reader must seek actively to be open to the working of the narrative information on his or her life (Sheely, 1992: 115-116).

In the above analysis we have established that Luke's preface is not to be aligned with the prefaces of the Greek historians, but with those of that miscellaneous tradition of technical prose which has been called "scientific" (Alexander, 1993: 169). The author of Lk 1:1-4 must have had some direct contact with Greek scientific literature, in which he felt at home, so much so that he naturally fell into its style and adopted its preface-conventions when he found himself at the beginning of a major literary undertaking.

Thus the style of the preface turns out to belong not to high literary historiography and provides no grounds for saying that with Luke the gospel is "leaving the milieu of 'ordinary people' and entering the world of literature, the cultural world of antiquity" (Haenchen, 1971: 136). In fact, once the preface is over, Luke reverts with startling suddenness to a "biblical" style with which he clearly feels much more at home (Alexander, 1993: 175).

There are significant pointers which link the early church with the crafts and professions of the Greek East, rather than with the status-conscious and culturally exclusive circles that were producing and reading the literary Greek of Luke's day. It seems only reasonable to conclude that Luke (the "beloved physician," Col 4:14?) and his readers do not belong to this group anymore than their "heroes" presented as artisans and traders (Acts 16:16; 18:1-3; Hock, 1980). Not only are many of the "heroes" of the New Testament story normal workers, there is also a strong current of respect in Christian ethics for "earning one's bread" by honest toil (e.g., 1 Thes 4:11; 2 Thes 3:6-13; Hengel, 1974: 60-73).

It is true that a number of recent studies have been concerned with correcting Deissmann's view of Christianity as "a movement among the weary and heavy-laden, men (sic) without power and position... the poor, the base, the foolish." Thus one can speak of a "new consensus... that the social status of early Christians may be higher than Deissmann had supposed" (Malherbe, 1983: 31-32). But current scholarship also produced estimates of the social constituency of early Christian groups in the cities of the Roman Empire, speaking of "the urban circles of well-situated handworkers, traders. and members of liberal professions" (Keissig), or describing the typical member of the Pauline churches as "a free artisan or small trader" (Meeks: 1983: 270). In social terms, these groups function at a level precisely analogous to the "intermediate" zone to which the linguistic and literary data point (Alexander, 1993: 178). But we should note the importance of nuancing our understanding of the "middle zones" of Greco-Roman society.

The above analysis of the literary affinities of Luke's preface is useful in defining where he and his work fit on the Greco-Roman axis. Lk 1:1-4 does provide a link with Greek culture, but not with the culture of the upper classes. Rather it reveals a connection with an "alternative" culture despised by its contemporaries and largely ignored by subsequent scholarship, a culture which consciously holds itself aloof from the prevailing passion for rhetoric, while admitting the usefullness of a limited number of rhetorical devices at certain formal points of composition (Alexander, 1993: 183).

Very recently some have taken a closer look at how Luke introduces his readers into his theological program (Dillmann, 1994: 86-93). To understand more precisely Luke's intention we have to establish which readers he intended to address, for while writing he had specific readers in mind. He did not only want to pass on tradition but also wanted to see that it was correctly understood and received, as suggested in the prologue (Lentzen-Deis, 1989: 18).

Lk 1:1-4 is not just a preface in which Luke gives information about his aim, his preliminary activities, and which contains his theological program. It is an invitation to get involved in Luke's presentation and to enter into a dialogue with him in order to align one's own Christian existence with the action model developed by him. The Gospel of Luke, then, presents itself as a work with a purpose (German: *Tendenzschrift*) that is more than an invitation to faith. It is an early church instruction that is concerned with the continuity of faith and therefore also with the warding off of other foundations of faith. To describe Luke as "very circumspect and in his time heaven-graced man" (Schürmann) is likely a personal opinion which the "I" of the narrator could accept without disagreement. It shows that Luke's guidance of his readers does not fail to affect also today's critical reader (Dillmann, 1994: 92-93).

THE INFANCY NARRATIVE OF LUKE (LK 1:5–2:52)

Introduction

Lk 1:5–2:52 as a self-contained narrative. The vast majority of scholars rightly recognize Lk 1:5–2:52 as the first major section of Luke's account. It is separated from the preface (Lk 1:1-4) by a shift from literary Greek to heavily Semitic Greek, and is distinguished from the beginning of Lk 3 by a fresh setting in world history provided at that point by the move from the infancy to the adult careers of John and Jesus, and by the total failure to play any role in the continuing story line from Lk 3:1 onward of the insight achieved by participants in Lk 1–2 (Nolland, 1989: 17-18). The latter is, of course, not true of the initiated reader.

Lk 1:5–4:44 as a preparatory section. Notwithstanding the observations mentioned above many scholars hold that there are sufficient thematic and structural reasons for taking the infancy narrative to form an integral part of Luke's work (O'Fearghail, 1989: 60; Strauss, 1995: 77-87). Indeed it is arguable that Lk 1:5-2:52 forms a literary unity with the following two chapters (Schmid, 1960: 33; Meynet, 1979: 149), and that Lk 1:5–4:44 acts as a preparatory section for the work as a whole (O'Fearghail, 1989: 60; Idem, 1991). The thematic importance of the first two chapters of Luke – the infancy narrative – has been noted by a number of scholars (Brown, 1977: 239-253). As an overture or prologue to the rest of Luke-Acts, certain motifs and themes first presented in the infancy narrative recur repeatedly in the following chapters (Tiede, 1980: 24; Jankowski, 1981: 9). It has been suggested that the songs, especially, express themes that are found throughout the author's work. The first theme listed is "God's classical action of raising the low and bringing down the lofty" (Drury, 1976: 50). But only the Magnificat expresses such a reversal pattern (York, 1991: 44).

Imitation of the Septuagint. The origin of the distinctive Jewish or Palestinian character of Luke's infancy narrative has long been subject to debate. Two main theories have dominated the debate, the Semitic source theory and the theory of the evangelist's imitation of the language and style of the Septuagint, with strong arguments being advanced in favor of both. But conclusive proof is difficult to find for either theory, and the debate continues. The theory of a Semitic original behind Lk 1–2 does not adequately explain the multitude of specifically Lukan vocabulary and grammatical constructions that are found in this section of the Gospel (Dawsey, 1985: 43). Nevertheles, taking seriously what Luke says in his prologue, namely that he did use sources, it has been suggested that Luke was not just imitating the Septuagint but was translating Hebrew (not Aramaic) sources, and translating slavishly (Most, 1995: 225).

In the present commentary we favor the imitation theory. There are a number of indications in Luke's work for the viability of this theory in Luke's infancy narrative. There is the evangelist's long recognized familiarity with the Septuagint and his frequent and varied use of it, whether in reminiscences or in exact, substantially faithful, or free quotations (Bock, 1987: 13-14). Luke belonged to a setting in which literary imitation was widespread, accepted and even warmly recommended (Brodie, 1986: 247-248).

There are a number of guidelines that may help to decide for or against possible imitation. Similarity in language, style or motif may indicate dependence, especially if the word, phrase or motif taken over is unusual or rare or if the language or style taken over is untypical of the later writer. Similarity in situation may also point in the direction of imitation. So too may similarity in the structure of a hymn, poem or narrative unit. Multiple points of contact between the texts increase the possibility of dependence. But the most informative clue to imitation is the presence of some awkwardness, incoherence, imprecision or lack of motivation in the later text. A recent study of Luke's use of the Old Testament concludes that Luke did not create the Old Testament colorings present in the infancy narrative, for had he done so in the manner which many suggest, his creations would have been very imprecise (Bock, 1987: 89). We accept that such imprecision is indeed present in Luke's account and is the result of imitation of the Septuagint. Some pertinent examples support this view (O'Fearghail, 1989: 61-70). The analysis of these examples and the concentration of "septuagintalisms" in Lk 19:43-44; 21:20-24 and Acts 26:16-18, for example, place a large question mark after the suggestions that Luke is using sacred prose to write "sacred history" or a "holy language" for a "holy apostolic age" (Haenchen, 1971: 74).

A number of points may be made in relation to Luke's imitation of the Septuagint in his infancy narrative. First of all, as in all literature, a certain amount of imitation may be due to the similarity of motifs or situations (see, e.g., Lk 7:11-17 and 1 Kgs 17: the raising of the son of the widow of Nain by Jesus and of the son of the widow of Zarephath by Elijah).

The second point that should be made concerns the many identifiable reminiscences that are found in the infancy narrative, especially in Lk 1. Some of these, to be sure, recall stories of barren women who conceived through divine intervention; others, the "infancy narratives" of Isaac, Ishmael and Samuel. But reminiscences associated with Noah, Abraham, Gideon, Samson, David, Deborah, Elkijah, Elisha and Daniel are also to be found. A certain consistent pattern emerges from this mosaic of identifiable allusions. It is that of the persistent recall of God's interventions in salvation history, whether in favor of individuals, of his people, or both. Its object is to characterize the present intervention in the light of these.

Thirdly, imitation placed at the service of comparison here, not just between the old and the new, but also between John and Jesus (George, 1970: 147-171). In both cases the conception of Isaac is recalled.

Fourthly, Luke uses an eclectic method of composition. In

the case of Elizabeth, for example, elements are used from various Old Testament stories of barren women who conceive through divine intervention; and we observe a similar approach regarding Zechariah. In these composite portraits of Elizabeth and Zechariah the reminiscences of the story of Abraham and Sarah are perhaps the most obvious. But Elizabeth is not a new Sarah, nor is Zechariah a new Abraham – certainly not in the matter of faith (O'Fearghail, 1989: 72).

Fifthly, there is the question of Luke's deliberate imitation of the language and style of the Septuagint, something that is additional to the reminiscences already mentioned. Its function is to intensify the recall of God's salvific interventions in the past by recreating the language and the style, the very atmosphere of the Bible that recounts them.

Finally, it may be argued that by plunging his reader into a Palestinian world straight after a Hellenistic proemium, Luke has both parts of his mixed audience of Gentile and Jewish Christians in mind. For the former, impressed no doubt by his prologue, this narrative stands as a reminder of the Jewish origins of the Christ and his message of salvation, and of the fact that they participate in the fulfillment of the promise made to Israel; for the latter, in need of reassurance perhaps, a timely reminder that Jesus is and remains the long awaited consolation and undeniable glory of Israel from which salvation came to all (cf. Lk 2:32; O'Fearghail, 1989: 73).

In Lk 1–2, Luke recreates for his readers the world of faithful Jews, anxiously awaiting the fulfillment of God's promise in the person of the Christ. But the setting is more than a repetition and recollection of the promises of the Old Testament. It portrays the promise *at the dawn of its fulfillment*. The role of the infancy narrative is not only to introduce themes which will be important later in Luke-Acts; it also forms a bridge between the Old Testament age of promise and the age of fulfillment, structurally setting the stage for the theme of promise-fulfillment which will run as a connecting thread throughout the whole of Luke-Acts (Strauss, 1995: 86).

The Form and Function of Lk 1-2. Attention has been drawn to the liturgical nature of these chapters (Minear, 1966: 111-130). One has indicated the prevalence of such words as "praise, glorify" (*doxazō*), "bless, praise" (*eulogeō*), and "joy" (*agalliasis*); of such themes as worship, the temple, fasting, prayer, joy and peace; the reliance in this section upon epiphany and angels; the use of hymns as "programmatic entrances." This insight into the tone of Lk 1–2 seems to fit nicely with the position that the Lukan septuagintalisms do not indicate a Hebrew source or a conscious attempt at imitation but rather a specialized language of worship (Horton, 1978: 1-23). The language of Lk 1–2 might well have originated and had its life in Greek worship. A liturgical setting also makes sense out of the poetic form of much material in Lk 1–2. It is common to refer to the Magnificat, the Benedictus, the Gloria in Excelsis, and the Nunc Dimittis as early specimens of Christian hymnody (Beare, 1972: 33-35) – and their liturgical use can in fact be traced back as far as the 6th century and probably goes back to the earliest church (Kuist, 1948: 288-298). The rhythmic patterns of Lk 2:14 in Greek indicate a liturgical setting for the Gloria exactly as it stands in Luke (Dawsey, 1985: 46). Again, the hymns in Lk 1–2 are of poetic form, which seems to indicate a proper setting in public worship. Finally, a liturgical setting for Lk 1–2 also makes sense of the familiarity which it must be assumed that Luke's early audience had with Jewish conventions and customs (Winter, 1954: 160-167,230-242)

In Mediterranean antiquity, stories of a hero's pre-public life were told as a way of explaining the hero's later life. It was a working out of the principle: the adult is foreshadowed in the child. Given this tendency, Luke's audience would hear the infancy narrative as the Third Gospel's answer to the question: How is such a life (like that recorded in Lk 4:16-24:53) possible? The distinctive way in which Jesus' birth is told would determine the auditor's perception of Luke's answer (Talbert, 1994: 393).

The form of the infancy narrative seems to link Lk 1–2 to

public worship. But what is the author's *purpose* in the special language of Lk 1–2? The author of the Gospel of Luke was a writer who could control his style (Cadbury, 1920; Strauss, 1995: 85-86). Even if he appropriated the form of Lk 1–2 from his sources, he did so consciously. But why, then, did he choose to begin his Gospel with hymnic material? It seems that the author must have wanted to set the proper mood for the story of salvation (Drury, 1977: 46-66). However, we must not be led astray by a modern concept of "private reader." Rather, we should think in terms of a community of Christians who heard the Gospel read in worship. Instead of a literary device, it seems that the form of Lk 1–2 served as a liturgical device. The form of Lk 1–2 indicates that it functioned liturgically to establish the atmosphere of joyous praise to God for his saving activity which is told in the Gospel story (Dawsey, 1985: 47).

1. The Annunciation of the Birth of John the Baptist (Lk 1:5-25)

Luke prefaces both annunciation accounts with an introduction of the parents-to-be. Both begin with chronological markers, followed by the introduction of the males and females in parallel formulae. Considerable attention is devoted to issues of status – with Zechariah and Elizabeth noted for their priestly lineage, advanced age (in a culture where honor comes with age), and exemplary piety. Joseph, too, has an enviable birthright. But Mary is young and no reference is made to her family. Finally, both introductions dwell on issues of childbearing status (Green, 1995: 51).

The account of the annunciation of John's birth is framed by references to Elizabeth's sterility in verses 7 and 25 ("barren" … "disgrace"), by the time indications in verse 5 and 25 ("in the days," not rendered in verse 25 by NRSV), and by the mention in verses 5 and 24 of Elizabeth herself, and the contrasting references to Elizabeth in verses 7 and 24 ("barren" … "conceived"; O'Fearghail, 1991:12).

Verses 5-7: (5) In the days of King Herod of Judea,
                  there was a priest named Zechariah,
                  who belonged to the priestly order of Abijah.
                  His wife was a descendant of Aaron,
                  and her name was Elizabeth.
            (6) Both of them were righteous before God,
                  living blameless according to all the commandments
                      and regulations of the Lord.
            (7) But they had no children,
                  because Elizabeth was barren,
                  and both were getting on in years.

Luke begins his narrative by going back to the days of King
Herod; but the retrospection is more contrived than this, since
both the style of introduction (compare, e.g., Esth 1:1, "...in the
days of Ahasuerus") and the language suggest not the reign of
Herod, but the more distant past of the Old Testament. Lk 1–
2 will understand the events narrated as fulfillments of past
promises. Therefore, in order to begin the narration of fulfillment, Luke turns back to the time of the promise, and that
means moving back beyond the line of Christian tradition evoked
in the prologue (Lk 1:1-4) into the world of the Old Testament. The implication is that the events of the narrative will
not be rightly understood unless seen as the fulfillment of past
promises; and the assumption is that the reader knows the Old
Testament well enough to recognize the echoes which the narrator now builds into the narrative. This is clearly no narrative
for beginners (Coleridge, 1993: 29-30). This is true for Luke's
time as well as ours.

So, from the beginning a pervasive typological connection
is established between the infancy narratives and the past saving acts of God by means of an "anthological style" (Nolland,
1989: 25). The echoes of the Old Testament and the mention
of Zechariah's and Elizabeth's childlessness stir in the reader
the memory of divine interventions of childless couples in the
Old Testament, stretching back to Abraham and Sarah at the
beginning of biblical history (Coleridge, 1993: 31).

In the days... The section opens in a way reminiscent of a number of Old Testament books. The temporal indication, "in the days of Herod King of Judea," recalls the manner of dating found in the opening verses of the book of Jeremiah, "in the days of King Josiah the son of Amon of Judah... in the days of King Jehoiakim son of Josiah of Judah..." (Jer 1:2-3); Amos, "in the days of King Uzziah of Judah" (Amos 1:1), and others (O'Fearghail, 1991: 24).

From the opening verse of the Gospel, we are aware that Luke is concerned with the *political world* and the *balance of power* in Greco-Roman Palestine. In fact, Luke's opening phrase, "in the days of King Herod of Judea" (Lk 1:5a), is far more than a vague chronological marker. Instead, it serves to draw attention to the social setting of these events in a particular period of political attention. Herod came to power despite strong anti-Idumaean feelings and, in particular, resistance to him among the Jewish elders in Jerusalem. His power base was purely secular, with no claim to God having chosen him for service as king of the Jews. This, together with the problematic economic and cultural affairs associated with his reign, must be considered important factors in any reading of "the days of King Herod." That these realities would not have been far from the minds of the narrator and his Greco-Roman audience is suggested not only by the notoriety of Herod's ignominious reign, but also by the pervasiveness of social-political concerns throughout Lk 1–2 (Green, 1995: 7).

The social world that Luke represents is also one in which *eschatological anticipation* is rampant. If we recall that eschatological hope in its many forms focused preeminently on the coming of God to rule in peace and justice (Beasley-Murray, 1986: 3-86), then we may also remind ourselves that eschatological hope within the Lukan narrative must be read against a socio-political backdrop. This is true inasmuch as the coming of God would bring an end to political dominance and social oppression. The world into which Jesus was born in Luke is shown to be rife with eschatological anticipation – an anticipation with clear ramifications for the cessation of Israel's subjection to its Herodian and Roman overlords (Green, 1995: 8-9).

It is also clear that the narrative to unfold will be concerned with issues of *social status and social stratification*. This is not to say that Luke is especially concerned with economic class – for example, as a function of one's relative income or standard of living, or as connected to one's relationship with the means of production (as in Marxism). Such matters of industrial or post-industrial society have little meaning in Greco-Roman antiquity. Rather, Luke's social world was defined around power and privilege, and is measured by a complex of phenomena – religious purity, family heritage, landownership, vocation, ethnicity, gender, education and age. Especially consequential in Luke is *status reversal*, together with Luke's concern to redefine the basis by which status is determined (Green, 1995: 9-12).

King Herod of Judea.

1. *Client-King of the Romans.* Herod the Great who ruled from 37 to 4 B.C., an Idumaean and hence hated by the Jews, was king by the grace of Rome, and he conquered the Jews with the help of Roman legions. By skillful and constant pro-Roman maneuvering, his father, Antipater, had become the ruler of Jewish Palestine under the nominal authority of the last Hasmonean high priest, Hyrcanus, after the Roman conquest under Pompey in 63 B.C. Herod thus got his start as a sort of governor of Galilee under his father's authority. Supported by Anthony, and granted the title "king of Judea" by the Roman senate in 40 B.C., he still had to win his kingdom and began to rule in 37 B.C. In order to feed his own and Roman troops, he raided the countryside for provisions. The slaughter of people in the villages and towns was extensive at points.

After this kingdom was confirmed by Augustus after the battle of Actium in 31 B.C., Herod set up a model client-kingdom in grand Hellenistic style. This was important in Roman imperial rule to ensure the security of the empire against the

Parthian empire to the east. Because the whole eastern Mediterranean was now pacified in subjection to imperial rule, much of Herod's energy as ruler went into what we would now call cultural activities, although the economic, political, and religious implications should be immediately obvious. He engaged in expensive building projects, magnificent palaces in Jerusalem and other cities, and fortresses around the country, the most famous of which were Herodium and Masada. The most famous project of all was the rebuilding of the temple in Jerusalem.

Many of Herod's building ventures were in homage of Caesar. The two most famous were named after the emperor – Sebaste (=Augustus) in Samaria, and Caesarea, which later became the governor's seat in the Roman province of Judea. Herod's munificence and benefactions were astounding even to the ancients, accustomed to such conspicuous display.

2. Exploitation and Tyranny. Herod's extraordinary expenditures for the massive building projects, the homages to Caesar, and the many impressive benefactions for foreign cities and imperial figures placed a heavy burden on the Jewish peasantry. But they also compounded what were already inordinately large demands for tithes, tribute, and taxes. A consideration of the politico-economic structure of imperial rule in Palestine once Herod was imposed as Roman client-king may help us appreciate the economic burden thus placed on Herod's subjects. In the ancient world the land and people controlled by a ruler such as a king or high priest was a basis of revenue. But no account was taken of the overlapping claims of various levels of rulers.

Under the Hasmonean high priesthood prior to 63 B.C., the principal demand for tithes was for the temple and the high-priestly governing apparatus. When Rome laid Jewish Palestine under tribute beginning in 63 B.C., an additional demand was thus placed upon the peasant producers. When Herod imposed his kingship, however, the high priesthood and the temple apparatus were not removed, nor did the Romans remit their demand for tribute. Structurally there was thus a triple demand for tithes, tribute, and taxes. The latter, however, must have been a tremendous burden just by themselves because of Herod's vast expenditures. Herod was in fact bleeding his country and people to death.

Besides bleeding his people dry, Herod was flouting their sacred traditions with many of his building projects – especially by erecting a golden eagle, symbol of Roman domination, and a violation of the commandment against images – over the great gate of the temple. The same was true for his dedications to Caesar and his institution of Hellenistic "cultural" activities.

Herod's own royal ideology, linked as it was with Hellenistic imperial ideology, was also surely offensive to his Jewish subjects. He claimed to be king and to have brought the long awaited peace and prosperity. He may even have made messianic claims in his royal propaganda. He appointed and deposed the high priests as suited his own policies, propaganda purposes, or whims, and his appointees were often accused of injustices or impieties.

3. *Resistance and Repression.* Herod must have seemed the very paradigm of tyranny to his Jewish subjects. Resistance to his tyranny did not altogether cease after his successful conquest of the countryside and Jerusalem. Little by way of effective resistance could get started, however, because Herod instituted what today would be called a police-state, complete with loyalty oaths, surveillance, informers, secret police, imprisonment, torture, and brutal retaliation against any serious dissent. One of the principal demands of the crowd after the death of the tyrant was "the release of prisoners who had been put in chains by Herod – and there were many of these and they had been in prison for a long time" (Josephus, *Antiquities*, 17.204). Many others had apparently simply been killed.

The resistance often took a messianic form. Some of the Pharisees who had always refused to make the loyalty oath to Caesar and Herod prophesied that the kingdom would be taken from Herod by a new king who would bring the restoration of wholeness, in some manner or form (*Antiquities*, 17.43-45). The visionary Pharisees were executed, of course. When Herod finally died, there were spontaneous insurrections in Galilee and

Judea which took a messianic form in which the people acclaimed one of their number as "king," but they were put down by the Romans (Horsley, 1989: 40-49).

Judea. Technically, Herod was king over all Palestine, not only over Judea, a smaller area eventually placed under the rule of his son Archaelaus (Mt 2:22). The use of "Judea," then, may be anachronistic, or perhaps simply the use of the part for the whole, as in Lk 7:17 and Acts 10:37, where "Judea" must include Galilee. [A modern equivalent would be the tendency to use "Holland," a province, as a name for the Netherlands]. The usage is explicable here since the action to follow takes place in Judea (Brown, 1977: 257-258). Both the Roman writer Tacitus (*Annals*, XII, 54) and the New Testament (Lk 4:44 compared to Mk 4:39) attest to a broad use of "Judea" as a term which includes Galilee (Marshall, 1970: 71). Moreover, "King of Judea" was the title that the Roman senate conferred on Herod upon the request of Anthony (Bovon, 1991: 54). Hence, Judea must be understood here generically as the land of the Jews (= Palestine) and is not restricted to the specific sense of "Judea," as it is used in Lk 1:65; 2:4 (Fitzmyer, 1981: 322).

There was a priest named Zechariah. The slant of this narrative is explicitly patriarchal from the very start: the divine message is addressed to Zechariah as the answer to his prayer, and the son who is promised is described as his own. God will overcome the hindrance that stood in the way of Zechariah's wish, that is, Elizabeth's barrenness and her advanced age (Seim, 1994: 199). Readers and hearers of ancient narratives are expected to put much stock in a character's lineage and culture – the familial and ethnic roots from which he or she grew. Descriptions of one's family or tribe are intended to inform us about a person's likely influences, tendencies and agenda. The portrait of John's family in Lk 1–2 is suggestive in this regard. Zechariah and Elizabeth are like an idyllic tapestry woven from colorful strands of Jewish tradition (Darr, 1992: 65).

Contrary to a possible first impression, the explicit statement of Zechariah's (and Elizabeth's) priestly descent does not seem to carry special import, either in the infancy narrative or in the Gospel as a whole. We could attempt to explain their priestly descent as either a literary device or a piece of Luke's theology of history. Some scholars have found considerable significance in the priestly origins and righteousness of Zechariah and Elizabeth. As representatives of the "institutions of Judaism" or "the temple/priesthood," they would be used to show that, despite the opposition which arose later, there was not "an inherent contradiction between Christianity and the cult of Israel" (Brown, 1977: 268).

The seemingly incidental information that John's parents were of priestly descent, however, might be significant in another respect: the socio-historical background and foreground of who stands where in the network of social relations presupposed and portrayed in these narratives. On the surface of things, it seems utterly incidental that John is born into a priestly family. Far more important are the traditions of resistance (Samson, Samuel, Elijah) and the revolutionary model (the spirit and power of Elijah) after which John the prophet is to restore Israel. Exploration of the social context, however, can perhaps lead us to an important point in the social dimension of the narrative: priests such as Zechariah (and Elizabeth and John) belonged with the people, as opposed to the high-priestly rulers, and may even have had a special sensitivity to and role in the fundamental conflict in Jewish Palestine under Roman rule.

In the standard treatments of the Jewish priesthood we learn that the priests were divided into twenty-four orders – of which the "order of Abijah" was the eighth – each of which provided in turn service in the temple for one week, twice a year. The priests, along with the Levites, were supported by tithes, although many had to supplement their income with other work.

But we need to explore more precisely the social relationships suggested by these distinctive aspects of the priesthood. Ideally, Jewish society was a theocracy, in which the people living under the rule of God brought sacrifices and offerings that the priests were specially designated to handle, and the priests were supported in their social service by tithes from the people's produce. Both the social structure and the temple in which the system was centered involved concentric circles of *purity* in which the ordinary peasants sent or brought offerings, the Levites attended to the temple courtyards, the priests attended to the service of God in the sanctuary itself, and only the high priest entered the holy of holies, once a year, on the Day of Atonement.

But this was also a system of *power*. Indeed, precisely because of their position at the center of the system religiously, the high priests dominated the whole society politically and economically as well. In effect, the significant division within Jewish society came not between the priesthood as a whole and the people, but between the ruling high priests and the people along with the ordinary priests. The high-priestly domination was rooted in the control of the tithes and offerings as well as in the imperial politico-economic order. Collection and distribution of the dues, including the tithes, were centralized in the Jerusalem temple.

While collection and administration of dues was centralized in Jerusalem, only a small percentage of priests could live in the city. The vast majority of the priests lived in various towns and villages around the country, as far as, for instance, Sepphoris in Galilee. Besides living among the people, the ordinary priests and Levites also apparently worked with them as well. As we have noted, the priests received tithes from the people, but this was not sufficient to support many thousands of priests and their families. Thus they had to have other means of support. We know of a priest who bought and sold oil; another priest was a stonecutter. Many priests, perhaps the majority, probably worked their own or others' fields alongside their non-priestly village neighbors, as is implied, for instance, by Neh 13:10, which states that the Levites and temple singers "had gone back to their fields" (Horsley, 1989: 91-95).

The combination of village residence with periodic service in Jerusalem, mentioned above, may be highly significant for two interrelated reasons. First, by serving in the temple in Jerusalem periodically, the priests had occasion to experience the *discrepancies* between the sacred covenantal traditions that featured ideals of egalitarian socio-economic relationships as well as independent life under the direct rule of God, and the actual state of affairs in the countryside. Second, the priests provided a *built-in network of communication* of the dominant capital and the local towns and villages. Social scientists attempting to understand how peasant revolts can be mobilized and sustained have noted that it is essential in such societies for a communication network to emerge. Native intellectuals or popular clergy are often the basis for the emergence of such a communication network between the central urban area and villages on the periphery.

There is every reason to believe that these country priests would have been in an uneasy and threatened position in Palestine. Josephus reports that in the late 50s A.D., "there was now enkindled mutual enmity and class warfare between the high priests, on the one hand, and the priests and the populace of Jerusalem, on the other..." (*Antiquities*, 20, 180.181). He also cites instances of high priests sending servants to forcibly confiscate the tithes which were due to the priests. The high-priestly families, apparently no longer having any pretense of legitimacy and rapport with the populace, had long since gathered gangs of ruffians to use in terrorizing the priests and people (Horsley, 1989: 96-99).

That John the Baptist's parents were from priestly families thus does not set him apart from the people in any usual or highly distinctive way. On the other hand, it is not surprising that one who assumed a distinctive prophetic role in biblical tradition would come from a priestly family in the hill country of Judea. Such a family, involved in the network of social relations sketched above, would be *unusually sensitive to the situation of the Jewish people under Roman rule*. This awareness can be seen no more clearly than in the longings expressed by Zechariah in the Benedictus: "that we would be saved from our enemies... Thus he has shown the mercy promised to our ancestors, and has remembered his holy covenant, the oath that he swore to our ancestor Abraham, to grant us that we, being rescued from the hands of our enemies, might serve him without fear, in holiness and righteousness before him all our days" (Lk 1:71-75; Horsley, 1989: 99-100).

Zechariah and Elizabeth. "There was a priest named Zechariah who belonged to... His wife... and her name was Elizabeth" recalls 1 Sam 1:1-2, "There was a certain man... whose name was Elkanah... he had two wives, the name of the one was Hannah,... but Hannah had no children." Inevitably, it was assumed that it was the woman who was infertile (Seim, 1994: 199). One has noted two inter-related features of Luke's presentation of Zechariah. In Lk 1:5 he is introduced as a *worshipper*. In Lk 1:6 the second characteristic is presented – together with Elizabeth, Zechariah is presented as *righteous*. The Semitic style of the indication of Hannah's childlessness (1 Sam) is recalled in the Lukan reference to the childlessness of Zechariah and Elizabeth: "they had no children" (Lk 1:7; O'Fearghail, 1989: 61; Jeremias, 1980: 24). A woman's position in her husband's family was never secure until she bore a son. Only then did she have a "blood" relationship that secured her place. Stories of barren women thus describe anguish of the deepest sort (Gen 11:30; 25:21; 29:31; Judg 13:2; 1 Sam 1:2; Malina-Rohrbaugh, 1992: 287).

The portrayal of Zechariah and Elizabeth as "righteous before God" may sound quite common, but this description is rare in the Greek Bible. It occurs, in fact, only once more, in Gen 7:1, where Noah is seen by God to be "righteous before me" and so was saved from the flood. Luke's predominant use of *dikaios* is to describe God's servants who do God's will. It is used of John the Baptist (Lk 1:17), of Simeon (Lk 2:25), of Joseph of Arimathea (Lk 23:50), and of Jesus (Lk 23:47; Acts 3:14; 7:52; 22:14). In this select company Zechariah and Elizabeth are placed, but their righteousness is not only established by association. Divine approval is expressed in the prepositional phrase "before God" (Carter, 1988: 240).

The rest of verse 6 establishes further the content of *dikaios*.

Elizabeth and Zechariah are said to be "living blameless according to all the commandments and regulations of the Lord" (more
literally "walking in all the commandments..."). For the reader,
the Deuteronomy phrase "all the commandments and regulations" has a familiar ring. But this stereotyped expression is usually constructed with "obey" or "observe," or both, as in Deut
30:10, never with "walk." So, strictly speaking, it is not a
septuagintal expression. It may, however, be described as a
septuagintal type phrase. "To walk" (*poreuesthai*) is used in a
ethical sense in the Septuagint, although usually with "the way(s)"
(*hodos, hodoi*; Deut 10:12; 11:22; 19:9; etc.). There are instances
of its use with "statutes/regulations" (Ez 36:27) and "commandments" (2 Chron 17:4) on their own (O'Fearghail, 1989: 61-
62).

Some scholars have opted to read the text as follows: "Both
were righteous, *walking before God*, blameless according to all
the commandments and regulations of the Lord" (Grundmann,
1961: 49; Meynet, 1988: 1:13; 2:19). The expression "to walk
before God" is widely attested in the Bible, e.g., in Gen 17:1,
"walk before me, and be blameless," addressed to Abraham, "the
father of us all" (Rom 4:16).

This is the first time that the word "God" occurs in the
Third Gospel. God himself does not come into view. Narra-
tively, therefore, God is not to be counted as one of the characters of Luke's gospel story. From another perspective, however, God is the chief "actor" throughout Luke-Acts. The very
name "God" occurs far more frequently than even the name
"Jesus," aproximately 122 times in Luke and 166 times in Acts.
As the creator of the universe and the ruler of the nations,
God guides the history of Israel, of Jesus, and of the church.
Although God himself may be hidden from view, Luke's entire
story is full of signs of his presence and guidance (Kingsbury,
1991: 11).

Verse 7 introduces a situation in which the two aspects of
Zechariah's character, worshipper and righteous one, are demonstrated. In the context of worship, God's call and mercy ef-

fect fecundity in barrenness as a child is promised (Lk 1:11-25), born and named (Lk 1:57-66; Carter, 1988: 241).

Elizabeth the Woman. The prominent position and roles of women in Lk 1–2 must be understood against the background not only of the androcentric attitudes and assumptions of modern and ancient culture, but against the context of patriarchal social systems which are at once political, economic and religious. One should also take into account the Israelite-Jewish tradition of leadership by women, particularly in situations of crisis in patriarchal institutions.

As in virtually all agrarian societies, in ancient Jewish Palestine the fundamental social unit of production as well as reproduction was the patriarchal family, whose head was evidently the "patriarch." Local patriarchal authority in the family and lineage or village was reinforced as well as reduplicated by patriarchal authority at the higher, governing levels of the society – in our case, the priesthood and high priesthood and scribes who assisted the priestly aristocracy in teaching, applying, and enforcing traditional customs and laws.

In circumstances of imperial subjection, such as prevailed at the time of Jesus, alien political-military rule and compounded economic exploitation intensified patriarchal domination. Besides sharpening patriarchal authority, imperial subjection also effectively caused local patriarchal forms to disintegrate under the pressure of intensified exploitation and relativized native authority. At one or several levels the traditional patriarchal authorities and institutions proved incapable of preserving the welfare and continuity of the people in its basic form of family and village. The patriarchs and the patriarchal forms had failed.

In such circumstances it is not surprising that women emerged in leadership roles. That women were prominent and instrumental in the Jesus movement in Galilee has been convincingly argued (Schüssler-Fiorenza, 1983: 138-140). The prominence of women in the infancy narratives, with Anna, the elderly widow and prophetess announcing the new salvation, and Elizabeth playing important roles alongside both Zechariah and Mary, thus parallels and reflects the importance of women in the Jesus movement. Elizabeth and especially Mary are represented in Lk 1 as active agents of their people's deliverance.

Women's prominence and assumption of leadership in the Jesus movement and in the infancy narratives are prefigured and almost certainly informed by long-standing traditions of women prominent in the redemption of people in times of crisis. The resistance to the Egyptian Pharaoh's oppression began not with Moses but with the Hebrew midwives, like Shiphrah and Puah (Ex 1:15-21). At points of crisis throughout biblical history, women emerged as inspired liberators, like Deborah (Judg 4–5), or prophetesses, like Hulda (2 Kgs 22). In the Song of Deborah (Judg 5), one significant element is the clear consciousness of class difference, manifested in the juxtaposition of Sisera's upper-class mother with the tent-dwelling Jael. The Song of Deborah expresses a popular tradition of Israelite peasants struggling against domination by foreign kings whose women live in finery and whose military conquests mean sexual abuse for the Israelite women.

Now it is evident in virtually all of these cases, where women played prominent roles in the people's deliverance from oppression or other crises, that they did not exert leadership in a traditional masculine role. Indeed, with the possible exception of prophecy, women exerted their leadership through traditional feminine roles or techniques. But ironically, the tradition that remembers these prominent women as leaders is patriarchal, and, notwithstanding the critique of patriarchal structures inherent in their stories and actions, they are remembered because they contributed mightily to the perpetuation of that same tradition.

It might be expected, therefore, that the infancy narratives, which stand in this same patriarchal tradition, would simply reaffirm and uncritically perpetuate traditional social forms. In the Jesus movement from which the infancy narratives originated, however, we find a clear challenge of those patriarchal forms. In exploring that challenge, we cannot separate the issues of patriarchal structures and poverty or socio-economic oppression, precisely because the patriarchal family and village were fundamental socio-economic forms of life, both reinforced and exploited by the patriarchal ruling structures. Any attempt to divide the issue of patriarchal culture and social structures from the economic issue tends to overlook the reality that in the first century – as today – the majority of the poor and starving were women, especially those women whose links with the basic patriarchal socio-economic units had been broken. In antiquity, widows and orphans were the prime paradigms of the poor and the exploited (Schüssler-Fiorenza: 1983: 140-141).[The U.N. Human Development Report 1995 states that of the 1.3 billion people living in poverty in the world, 70% are women.]

It is often remarked that Luke accords a special place in his narrative world to women, and this is certainly true of the infancy narrative where Elizabeth, Mary and Anna (Hannah) all play important roles. He seems quite deliberately to overturn the patriarchal hierarchy which would have woman as supplement to man (Kearney, 1984: 121). Joseph is therefore a very shadowy figure who never once speaks in the narrative and only takes initiative once, at a point where Luke wants to evoke a world of patriarchal authority (Lk 2:4). For the most part, Joseph is made to lurk so deep in the shadows that he seems a supplement to Mary, with Luke merely substituting one hierarchy for another, leaving the category of opposition intact. A new matriarchal hierarchy replaces the old patriarchal hierarchy.

Or does it? Although women (especially Mary) play an unusually key role in the infancy narrative, the last word is left with the male Jesus. Luke may want to say that the divine liberation worked in Jesus is symbolized by the overturning of patriarchal hierarchy; yet the one in whom this liberation is worked is himself male and in the narrative will perform roles and functions that only a male could perform. Moreover, when he speaks for the first time in the narrative (Lk 2:49) Jesus speaks of a God who he names "father." Luke puts in the mouth of Jesus the language of patriarchy to describe the God who overturns patriarchal hierarchy. He reverses the hierarchy only in the end to leave it intact. In cases like this, we see the gap between what Luke intends to say and what he actually says. And if true liberation consists in the *undoing* of hierarchy, mere substitution of one hierarchy for another cannot be the liberation that God works in Jesus (Coleridge, 1992: 141-142).

In circumstances of widespread disintegration of traditional institutions, particularly in the patriarchal family but also in the ruling mechanics of temple and Torah-enforcement through the "scribes and Pharisees," Jesus and his movement appear to have fostered alternative non-patriarchal but familial communities (Schüssler-Fiorenza, 1983: 143-151; Horsley, 1987: 232-245). The true family is now constituted not by physical kinship or blood relationships, but by "whoever does the will of God is my brother and sister and mother" (Mk 3:35). Within the new, egalitarian familial community, moreover, the followers of Jesus were to call "no one father on earth, for you have one Father — the one in heaven" (Mt 23:9; Horsley, 1989: 81-91).

Verses 8-10: (8) Once when he was praying as priest before God
                       and his section was on duty,
             (9) he was chosen by lot,
                       according to the custom of the priesthood
                       to enter the sanctuary of the Lord
                       and offer incense.
             (10) Now at the time of the incense offering,
                       the whole assembly of the people were praying out-
                       side.

It is Luke the writer and not the specialist in liturgy who de-scribes Zechariah in the exercise of his temple functions. Litur-gical exactness gives way to the narration (Bovon: 1991: 55).

Luke uses here for the first time the expression *egeneto de*, "it came to pass that," often not translated in English, which, together with the expression *kai egeneto*, is characteristic of Luke's style (he used the simple *egeneto* already in Lk 1:5; Neirynck, 1989: 94-103). His use of this Hebraism is usually attributed to his conscious adoption of the Hebrew style in order to lend

greater acceptability to his work, or to his unconscious incorpo-
ration into his work of elements of the religious language of the
Septuagint with which he had become so familiar. But this does
not answer the question why Luke chose to use the *egeneto*
expression where he did, and why he used *kai egeneto* in some
places and *egeneto de* in others.

The source of the *egeneto* expression used by Luke was clearly the
Septuagint. This expression in the Septuagint is the translation of the Hebrew *wayehi*. The function of *wayehi* in Hebrew narrative was to introduce a
temporal or circumstantial setting for the event that followed. In the Joseph
story (Gen 39–50), for example, the expression occurs fourteen times in the
narrative portions. It appears to have two discourse functions: to resume the
narrative after a time lapse and to mark significant events. These two discourse functions of *wayehi* are reflected in Luke's use of *egeneto* (Gault, 1994:
388-390). The *egeneto* expression functions on different levels. At the highest level, it marks major divisions of the total narrative. It marks the beginning of the travel narrative in Lk 9:51. The birth narrative's beginning in
Lk 2:1 may also be in this category. On a lower level, the expression may
mark individual episodes. Each episode may be viewed as a stage in the
narrative, though on a lower level than the major divisions, such as Lk
6:12. Lastly, the expression may mark a particular event or movement, as
Lk 2:46. These events may be viewed as a stage within an episode. As an
episode marker, the *egeneto* expression functions in two ways. It may introduce a whole episode, or it may introduce the event line after a setting.
When it introduces a whole episode, that episode may or may not be isolated chronologcally from the preceding episode. When it does follow the
preceding episode in time, the time period is usually vague. Luke has adapted
the *egeneto* expression well to indicate episodes that are isolated chronologically (Lk 5:1,12.17; 6:1,6,12). When Luke uses *egeneto* to introduce a preceding episode chronologically, the background material is limited to a temporal or circumstantial phrase, such as Lk 9:28, "and it came to pass about
eight days after these words." Luke also uses *egeneto* to begin an event line
after a setting. In this case, only *egeneto de* is used, consistent with the function of *de* as marking a shift in focus. Within an episode, the *egeneto* expression can mark a particular event, either a second stage in the episode, or
rarely, a climax or closing. In every one of these cases in the Gospel, *egeneto*
occurs with *kai*. In Lk 1:23 *kai egeneto* marks Zechariah's return home to
Elizabeth and the fulfillment of the angel's promise. In Lk 2:46 it marks the
discovery of Jesus in the temple, the first indication of Jesus' own awareness
of who he is. *Egeneto* may also be used as a climax. In Lk 24:30 Jesus has
been walking along with the two disciples on the road to Emmaus. *Kai egeneto*

marks the blessing of the meal when the disciples recognize Jesus. In Lk 24:51 *kai egeneto* marks Jesus' ascension. All these occurrences seem to be climactic rather than a development in the episode (Gault, 1994: 390-393).

What is the difference between *egeneto de* and *kai egeneto?* It would appear that *egeneto de* should occur with episodes that are a definite shift from the preceding material, whereas *kai egeneto* should occur within episodes or beginning episodes that in some sense are a continuation of the preceding narrative. That is, in fact, generally the case (Gault, 1994: 395-396). The *egeneto* expression should not be ignored in exegesis or translation. This is not to say that the form of the expression should be translated literally, for obviously "and it came to pass" is not normal English usage and does not have the same function in English as the *egeneto* expression had in biblical Greek. The alternate translation "and it happened" is worse because it includes the connotation of "happenstance," an aspect of meaning totally foreign to *egeneto*. The translator must be sensitive to the function of the *egeneto* expression in each occurrence and choose, in each case, the element of his language which has the same function that *egeneto* does in the particular context in the Greek text. It will not always be translated the same way in every language, and the translation may not always be lexical. It may be a change in word order or a change in clause type or verb aspect. The translator must use whatever the receptor language signals to get the same meanings that the *egeneto* expression signals: "This is the beginning of a new episode" or "this is where the action starts" or "this is an important event in the story." If the translator is sensitive to these various functions, he/she will go a long way toward achieving his/her purpose of communicating the total message of Luke-Acts (Gault, 1994: 398).

Verses 8-10 provide the immediate setting for the angelic announcement that is to come to Zechariah. These verses emphasize the cultic context for the angelic appearance and message. The time is clearly indicated: during the week of temple service performed by the section of Abijah to which Zechariah belonged. As mentioned above, each of the twenty-four sections served one week every half-year. This indication of time is further specified in verse 10: "at the time of the incense offering," which took place in the afternoon.

God's providence has been at work in the choice of Zechariah to be the one to offer incense. There were eight hundred priests in the division of Abijah; hence, being chosen by lot to burn incense could be a once-in-a-lifetime experience. Incense was burned in the morning and in the evening, though "the whole assembly of the people" here suggests the more widely attended evening rite (Malina-Rohrbaugh, 1992: 284). Zechariah was not elected, but designated by lot (just as Matthias was designated by lot in the reconstitution of the Twelve in Acts 1:26).

The place is also clearly indicated: "the sanctuary of the Lord," that is, the holy place, not the inner Holy of Holies entered only by the high priest on the Day of Atonement (cf. Heb 9:1-7). Omitting the prologue (Lk 1:1-4) from consideration, fifty-two of the 128 remaining verses of Lk 1–2 describe activity that takes place in the temple. Thus, almost forty percent of the first two chapters is devoted to the setting of the temple (Chance, 1988: 48). Luke speaks here of the "sanctuary" (*naos*) as opposed to the *hieron*, usually translated as the "temple" (Lk 2:27 etc.), that is, the whole complex of temple buildings. The temple had asserted itself as a major economic and political force within Second Temple Judaism and thus throughout the "land of the Jews" with which Luke's Gospel is concerned. But Luke's presentation of the temple almost completely sidesteps this historical reality. Instead, Luke actualizes other important aspects of the place of the temple in the life of the Jewish people. He portrays the temple as the locus of God's presence, a place for prayer, and an institution that served to perpetuate distinctions between Jews and non-Jews, priests and non-priests, men and women, and so on (Green, 1995: 4-5). Although the Jerusalem temple functioned as a vital economic center in the world of Jesus, Luke has very little to say on this matter. This is because, on the one hand, the economic issues Luke wants to address are far bigger than the temple; in fact, questions of economic exchange and economic power were integral to the Mediterranean world of which Jerusalem was a part; these Luke will work to undermine in his account, but not by an all-out attack against the temple. On the other hand, Luke does not elaborate on the politico-economic power of the temple because for him the primary importance of the temple lies elsewhere, on its role as "cultural center" (Geertz). Cultural centers are the active centers of social order: essentially concentrated loci of serious acts, they consist of the point or points in a society where its leading ideas come together within its leading institutions to create an arena in which the events that most vitally affect its members' lives take place. They mark the center of the social world as center and give what goes on there its aspect of being not merely important but in some fashion connected with the way the world is built (Geertz, 1983: 122-124). Luke's narrative undermines this key role of the temple first by acknowledging it, and then by means of a slowly evolving, increasingly negative characterization of the temple, transforming the initially positive conception of the temple in Lk 1–2. In the Third Gospel, finally, at Jesus' death, Luke narrates in proleptic fashion, the thorough-going theological critique of the temple which will follow in Acts 7 (Green, 1995: 5-6).

Zechariah is located at the socio-religious center of the Jewish world, on duty in the Jerusalem temple (Green, 1991: 550-557). Moreover, he has been chosen by God – for so the casting of lots was understood (see Acts 1:26; Godet, 1981: 46; Johnson, 1991: 32). The priest would take the incense from a bowl, put it on the burning coals, and scatter it. From the large number of people mentioned it has been argued that we are dealing here with the evening incense offering, which took place at approximately 3:00 p.m. That hour, the ninth hour in the Jewish time reckoning, is called by Acts 3:1, the "hour of prayer." The second Old Testament appearance of Gabriel (Dan 9:21) took place at the time of the evening sacrifice. Presumably the smoke of the incense was the signal for prayer (Brown, 1977: 259-260; Fitzmyer: 1981: 323-324).

The whole of the people. The term "assembly/multitude" is so stereotyped a Lukan expression (twenty-five times) that one may wonder whether it constitutes any estimate of number. It should probably be understood to mean, "the people who were assembled outside were all praying" (Brown, 1977: 260; Fitzmyer, 1981: 324).

"The whole people" were predominantly peasants. In any traditional agrarian society, the peasantry represented of 90 percent or more of the population and included all those living in towns and villages who engaged in working the soil or related activities. Peasants are rural cultivators whose surpluses are transferred to a dominant group of rulers that uses the surpluses both to underwrite their own standard of living and to distribute the remainder to groups in society that do not farm but in turn must be fed for their specific goods and services (Wolf, 1966: 3-4).

This definition fits the Palestinian situation well. Most peasants were and are economically marginal. After the demands for rents and taxes, most peasants were and are left with a minimal subsistence living. The peasants' own needs for survival often conflict with the demands of their rulers. Their consumption obviously cannot be curtailed below the caloric minimum needed to maintain human life. And production cannot be increased if the soil will not sustain higher yields or if there is not sufficient land to support the peasant population as well as the ruler's demands. Given the structure of politico-economic domination in Palestine at the time of Jesus' birth, with a double or triple layer of rulers' demands to be met, it is clear that the vast majority of the people would have been poor. Even Herod knew that his heavy demands on his subjects were becoming counter-productive and were simply killing his peasant producers (Applebaum, 1976: 631-700).

Peasants unable to meet the heavy demands for tithes, taxes and tribute would be driven increasingly into debt and might eventually be disinherited and displaced. A number of factors indicate that many Jewish peasants were indebted or displaced already during Herod's reign and that the problems of debt and displacement became steadily worse during the first century A.D. The devastation, slaughter, and enslavement involved in a generation of conquest and civil war, from 63 to 37 B.C., would have depleted or decimated some families and villages. On a lesser scale, but nevertheless serious in its impact, when Herod sent raiding parties out into the countryside to commandeer provisions for the Roman troops, some families or whole villages would have been left destitute. Then the structure of the imperial situation would have forced many to borrow in order to make it through to the next harvest after rendering to temple and Herod as well as to Caesar. There was a severe draught and famine near the midpoint of Herod's reign, with its obvious consequences for farmers already at the subsistence level. It is not surprising that the people clamored for reduction of taxes (Josephus, *Jewish War*, 2.4; *Antiquities*, 17.204). The escalating banditry and large numbers of people ready to abandon their homes and lands to join one of the popular prophetic movements at mid-first century A.D. are telling indicators that the economic and social viability of many peasants was in serious jeopardy. Not surprisingly, one of the first acts of the rebels who took control of Jerusalem in the summer of 66 A.D. was to burn the public archives where the debt records were kept (*Jewish War*, 2.427).

Once we are more familiar with the general situation of the Jewish peasantry, we can appreciate the likely reflection of that situation in the infancy narratives. Thus, for instance, instead of pondering why the Romans would be expecting people such as Joseph to go from their place of residence to the place of their ancestral origin, we should perhaps inquire why Joseph was no longer in his ancestral town in the first place. In Jewish Palestine, as in any traditional agrarian society, the vast majority of the peasants would have been working their ancestral lands and supporting the ruling groups with a portion of their produce. How did it happen that Joseph now lived nearly a hundred miles from his "house and family" of origin and even in a different district of Palestine? Tradition has it that Joseph was a "carpenter." How did a carpenter make a living, especially in a village such as Nazareth? Was he perhaps a wage laborer in a nearby town such as Sepphoris? How did people become carpenters or wage laborers in the first place? Almost certainly because of some displacement from their ancestral land, because of debts, famine, war, and so forth. Thus Joseph and Mary represent the thousands of rootless people in ancient Jewish Palestine cut loose from their ancient lands and villages by the Roman conquest or by indebtedness resulting from the intensive economic exploitation by Herod that compounded the demands for temple dues and Roman tribute. The Roman and Herodian troops would have created refugees virtually everytime they took military action to maintain or reassert their domination in a given area. Even without war, however, the Roman imperial system was creating plenty of refugees. Simply because of the steady economic pressures, peasants who could no longer squeeze out a subsistence living from the soil would have fled the land (Horsley, 1989: 68-73).

In contrast to most other peoples subjected to the *Pax Romana*, the Jewish people were not docile and passive, and resistance took a variety of forms. We should note here the importance of people's memories of past liberation and longing for future deliverance.

"The whole assembly of the people" is both a rhetorical and theological exaggeration. It is not only the entire biblical past, stretching back to Abraham, that provides the context for the introduction of Zechariah and Elizabeth and the narrative's beginning, but also the present hope of the entire people, grounded upon the biblical past and implied in their prayer. Whatever the story of Zechariah and Elizabeth may be, it will unfold within the twin context of Israel's biblical past and the life of the people now. Whatever the private future of Zechariah and Elizabeth may be, it will touch the very public future of "the whole assembly of the people" (Coleridge, 1993: 32).

Prayer notices without any content are common in Luke-Acts. Prayer has been identified as one of the themes of Luke's epiphany narratives, that is, narratives in which God manifests himself (Hubbard, 1977: 121-122); the individual who receives such an epiphanic vision is often praying when it takes place (Crump, 1992: 114). "Outside" would refer to the courts of the men and women that were separated from the temple sanctuary by the court of the priests (Brown, 1977: 260).

Verses 11-12: (11) Then there appeared to him an angel of the Lord,
                         standing at the right side of the altar of incense.
                    (12) When Zechariah saw him, he was terrified,
                         and fear overwhelmed him.

The language of "appearance" is not uncommon in Luke-Acts
(four times in Luke and nine times in Acts), and it is not infrequently used in connection with prayer related events (Crump,
1992: 46). Up to this point everything narrated is in line with
convention. But as soon as Zechariah enters the sanctuary the
unconventional erupts. The temple and its cult are immediately
transcended as the angel appears in verse 11. The cultic action
is never narrated, since, as the narrator has it, it is not through
the temple cult that God visits his people. The narrator locates
the divine visitation in the temple, but does not link it to the
cultic action (the burning of incense is never narrated; Coleridge,
1993: 33).

With these verses begins what has been called the "biblical
annunciation of birth," a literary genre found in the Old Testament as well as in the New Testament and consisting of the
following "five steps":

(1) The appearance of an angel of the Lord (or of the Lord).
(2) Fear or prostration of the visionary confronted by this su-
    pernatural presence.
(3) The divine message:
    a. The visionary is addressed by name.
    b. A qualifying phrase describing the visionary.
    c. The visionary is urged not to be afraid.
    d. A woman is with child or is about to be with child.
    e. She will give birth to the (male) child.
    f. The name by which the child is to be called.
    g. An etymology interpreting the name.
    h. The future accomplishments of the child.
(4) An objection by the visionary as to how this can be or a
    request for a sign.
(5) The giving of a sign to reassure the visionary (Brown, 1977:
    156).

It has been argued that Brown's understanding of the structure of the "biblical annunciation of birth" needs to be amended and that a somewhat larger list of Old Testament texts will clarify the model followed in the New Testament tradition. Following Robert Neff (1972), Conrad has suggested an alternative to the structure of the genre:

(1) The announcement of birth introduced by the particle *hinneh*.
(2) The designation of the name.
(3) The specification of the child's destiny.

The Old Testament representatives of the genre are Gen 16:11-12; 17:19; 1 Kgs 13:2; Isa 7:14-17; 1 Chron 22:9-10. The form is directly or indirectly used to announce a Davidic king.

The suggested alternative to the structure of the genre as well as the qualified list of Old Testament representatives of the genre strengthen a major thesis of Brown's argument, namely, that the "biblical annunciation of birth" was a form which carried a pre-Lukan tradition of the birth of Jesus as Davidic Messiah (Brown, 1977: 159). It will be observed that while the phrase "fear not" does occur in the Old Testament annunciations of birth, it does occur in an Old Testament form that announces "offspring" especially to the patriarchs. This observation undergirds another primary thesis of Raymond Brown's argument that the New Testament annunciations of birth, especially in Luke, are strongly evocative of patriarchal narratives (Brown, 1977: 279-281; Conrad, 1985: 657).

It has also been pointed out that several of the elements found in Brown's schema can also be found in the call narratives as, for instance, in the call of Gideon (Judg 6:14-18). Elsewhere we have suggested that Lk 1:8-23 and 1:26-38 may be a combination and overlapping of two Old Testament patterns, that of the birth of an important person and that of the call to mission (Hendrickx, 1984: 57-58). We also noted that Luke is giving the annunciation narratives a strongly apocalyptic setting, having at least thirteen features in common with the Book of Daniel (Ibidem: 54-56).

There appeared... There appeared, literally, "was seen." The expression is a favorite of Luke's. It is used for the appearance of the "tongues of fire" (Acts 2:3), the appearance of God to Abraham (Acts 7:2), of Jesus to Paul (Acts 9:17), and for other Pauline visions (Acts 16:9); and so one can draw from it nothing special about the manner or reality of the appearance (Brown, 1977: 260).

An angel of the Lord. As in the Old Testament, "the angel of the Lord" is presented as a special agent of God, who helps God to accomplish his will (Ex 3:2; Judg 6:11-16). In particular, this divine servant serves here as a surrogate for the presence of God (in the Holy Place) and so as God's mouthpiece. In this role, Gabriel's words are set alongside the words of Scripture as expressions of the divine purpose (Green, 1995: 40). This is the exalted Old Testament figure who appears at times to be indistinguishable from Yahweh himself (Gen 16:7-13; 21:17; Ex 14:19-24; Judg 2:1-5). It is not usually a personal, spiritual being between God and people, but a way of describing God's presence to human beings. But in the course of time it becomes a definite heavenly being (Zech 1:11-14). Especially after the Babylonian exile (587-538 B.C.) Jewish angelology developed, mostly owing to contact of exiled Jews with other cultures in which lesser gods and divine heroes were commonplace. To preserve the transcendence of Yahweh, angels of various types were introduced, and there developed names for specific angelic beings, especially in apocalyptic and related literature. The only angels named in the Old Testament are Michael and Gabriel in the Book of Daniel, written in about 175 B.C. In Lk 1:19, Luke will identify the angel of the Lord as Gabriel; and so he is writing in the context of post-exilic angelology with the concept of personal, intermediate beings. This new concept in Judaism had been accepted by the Pharisees but rejected by the Sadducees (Acts 23:8; Brown, 1977: 260; Fitzmyer, 1981: 324).

The "angel of the Lord" also appears to the barren wife of Manoah, the father of Samson in Judg 13:3. "The angel of the Lord" further appears in Lk 2:9; Acts 5:19; 8:26; 12:7,23.

Standing at the right side of the altar of incense. The altar of incense is described in Ex 30:1-10. In the ancient world the right side was considered the favorable side, here fitting for the delivery of good news (see verse 19; C.F. Evans, 1990: 148).

Zechariah... was terrified, and fear overwhelmed him. "To terrify" is often used for fear falling on a person (Acts 19:7; Dan 4:2LXX; 10:7LXX). We probably have here an allusion to Dan 10:7. Throughout the Bible "fear" is the standard reaction in the presence of the divine, whether encountered directly, through an angel, or through an exercise of some extraordinary power (Brown, 1977: 260). Zechariah's fear implies a recognition of what is happening, but he cannot yet know why. He stands before a sign which demands interpretation. At this point the narration is set in a strong visual key: the angel remains silent, but his location is visualized with surprising detail ("standing at the right side of the altar of incense"), and the narrator has Zechariah upset by what he *sees*. In order to know why the angel has appeared, Zechariah needs to *hear*: the narration needs to move into an aural mode. The sign must be interpreted (Coleridge, 1993: 34-35).

Verses 13-14: (13) But the angel said to him,
"Do not be afraid, Zechariah,
for your prayer has been heard.
Your wife Elizabeth will bear you a son,
and you will name him John.
(14) You will have joy and gladness,
and many will rejoice at his birth,

The angel, silent until now, speaks in verse 13. For the first time the narrator has one of his characters move into direct speech. He retires behind the veil of direct speech as heaven speaks for the first time. It is better that the heavenly messenger be allowed to speak in his own right, lest there be any suggestion that he speaks, not so much as God's messenger but as the narrator's mouth-piece. In the angel's speech we have the rudiments of a biblical hermeneutic which will come to full flower later in the Lukan narrative. Placing the speech in the mouth of an angel gives the hermeneutic an authority transcending the narrator's authority. It bears the authority of heaven itself (Coleridge, 1993: 35-36).

The first four lines of the message delivered by the angel concern participation in and reaction to the birth of John the Baptist, primarily on the part of Elizabeth and Zechariah, but then also on the part of "many." The opening words, "Do not be afraid, Zechariah, for your prayer has been heard," recall Dan 10:12, "Do not fear, Daniel,... for your words have been heard," and Dan 10:19, "Do not fear, greatly beloved..." The phrase is repeated by the evangelist in Lk 1:30, "Do not be afraid, Mary...," and in Lk 2:10, "Do not be afraid," addressed to the shepherds.

The object of Zechariah's prayer is not specified, but the immediate context and the following words of the angel would imply that he had been praying for the good of Israel but also for a child (verses 6-7; Fitzmyer, 1981: 325). According to the immediate situation, Gabriel's promise that "your prayer has been heard" appears to refer to the priestly prayer being offered in conjunction with the burning of incense. But the message that Gabriel actually brings indicates that it is Zechariah's personal prayer for a son which God is now about to answer. The details of the narrative seem to indicate that it is Zechariah's and Elizabeth's past prayers for a child which are now being answered, and these personal prayers have meshed with God's plans for the entire nation in a way which will thoroughly supersede their limited expectations (Crump, 1992: 63-64). Given the domestic, economic, and religious benefits a family derived from a male child, boys were often considered a gift from God (Malina-Rohrbaugh, 1992: 284). Indirectly, the prayer for Israel is also heard, since the child "will turn many of the people of Israel to the Lord their God" (Lk 1:16). For the rest, the format in verse 13 is almost totally that of the standard annunciation pattern presented above. Specifically, we may compare the words addressed to Abraham in Gen 17:19, "your wife Sarah shall bear you a son, and you shall call him Isaac," with "your wife Elizabeth will bear you a son, and you will name him John." The name "John" is given before birth to signify that God has a special role for this child. Like other heaven-imposed names (Gen 16:11; Isa 7:14), it implies that the child will have a role in the drama of God's saving history. A link between "your prayer has been heard" and the meaning of the name "John" would not be intelligible in Greek (Marshall, 1978: 56). The Greek reader is unlikely to have known that *Yohanan* meant "Yahweh has shown favor."

In both the divine designation of a name and the angel's description of the child to be born, honor is being ascribed. The pivotal focus of the Mediterranean society of the first century was honor-shame. As in the traditional Mediterranean and Middle Eastern society of today, so also in biblical times, honor meant everything, including survival. Note Rom 12:10, where Paul admonishes Christians to outdo one another in showing honor. Honor can be understood as the status one claims in the community together with the all-important recognition of that claim by others. It thus serves as an indicator of social standing, enabling persons to interact with their social superiors, equals, and inferiors in certain ways described by society. Honor can be ascribed or acquired. Ascribed honor derives from birth; being born into an honorable family makes one honorable in the eyes of the entire community. Acquired honor, by contrast, is the result of skill in the never-ending game of challenge and response. Not only must one win to gain it; one must do so in public because the whole community must acknowledge the gain. To claim honor that the community does not recognize is to play the fool. Recognition by onlookers is anticipated in Lk 1:14 and then seen in Lk 1:59-66 (Malina-Rohrbaugh, 1992: 284,310).

"You shall have joy (*chara*) and gladness (*agalliasis*)." The first is repeated in Lk 1:28,46,58; 2:10. The second in Lk 1:44; Acts 2:46. The latter is a forceful word denoting spiritual exaltation, as does the corresponding verb in Lk 1:47; 10:21; Acts 16:34. For the two words in combination see Mt 5:12. The joy and gladness are both for Zechariah and Elizabeth and for the rest of Israel in the future when John fulfills his divine destiny ("for he will be"; C.F. Evans, 1990: 149). This is the first indication of the atmosphere which pervades the Lukan infancy narrative. Verse 15 will give the reason for the joy, which is not limited solely to John's parents, but will also come to "many" (Fitzmyer, 1981: 325).

Verses 15-16: (15) for he will be great in the sight of the Lord.
He must never drink wine or strong drink;
even before his birth
he will be filled with the Holy Spirit.
(16) He will turn many people of Israel
to the Lord their God.

From verse 15 onwards, it is John who is the focus of the speech, though in the climactic "to make ready a people prepared for the Lord" of verse 17, it is God whose shadow moves fleetingly to center stage (Coleridge, 1993: 37).

The second four lines of the message concern the future career of the child and what he will do. The first clause, "for he will be great...," is an echo of Lk 7:28, where Jesus is quoted as saying, "among those born of women no one is greater than John." That John the Baptist will be great "in the sight of the Lord" may be echoing the prophecy of Mal 3:1 applied to John the Baptist in Lk 7:27, "See, I am sending my messenger ahead of you, who will prepare your way for you." The statement that John "must never drink wine or strong drink" is an echo of Lk 7:33, "For John the Baptist has come eating no bread and drinking no wine." Two of the most famous Old Testament birth annunciations concerned Samson and Samuel. To the mother of Samuel it was said by the angel, "Now be careful not to drink wine or strong drink... for you shall conceive a son" (Judg 13:4-5). When the mother of Samuel prayed "before the Lord" (compare Lk 1:15a), she promised that, if God would give her a son, she would give him to the Lord all the days of his life; and that "he shall drink neither wine nor intoxicants" (1 Sam 1:8-11). A bit later she insists that she had "drunk neither wine nor strong drink" (1 Sam 1:15). So, using this stereotyped language, Luke is portraying John the Baptist as an ascetic, as a Nazirite (Brown, 1977: 273). The allusion to the Samuel story is but part of the larger Lukan dependence on that story in the infancy narrative. In depicting John thus, Luke is hinting at his prophetic role (Lk 1:76; 7:26-27; Fitzmyer, 1981: 326).

The idiom "to be filled with the Holy Spirit" is found three times in the infancy narrative (Lk 1:15,41,67) and five times in the Acts of the Apostles (Acts 2:4; 4:8,31; 9:17; 13:9) and not in the rest of the New Testament or in the Septuagint (Nolland, 1989: 30). Here the Spirit is depicted as the impetus of John's prophetic ministry. This judgment is confirmed by the immediate context: John will go before the Lord "with the spirit and power of Elijah" (Lk 1:17). John's unique reception of the Spirit while still in the womb points to John's special status and role: he is "more than a prophet" (Lk 7:26,28) and "shall go before the Lord" (Lk 1:17). Luke has placed the references to the Spirit (Lk 1:15,17) in the narrative in order to emphasize the pneumatic and prophetic character of John's ministry and to strengthen the links between John and Jesus (Menzies, 1991: 118-119).

In verse 16 Luke begins to specify the role that this forthcoming prophet will have: "He will turn many people of Israel to the Lord their God." The idea of "turning" or "returning" to the Lord God is standard Old Testament language for the repentance of a people (Deut 30:2; Hos 3:5; 7:10); and sometimes such a "turning" is proclaimed by a prophet upon whom the Spirit of God has come (2 Chron 15:1,4). Some see here an allusion to Mal 2:6 where it is said that Levi, with whom God had entered into a covenant, "turned many from iniquity."

Verse 17: With the spirit and power of Elijah
   he will go before him,
   to turn the hearts of parents to their children,
   and the disobedient to the wisdom of the righteous,
   to make ready a people prepared for the Lord.

The final strophe of the angelic oracle proclaims that John the Baptist will carry out his prophetic mission of repentance and reconciliation "with the spirit and power of Elijah." Again we seem to have an anticipation of the theme that is common in the synoptic accounts of Jesus' ministry. For instance, Mk 9:13 quotes Jesus as saying, "I tell you that Elijah has come, and they did to him whatever they pleased, as it is written about him." Whatever Jesus himself may have meant by these words, it is probable that Mark interpreted it as a reference to John the Baptist, since he described him as wearing Elijah-like clothing (Mk 1:6; cf. 2 Kgs 1:8), and he has dramatized the violent death of John the Baptist, a death suffered precisely because, like Elijah, John the Baptist dared to challenge kings (Herod and Herodias resemble Ahab and Jezebel, 1 Kgs 21). John will go before God in the sense of Mal 3:23-24 (ET: 4:5-6): he precedes the great and terrible day of the Lord which means both salvation and judgment (Nolland, 1989: 31). John is not directly identified with Elijah, but is simply to be inspired by the same spiritual power as Elijah (Marshall, 1978: 59). The association of John the Baptist and Elijah is echoed in the other lines of verse 17. The texts to be remembered here are Mal 3:1, "See, I am sending my messenger to prepare the way before me," in which the "messenger" may originally have meant an angel, but by the time Mal 3:23-24 (NRSV 4:5-6) had been appended he was identified with Elijah: "I will send you the prophet Elijah before the great and terrible day of the Lord comes. He will turn the hearts of parents to their children and the hearts of children to their parents, so that I will not strike the land with a curse." Finally, Sir 48:10, "At the appointed time, it is written, you [Elijah] are destined to calm the wrath of God before it breaks out in fury, to turn the hearts of parents to their children, and to restore the tribes of Jacob." Both Mal 3:24 and Sir 48:10 gave Elijah a task of reconciliation before that terrible day (Brown, 1977: 276-277).

In the continuation of verse 17, which resumes verse 16, the mode in which the turning to the Lord is to happen is made specific. The first specification mentions only one form of conversion mentioned in Mal 3:24, leaving out the turning of children to their parents. The conversion is to remedy the parental neglect of the young in Israel. In adopting this phrase, Luke may be hinting at the neglect shown by Israel of old toward those who are to become children of Abraham (Lk 3:8). The second specification is a turning of the disobedient to the "wisdom" or "understanding" of those who stand upright in the sight of God, the way of thinking of the just. The third specification of the turning emphasizes John's role in preparing Israel for the coming of the Lord (Fitzmyer, 1981: 320).

The somewhat tautologous statement, "make ready a people prepared for the Lord," concludes and summarizes the role of the eschatological prophet. The verb "make ready" (*hetoimazein*). is used in Isa 40:3 with a "way" and in 2 Sam 7:24LXX with a "people" (C.F. Evans, 1990: 150-151).

Throughout this thoroughly scriptural oracle, the message of joy and divine promise is constant. This is the same God who spoke through the prophets of old, and God's word abides forever. God is even providing the messenger to bring the children of Israel back into the obedience of the wisdom of the just: The destiny of this child is described in wholly positive terms, giving expression to God's determined purpose to restore his people in faithfulness, wisdom, and righteousness (verses 16-17). Even when John's preaching will become stern or threatening (see Lk 3:7-19), God's gracious resolve for the people must never be obscured (Tiede, 1988: 43).

Verses 18-20. (18) Zechariah said to the angel,
"How will I know that this is so?
For I am an old man,
and my wife is getting on in years."
(19) The angel replied, "I am Gabriel,
I stand in the presence of God,
and I have been sent to speak to you
and to bring you this good news.
(20) But now,
because you did not believe my words,
which will be fulfilled in their time,
you will become mute, unable to speak,
until the day these things occur."

The basic pattern of biblical annunciation of birth is continued in verses 18-20: the objection as to how this can be, and the giving of a sign. Both elements have Old Testament anteced- ents. Zechariah echoes Abraham's objection, "How am I to know that I shall possess it?" (Gen 15:8, when God promised him a progeny as numerous as the stars of heaven). This is followed by a reminder of Zechariah's and Elizabeth's age in which they most resemble Abraham and Sarah (Gen 17:17; Jegen, 1992: 335-340). Zechariah questions the announcement (see Gen 17:17- 18; 18:11-15), though here in the mild form of requesting a verifying sign (see Gen 15:8; Judg 6:36-40; 2 Kgs 20:8-11; Isa 7:11), such as is given without request in Lk 2:12 (C.F. Evans, 1990: 151).

The angel identifies himself as "Gabriel" thereby again sug- gesting the Danielic background of the annunciation (Dan 8:16; 9:21), where he is described as a human being. The name *Gabri- el* means "God is my hero/warrior" (Fitzmyer, 1981: 328; for the idea of angels standing before God, see Job 1:6; Dan 7:16).

"I have been sent" is a so-called theological passive and stands for "God has sent me." The word for "angel" in Hebrew has the sense of messenger. "To bring you this good news": *euangelizesthai* is a verb related to *euangelion*, "good news," "gos- pel," which is, however, avoided by Luke in the Gospel, but introduced in Acts 15:7, on the lips of Peter, and in Acts 20:24, on the lips of Paul. In view of Luke's attitude towards *euangelion*, it is highly improbable that Luke would think of Zechariah as the first to whom the gospel is preached (Fitzmyer, 1981: 173, 328; against Rengstorf, 1969: 22). "But now" (RSV: "and be- hold," a more literal translation of *kai idou* that occurs twenty- seven times in Luke and nine times in Acts) a sign is added to confirm the angelic message. Indeed, especially if we suppose here an underlying Aramaic story, and no matter what the fea- ture means for Luke now, the original meaning of Zechariah's dumbness seems to have been a sign rather than a punishment. The following reasons may be adduced for this opinion:

(1) At this stage of the pattern of the biblical annunciation of birth we expect a sign (Isa 7: 10-14; Lk 1:36; 2:12).

(2) It is improbable that Zechariah, who has been described as "righteous before God, living blameless..." (Lk 1:6), would now have to be punished for lack of faith.

(3) In fact, only two verses before Abraham asks a very similar question, "How am I to know that I shall possess it?" (Gen 15:8), Gen 15:6 states: "And he believed the Lord; and the Lord reckoned it to him as righteousness." And Mary who asks, "How can this be, since I am a virgin?" (Lk 1:34) is addressed by Elizabeth as "blessed is she who believed..." (Lk 1:45).

(4) Moreover, it is highly improbable that the father of the great prophet whose birth is announced would be presented as lacking faith.

(5) In Dan 10:15 the visionary also becomes speechless. It seems to be a feature linked with visions.

(6) This would explain why, upon realizing that Zechariah cannot speak, the people "realized that he had seen a vision" (Lk 1:22).

(7) Requesting a sign is not necessarily an indication of lack of faith (see the case of Abraham and Mary). The visionary does not express doubt in God's capability but his/her incapability to fulfill his/her role/mission.

(8) A sign of confirmation is needed only as long as the things to be confirmed are not yet fulfilled. That explains why Zechariah's dumbness ceases as soon as the child has received his name (Lk 1:46).

The above refer to the probable original meaning of the dumbness of Zechariah in the account. But there is no doubt that Luke himself presents the dumbness as a punishment. It has been suggested that Luke may not have been aware of the function of signs of confirmation, freely given or requested, in Hebrew/Aramaic stories of annunciation of birth or call to mission (see Judg 6). And he was no doubt aware of Jesus' negative attitude towards asking for signs (see, e.g., Lk 11:16,29). He may also have been unaware of the fact that, in Daniel, incapability to speak is linked up with visionary experience. Moreover, in his overall plan of the infancy narrative and the Gospel as a whole, Luke may have considered this feature part of the presentation of Jesus as superior to John the Baptist. The superiority started already with the parents. Indeed, Zechariah's unbelief is later contrasted with Mary's belief (Lk 1:45).

In a recent literary approach it has been pointed out that – in the final redaction – while there are some obvious similarities between Abraham and Zechariah (Aletti, 1989: 64-70, especially 68), there are considerably more differences, and that Zechariah's question, although almost identical in form, moves in a direction quite different from Abraham's question in Gen 15:8. He repeats the words of Abraham, but fails to remember the events of the biblical story which would answer his question. Abraham was the first of the line of Old Testament figures who were given offspring by divine intervention; Zechariah is the last. The question makes sense for Abraham since the promise to him is a totally new event, a new and unforeseeable beginning. But the promise of a son to Zechariah is not a totally new event, nor a new and unforeseeable beginning. Scripture offers evidence of God's power to bring babes from barren wombs, and this is a moment of fulfillment rather than a new beginning.

The angel's answer shows that God's plan transcends human doubt. God looks to the human being to accept his plan, but does not depend upon the human being for its implementation. The angel has stated what *will* happen, and he repeats that assurance in verse 20. Gabriel's second speech underlines the dynamic of promise – fulfillment. The fact that he introduces himself and states his credentials emphatically, "I am Gabriel, I stand in the presence of God and I have been sent...," confirms the suspicion that Zechariah's question implied doubt as to the authority and reliability of the messenger. This is Gabriel, fresh from the Book of Daniel, though speaking now in different accents. Indeed, though the sweep of his speech is grand enough, it is less elevated and more personal than in Daniel, where he is also never as stern as he proves to be in Lk 1:19-20. He begins to speak and act in his own right and even refers in verse 20 to the oracle as "my words," and acts without reference to heaven by imposing silence on Zechariah.

Where Zechariah has spoken in terms of *knowledge*, "how will I *know*," Gabriel speaks of *faith*, "because you did not *believe* my words." The narrator makes it clear that the key to an understanding of what is required for the recognition of the divine visitation is faith. Knowledge, though necessary, is never adequate (Coleridge, 1993: 37-44).

Verses 21-23: (21) Meanwhile the people were waiting for Zechariah,
and wondered at his delay in the sanctuary.
(22) When he did come out,
he could not speak to them,
and they realized
that he had seen a vision in the sanctuary.
He kept motioning to them
and remained unable to speak.
(23) When his time of service was ended,
he went to his home.

The narrator leaves Zechariah and Gabriel in the sanctuary and turns his attention again to the people (see verse 10), suggesting that the unfolding drama does not concern only Zechariah and Gabriel. That they "were waiting for Zechariah" may seem to imply that Luke was unaware that several priests were supposed to enter the sanctuary, but it could simply be due to Luke's intention to focus on the main characters of his account. Normally the priest(s) remained inside for a short time. When Zechariah failed to appear, they were surprised at his delay.

Once Zechariah did emerge, the people were no longer at prayer (as in verse 10), but were faced instead with a puzzling sign, the dumb-struck Zechariah, who constitutes the narrative's *first sign* of fulfillment. The irony is that he who sought a sign from the angel becomes himself a sign (Coleridge, 1993: 45). Zechariah (and the assisting priests) should have pronounced the Aaronic blessing (Num 6:24-26) from the steps of the sanctuary building, but "he could not speak to them."

Zechariah is incapable of discharging his duties as a priest; he is unable to bless the people who await his service. He returns home, unable to speak, task unfinished (Lk 1:23). At the end of the Gospel Jesus raises his hands in a levitical fashion and blesses his disciples (Lk 24:50-51). Scholars pointing out a "circularity" between the beginning and the end of the Gospel have suggested that Jesus completes what Zechariah could not do; he blesses the people of God. Then, in a sense, Jesus too returns to "his own home" (Schweizer, 1984: 378-379; Hendrickx, 1984b: 98; Parsons, 1987: 74).

Luke does not tell us how the people came to realize that Zechariah had seen a vision in the sanctuary; but to ask how they do reach this conclusion may be missing the point of this story (Fitzmyer, 1981: 329). There may be an echo here of Dan 10:15 where Daniel is left speechless during a vision. Moreover, the seeming illogic of the people's guess may be solved if there was a tradition of appearances in the sanctuary. Josephus relates a vision which came to the high priest John Hyrcanus (134-104 BC) while offering incense in the temple sanctuary (*Antiquities*, 13.10.3; Brown, 1977: 263). So Zechariah "kept motioning to them," that is, he tried to explain with gestures what he could not explain by speech. "He remained unable to speak" translates the term *kōphos*, which can have several meanings, and since Lk 1:62 implies that Zechariah could not hear either, perhaps one should translate "deaf and dumb."

"When his time of service was over," that is at the end of the one week of service of his section, (it happened that) "he went to his home," referred to as "a Judean town in the hill country" in Lk 1:39. A theme or refrain of departure concludes six of the seven scenes of Luke's infancy narrative (Lk 1:23,38,56; 2:20,39,51). They are to be seen more as a literary device to conclude these scenes rather than as historical information.

In light of the importance of the temple in the Third Gospel, the balance between the temple and the house (*oikos*; NRSV translates here: home) in Lk 1–2 is noteworthy. Both function as space for divine revelation and the praise of God. As the narrative develops, a similar pairing of synagogue and house will occur. In the end, temple and synagogue will present themselves as antagonist to Jesus and his message, and the house will become more and more the center of Jesus' movement (Green, 1995: 12).

Verses 24-25: (24) After those days his wife Elizabeth conceived,
and for five months she remained in seclusion.
She said,
(25) "This is what the Lord has done for me
when he looked favorably on me
and took away the disgrace
I have endured among my people."

Zechariah disappears from the narrative, and Elizabeth, who has been only a name until now, moves to centre stage. As Hannah conceived a son after her visit to the sanctuary at Shiloh (1 Sam 1:19-20), so now on the return of her husband from the temple, Elizabeth conceives a son in fulfillment of God's promise. Her pregnancy is the narrative's *second sign of fulfillment*.

There does not seem to be any need to posit an obscure purpose in the Lukan mention of Elizabeth's seclusion for five months, or to explain it psychologically as the result of some modesty or shame, since it is probably a literary device in relation to the annunciation to Mary, which prepares for the sign to be revealed to Mary in Lk 1:36. Indeed, if Elizabeth hid for five months, her pregnancy could still operate as news and, therefore, as a sign "in the sixth month." At any rate, Elizabeth thus joins her husband in remaining incommunicado (Kozar, 1990: 215).

"This is what the Lord has done for me" expresses Elizabeth's joy over the divine removal of her embarrassment, in a way similar to the jubilation of Sarah, "God has brought laughter for me" (Gen 21:6), and Rachel, "God has taken away my reproach" (Gen 30:23), especially echoed in Elizabeth's words, "and took away my reproach." "Reproach" (*oneidos*) is used only here in the New Testament. Elizabeth's words have been compared with those of Mary in the Magnificat, and at least one author refers to them even as a "short Magnificat" (Bovon, 1991: 62). It has also been noted that Elizabeth's words disclose the humiliations which this woman endured from her neighbors during her long years of barrenness (Godet, 1981: 53). The disgrace would have been both within the husband's family, where a childless woman would have been considered a stranger, and in the village or town, where barrenness would have dishonored the family (Malina-Rohrbaugh, 1992: 285).

Having conceived, Elizabeth's response centers on the consequences of her pregnancy for her interaction in the community (Lk 1:25). As in Israel's Scriptures, wherein is firmly embedded the idea that God controls the womb (Trible, 1978: 34-38), so here childbearing is understood as a manifestation of divine blessing, and so a marker of social status. Her weighty claims to honor reported in Lk 1:5-7 had been compromised by her childlessness; God's intervention, then, was experienced by her as a way of removing shame, of gaining honor (Green, 1992: 463-464).

2. The Annunciation of the Birth of Jesus (Lk 1:26-38)

The second episode of the Lukan infancy narrative is parallel to the first. [For a detailed comparison see Brown, 1977: 294-297]. There can be little doubt that throughout the Gospel Luke deliberately multiplies stories about women and that these stories function as "pairs" to stories about men. In the infancy narrative we have two annunciations to Zechariah and Mary (Lk 1:5-25; 1:26-38); two hymns of Mary and Zechariah (Lk 1:46-55; 1:67-79); and two prophets: Simeon and Anna (Lk 2:25-35 and 36-38; D'Angelo, 1990: 443-444). The forms of the two narratives are so similar that it cannot be doubted that they were consciously arranged to bring out the parallelism between them. Most scholars hold that the present story has been modeled on that of John, but the opposite view, that the story of John was modeled (by Luke) on that of Jesus, is also defended by some. Since, however, the story of John displays a greater dependence on Old Testament types, it is unlikely that it was modeled on that of Jesus. On the other hand, the story of the annunciation of Jesus displays such a wealth of individual features that a number of scholars think that it cannot be simply regarded as an imitation of the story about John, and that it is best, therefore, to postulate mutual dependence between the two stories (Marshall, 1978: 62-63).

At first glance, the two episodes seem very similar, but it remains to be seen whether the similarity is superficial or more thoroughgoing. There is a range of opinion on this. Fitzmyer says that "the second episode of the Lukan infancy narrative is parallel to the first" (1981: 334), and Lucien Legrand by contrast claims that "the parallelism of composition is only superficial. The narrative structures are different" (1981: 75). We are dealing with a technique not of *repetition* but of *reprise*; the narrator resumes elements of the previous episode but modulates them by means of variation and addition, at times subtle, at other times less so (Coleridge, 1993: 52).

The infancy narrative in Luke is focused on Mary in a way that puts Joseph in the shadow. This becomes clear both when compared with the parallel of Zechariah and Elizabeth, and also when compared with the infancy narrative in Matthew's gospel, which gives more weight to Joseph's role. Zechariah's temporary dumbness gives Elizabeth a certain scope for action, and she is presented positively. But she still has her place in a pattern that is very largely conventional; she bears Zechariah his promised son, and it is he who praises God when the power of speech is restored after the birth of John. Only in her relationship to Mary does Elizabeth play an independenrt role. Mary's independence is much greater. She is the protagonist, while Joseph is almost to be considered an extra throughout the narrative (Seim, 1994: 201-202).

Verses 26-27: (26) In the sixth month
                     the angel Gabriel was sent by God
                     to a town in Galilee called Nazareth,
               (27) to a virgin
                     engaged to a man whose name was Joseph,
                     of the house of David.
                     The virgin's name was Mary.

The narrator's introduction in verses 26-27 serves two purposes. First, it links the pericope with the annunciation to Zechariah in the preceding episode: the time reference "in the sixth month" refers to the sixth month of Elizabeth's pregnancy, and again it is Gabriel who brings the message from God. Secondly, the introduction shows main interests in the story: (1) Gabriel appears "to a virgin"; (2) Mary is engaged to a man whose name is Joseph, "of the house of David." The reader is thus prepared for both the divine conception and the Davidic-messianic role of the child (Strauss, 1995: 87; Ellis, 1966: 71, 84).

The dating, "in the sixth month," also prepares for the announcement to be made in Lk 1:36. Elizabeth's pregnancy will be revealed to Mary before it becomes public. The mention of the angel Gabriel also effects continuity with the previous section, though here he does not announce himself by name. Indeed, while in the first episode Gabriel did not name himself until verse 19, now the narrator mentions him in verse 26, making a strong and immediate link with the preceding episode. Gabriel is named not simply as "Gabriel," but as "the angel Gabriel." The narrator insists on his link with God who sent him. This will remain so throughout the episode with Gabriel referred to as "the angel" in verses 30,34,35,38. Gabriel is not important in himself, but as servant of God whose messenger he is (Coleridge, 1993: 53).

Before we are told to whom the angel is sent, we are told where: "to a town in Galilee called Nazareth." The Greek word here translaterd "town" (*polis*) is the common Hellenistic term for "city." Yet Nazareth in Jesus' day could hardly be described in that way. It was a small village of a little more than a hundred people, perhaps belonging to the nearby city of Sepphoris

(Malina-Rohrbaugh, 1992: 288). Attention has been drawn to the emphasis Luke places on rural and urban life. Galilee is the locus of Jesus' ministry until he begins the long, wandering journey to Jerusalem in Lk 9:51. "Galilee" is more than a geographical location, and it is important to ask how this spatial marker locates the story on the cultural map. Galilee (together with Jericho) was the heart of agricultural production in Palestine. Its fertile soil contributed to the growth of such crops as grapes for wine, figs, olives, and wheat, as well as to pasturage, while the Sea of Galilee served as the hub of an important fishing industry (Oakman, 1988: 90-115). This was an agrarian society marked by many features of peasant culture. Socio-economic realities among Galilean peasantry, in part grounded and fueled by disaffection toward Roman occupation, contributed to social unrest in the region. Although Hellenization was influential throughout the land of the Jews by the first century A.D., this was apparently less so in the sparsely populated area of upper Galilee. In some ways, then, this area was "beyond easy reach" of a more pervasive Hellenism and, for practical purposes, was outside the firm grip of Roman overlordship. Historically, the story here was one of stubborn resistance to alien cultural influence and foreign domination (Green, 1995: 12-13).

Luke's narrative reflects what would be expected in an agrarian culture, especially as it relates to economics. First, peasant existence generally is characterized by the ever-present demands of one's family, the needs of one's ongoing agricultural operation, and the requirements of the state, in this case Rome. Peasant life, then, rests on a narrow margin between subsistence and abject poverty. Second, we may refer to systems of economic exchange within the peasant village, of which two sorts were operative. The first is generalized reciprocity – that is, a transaction characteristic of those who share close kinship ties, whereby the exchange is essentially one-sided, altruistic, the giving of a gift without explicit stipulations for reciprocation of any kind. The second is balanced reciprocity – the direct exchange of goods of approximately equal value within a relatively short period of time. Concerns with reciprocity are present in Luke's account – e.g., "the measure you give will be the measure you get back" (Lk 6:38c) – and can be brought to the forefront in order to be dismissed or parodied. Here it is important to observe the central role allotted to kinship relations, evaluations of social distance and nearness in peasant life. Characters in Luke's account show a marked concern for determining the boundaries of "our group" and stipulating the nature of appropriate interaction with those outside the group (e.g., Lk 4:23-29; 9:49-50). Third, and closely related, Luke's narrative reflects the patronage system characteristic of the Mediterranean world – a system of relationships grounded in inequality between two principals: a patron has social, economic, and political resources that are needed by a client. In return, a client can give expressions of loyalty and honor that are useful for the patron (Moxnes, 1991: 242). A textbook case example of patronage appears in Lk 7:1-10. Overall, however, Luke's accounts are less focused on individual patron-client relations and less friendly toward the institution of patronage. In fact, Luke's material is more concerned with the patronal system as such, a system by means of which those in need (clients) are controlled by those (patrons) to whom they are indebted (Green, 1995: 14-16).

Now we have not the sacral space of the temple, as in the previous episode, but far-flung Nazareth, which is nowhere mentioned in the Old Testament, Josephus, or rabbinical writings. The existence of this insignificant Galilean hamlet is known, however, from a Hebrew inscription found in 1962 at Caesarea Maritima (Fitzmyer, 1981: 343). The goal of the divine action is not a place but a person.

Indeed, the angel is sent "to a virgin." Luke does not call Mary "girl" (*pais* as in Lk 8:51), but rather *parthenos*, the normal understanding of which is "virgin" (Fitzmyer, 1981: 343). She is further described as "engaged to a man whose name was Joseph." The translation "engaged" used here in the NRSV is inappropriate. It suggests to the reader our modern custom of pre-marriage engagement, though that is nothing like the ancient custom of betrothal. It is anachronistic to assume that "betrothal" is akin to our notion of "engagement" before marriage. Marriages in antiquity were between extended families, not individuals, and were parentally arranged. Marriage contracts required extensive negotiation in order to ensure that families of equal status were being joined and that neither took advantage of the other. In Middle Eastern villages even today such contracts are negotiated by the two mothers, but require ratification by each family patriarch. A village would be involved as well. The signing of the contract by the village leader, witnessed by the whole community, sealed the agreement and made it binding (Malina-Rohrbaugh, 1992: 288-289).

The fact that Mary is referred to as a virgin and betrothed means that she has exchanged consent with Joseph but has not yet been taken to live with him. Jewish matrimonial procedure consisted of two steps: a formal exchange of consent before witnesses (Mal 2:14) and the subsequent taking of the bride to the groom's family home (Mt 25:1-13). While the term marriage is sometimes used to designate the second step, in terms of legal implications it would be more properly applied to the first step. The consent, usually entered into when the girl was between twelve and thirteen years old, would constitute a legally ratified marriage in our terms, since it gave the young man rights over the girl. She was henceforth his wife (notice the term *gynē*, "wife," in Mt 1:20,24), and any infringement on his marital rights could be punished as adultery. Yet the wife continued to live at her own family home, usually for about a year. Then took place the formal transferal or taking of the bride to the husband's family home where he assumed her support. It is clear, explicitly in Matthew and implicitly in Luke, that Joseph and Mary are in the stage of matrimonial procedure between the two steps (Brown, 1977: 123-124).

Mary holds no official position among the people, she is not described as "righteous" in terms of observing the Torah, and her experience does not take place in a cultic setting. She is among the most powerless people in her society: she is young in a world that values age; female in a world ruled by men; poor in a stratified economy. Furthermore, she has neither husband nor child to validate her existence. That she should have found "favor with God" and be "highly gifted" (verse 28) shows Luke's understanding of God's activity as surprising and often paradoxical, almost always reversing human expectations (Johnson, 1991: 39). Based on studies made of that period, we can say with relative certainty that Mary was a peasant woman, probably illiterate, as most women of her time were because opportunity to study scripture was a man's domain. She was occupied with domestic chores of village life and her religious observance centered on her home. Thus from the perspective of the unschooled, poor women from *barrios* (Filipino word for "village"), Mary was someone with whom they could identify in their daily hard work. Re-read from the perspective of poor and homeless people, of the rejected and the marginalized, Mary becomes a sister and companion to them with whom they can identify, a village woman who understands their poverty, a peasant woman who knows what it is to suffer from social oppression. She is one who knows the poverty of unfulfilled longings and in her emptiness is filled by God's promise. She is one who has been empowered by the Spirit to stand up and reclaim for herself and for all women the dignity of womanhood and personhood (Gallares, 1995: 276, 282).

Following his introduction of Zechariah and Elizabeth, and the accounts of the annunciation to Zechariah and Elizabeth's response to her conception, Luke directs our attention from the home and concerns of this priestly couple to a virgin, Mary, in Galilee. This introduction of Mary stands in stark contrast to the expectations that we have built by the time we reach this narrative segment. In introducing Zechariah and Elizabeth in Lk 1:5-7, Luke had devoted considerable attention to issues of status, piling up data in an economic way to accentuate their socio-religious status, their purity (Douglas, 1966) and their righteousness. In so many ways Luke shows himself to be a person of the honor/shame-oriented culture of the Mediterranean world. Having accentuated these cultural values so transparently in the opening account of his birth narrative, we expect more of the same when the scene changes. Indeed, even Joseph, who appears infrequently in Luke's infancy narrative and has almost no active role at all, is characterized by his enviable birthright (Lk 1:27, "of the house of David"; Green, 1992: 461-462, 464). The stature of important persons in Luke-Acts is communicated by special note of their pedigree, both kin and clan, thus extending the honor and identity of the ancestors to the contemporary individual (Malina-Neyrey, 1991: 86). This is true of Elizabeth, Zechariah, and Joseph. Why not Mary?

Mary is portrayed as a young girl, not yet or recently having achieved puberty, in an insignificant town in a radically mixed region. Joseph is a son of David, but Mary has not yet joined his household and thus has no current claims on his inherited status (Malina-Neyrey, 1991: 61). Mary's family is not mentioned. Indeed, she is not introduced in any way that would recommend her to us as particularly noteworthy or deserving of honor. It is significant that Mary is introduced without a set of respectable credentials corresponding to the detailed social and religious presentation of Zechariah and Elizabeth in Lk 1:5-7 (Seim, 1994: 203). In light of the care with which other characters are introduced and portrayed as women and men of status in Lk 1–2, this is remarkable. Mary's insignificance seems to be Luke's primary point in his introduction of her here. The subsequent characterization of Mary as a "relative" of Elizabeth in Lk 1:36 does not in any way transform this image. *Suggenis* is sufficiently vague not necessarily implying anything about Mary's participation in the priestly line for which Elizabeth is noted. With the onset of the interchange between Gabriel and Mary, the concern with status honor in Lk 1:26-27 will be further advanced (Green, 1992: 465-466).

Nothing is said of Mary's lineage or piety. Indeed, whereas

the piety of Elizabeth and Zechariah is told to the reader (Lk 1:6), the quite different piety of Mary is shown as the episode unfolds (Carroll, 1988: 41).

The narrator says nothing of what Mary is doing when Gabriel enters. Whereas Zechariah, if alone in the sanctuary, is still surrounded by the people at prayer, Mary is presented as physically alone. The narrative discourse on Mary is reduced to a minimum (Legrand, 1981: 73). Mary is not named immediately, but is referred to twice by the narrator as "a virgin" to prepare for what is to come in verses 34-35. Whereas in Mt 1:22-23 the reference to Isa 7:14 is explicit, here in Luke it is not. Some scholars (Laurentin, Schürmann, Marshall) consider Lukan dependence on the Isaian text probable, but others, e.g., Fitzmyer (1981: 336) reject it, saying that the description of Mary in Lk 1:27 is far closer to Deut 22:23, "If there is a young woman, a virgin already engaged to be married...," while others agree that there is no way of knowing that Luke was drawing upon Isa 7:14 (Brown, 1977: 300). Joseph too is mentioned, but only as a name and in terms of status as a Davidide, and he will play no role at all in the episode (Coleridge, 1993: 54-55). The phrase "of the house of David" prepares for Lk 1:32-33, where Jesus will be related to the Davidic dynasty.

Verse 28: And he came to her and said,
         "Greetings, favored one!
         The Lord is with you."

The greeting is ambiguous because it is not immediately clear what either, "greetings, favored one!" (NRSV, RSV: "Hail, O favored one") or "the Lord is with you" might mean. Evidence of this is the diversity of opinion among scholars. On *chaire* ("greetings, hail"), some claim that it is best understood as the standard Greek salutation and should, therefore, be translated as "Hail!" or something similar. Others argue for a more theologically charged sense, and for a literal translation ("Rejoice") which would suggest a link with the Old Testament Daughter of Zion (see especially Zech 3:14). But, socially speaking, Mary's virginal status implies a situation in which a pregnancy provides neither happiness nor blessing, but an unseemly moral and legal offence. In fact, in Matthew's version of the story, the socially problematic element in the event is explicitly dealt with. In keeping with Matthew's focus on Joseph, the social scandal is reflected as his problem (Mt 1:19; Seim, 1994: 203-204). Therefore, the interpretation of the greeting, *chaire*, as an allusion to Zech 3:14-17 is criticized (Brown, 1977: 320-324; Carroll, 1988: 43 note 22). On *kecharitōmenē* ("favored one") some have argued that it should be understood as referring to Mary's future role as mother of the messiah, while others see it as referring rather to a pre-existing state of grace in Mary herself, with one scholar favoring the translation, "Rejoice to have been transformed by grace" (de la Potterie).

Though greeted as "favored one," Mary herself is not named by Gabriel. She is greeted not so much in her own right, but in terms of what God has done for her, in a way that paradoxically focuses on both God and her. Some manuscripts "import" Elizabeth's words from Lk 1:42, "blessed are you among women," as a way of dealing with a text considered too elliptical and wanting therefore to focus more on Mary and her privilege than on God and his grace as the narrator does (Coleridge, 1993: 55-56). This is almost certainly a scribal borrowing from Lk 1:42, but it has influenced the "Hail Mary" prayer (Brown, 1977: 288).

While the phrase "the Lord is with you," assures Mary of God's support, it does not mean that the Lord Jesus is within Mary's womb. It is a formula used with reference to a person chosen by God for a special purpose in salvation history. In fact, this is a frequently used Old Testament phrase (e.g., Gen 26:24; 28:15; Ex 3:15; Acts 18:9-10), but it occurs as a greeting only in two places in the Old Testament, namely, Ruth 2:4 and Judg 6:12. Obviously, "Lord" is here to be understood as God.

Verse 29: But she was much perplexed by his words
          and pondered what sort of greeting this might be.

At first, verse 29 seems very much like verse 12, again a standard element of the Old Testament annunciation scheme; and linguistically there is the link between "he was terrified" (*etarachthē*) in verse 12 and "she was much perplexed" (*dietarachthē*, the compound adding intensity without changing the sense) in verse 29. Disturbance is part of the literary pattern of an angelic annunciation of birth. Yet the similarities become less impressive upon closer scrutiny. First, Zechariah was upset by what he *saw*, and Mary is upset by what she *hears*. Secondly, the report of the reaction is less stereotyped. Where verse 12 mentioned the fear which is standard Old Testament reaction of the human being to the irruption of heaven, verse 29 refers instead to puzzlement: "she pondered what sort of greeting this might be." This suggests that Mary's problem is not the apparition, as it was for Zechariah, but the greeting and what it meant. Mary's reaction is less a reaction to a theophany than a need for clarification (Legrand, 1981: 74).

Verses 30-33: (30) The angel said to her,
                     "Do not be afraid, Mary,
                     for you have found favor with God.
               (31) And now, you will conceive in your womb
                     and bear a son,
                     and you will name him Jesus.
               (32) He will be great,
                     and will be called the Son of the Most High,
                     and the Lord will give him
                         the throne of his father David.
               (33) He will reign over the house of Jacob forever,
                     and of his kingdom there will be no end."

"Do not be afraid" is a standard Old Testament reassurance given by heavenly visitors (Gen 15:1; Dan 10:12,19). We found it already in Lk 1:13. Now the angel addresses Mary by her name. The expression "to find favor" is also an Old Testament expression found, e.g., in Gen 6:9LXX, "Noah found favor in the sight of the Lord." It explains the real sense of "favored one" in verse 28.

As in verses 13-17, Gabriel announces a birth and then offers an interpretation of it framed in language drawn from the Scripture. As in the previous passage, understanding comes from looking backwards. In contrast to what was said of Zechariah, nothing is said of Mary's desire to be the mother of the Davidic messiah nor of any prayer on her part. That nothing is said of any desire or prayer on Mary's part leaves the initiative firmly with God. This is further emphasized by the three references to God in verses 30-33. In verse 30, Gabriel specifies what was not said in "favored one," that Mary has found favor *with God*; and in verse 32 it is said of Jesus that he will be called "son of the Most High" and that "the Lord God" will give him the throne of David. God is named in three different ways to ensure that he appears as prime mover (Coleridge, 1993: 58-59).

Verses 31-33 represent the traditional pattern for the biblical annunciation of birth: pregnancy, birth, name giving, future of the child. The angel introduces the annunciation proper by "and now" (literally, "and behold," see above verse 20). "You will conceive in your womb" is based on Old Testament accounts, for instance, Gen 16:11, "Now you have conceived and shall bear a son"; Judg 13:3-5: "you shall conceive and bear a son." [It is not indicated *when* Mary will conceive]. Likewise the name giving has many counterparts in the Old Testament, for instance, Gen 16:11, "you shall call him Ishmael."

As in the case of John, the child's name is given by God. The fact that the mother is to confer the name has been taken as an indication that the child will have no human father (the father normally being the one to confer the name), but in view of Gen 16:11, where practically the same words are addressed to Hagar, the mistress of Abraham, the point cannot be pressed (Marshall, 1978: 67).

Verses 32-33 describe the role that the child born to Mary is to play. What Gabriel says echoes the great Davidic covenant of 2 Sam 7 in which King David is promised that his throne and kingdom would be established forever. The following parallels have been listed:

2 Sam	Luke
7:9 "a great name"	1:32 "he will be great"
7:13 "the throne of his kingdom"	1:32 "throne of his father David"

7:14 "he will be my son"	1:32 "son of the Most High"
7:16 "your house and your kingdom"	1:33 "he will reign over the house of Jacob forever."

These parallels indicate that Luke sees in the birth of Jesus the fulfillment of the hope that a descendant of David would some day arise, as promised in 2 Sam 7:9-16; Isa 9:1-7; 11:1-3. There are also interesting parallels with Ps 89:26-36 (Strauss, 1995: 88-89). Although there was no uniform concept of messiah, the most popular view was that he would be a "son of David" who would liberate Israel (C.A. Evans, 1990: 25-26).

There is nothing exceptional in the way the Davidic messiah's coming is announced, even if the choice of a woman of un-distinguished provenance as mother seems odd. The announce-ment is couched in traditional language, and Mary has already been introduced as a woman betrothed to a Davidide. There is nothing, then, to suggest that a Davidic messiah matching customary expectation will not be born in the usual way. For all the diversity of Jewish expectation, it was never believed or suggested that the messiah – Davidic or otherwise – would be born in any other than the normal way (Coleridge, 1993: 58-59). There was nothing in Jewish expectation to suggest that the Davidic messiah would be God's Son in the sense of having been conceived without a male parent (Brown, 1977: 312).

Jesus becomes subject only in verse 33 with the reference to his rule: "he will reign." The revelation concerns Jesus, but God and Mary take the leading parts in the action described by the oracle. God has taken the initiative by approaching Mary; she will now conceive, give birth to and name Jesus. Once that has happened God will again intervene and give to Jesus the throne of David; and only then will Jesus assume the initiative. John will be great because of what he *does*, Jesus because of what he *is*. John is defined by his action. Jesus is the ultimate act of God, resuming and bringing an end to all human action (Legrand, 1981: 78). Gabriel has announced the "what" of Jesus' role and identity but has said nothing of the "how," so that the reader now faces the question, "how will this happen?" (Coleridge, 1993: 60).

Lk 1:26-38 has distinct political overtones which may not have been sufficiently perceived. This political trend is particularly explicit in verses 32-33. "Throne," "reign," "kingdom," "davidic lineage" are terms clearly belonging to political language. In this context "Son of the Most High" is also likely to be taken in the messianic sense. In fact, it is the whole background of Jewish royal messianism which is evoked in the first part of the angel's message. What are we to make of it? Does messianic language retain its obvious political significance in the context of the annunciation and of the Third Gospel? Or are we to presume that, in its Christian context, it has evaporated into mere religious significance? (Legrand, 1989: 1).

The words of Gabriel resume the main lines of the great messianic prophecies of the Old Testament, beginning with the oracle of Nathan to David in 2 Sam 7:14-16. Similar words can be found in Isa 9:6-7:

> For a child has been born for us, a son given to us;...
> and he is named...
> His authority shall grow continually,
> and there shall be endless peace
> for the throne of David and his kingdom.
> He will establish and uphold it
> with justice and with righteousness
> from this time onward and forevermore.

Almost every word of Gabriel's message resumes a term of the great messianic prophecy of Isaiah. There can be no doubt that Isaiah's messianic oracles implied a definite political programme. The messiah, anointed of the Lord, was to be a king to whom a set prophetical programme was assigned. But it is commonly presupposed, at least implicitly, in our Christian reading of the Bible that the earthly messianic perspectives of the Old Testament have been "spiritualized" in the New Testament, that the

Davidic themes of the "throne" and of the "reign" have become mere metaphors of a spiritual salvation, that Jesus' Davidic sonship, in short, that the message of the annunciation is basically "christological." The very shift from the terminology of "messianism" to that of "christology" is significant and reveals the implicit but quite effective "spiritualization" of the perspectives (e.g., Laurentin, 1957: 72-73). But theologically, there is little to support the idea that Jesus' divine sonship would neutralize his human ancestry and the promises attached to it. Exegetically as well, it would be quite a rash hypothesis to presume a priori that verses 32-33 have no consistence of their own, that they are nothing but an insignificant backdrop to verse 35, a gratuitous concession to the early Christian interest in the Old Testament formulas (Legrand, 1989: 2-3).

A study of the form of annunciation and of the "two stage christology" [that is, a christology in which Jesus is introduced in two stages] of Lk 1:32-35 as well as the different language of Lk 1:32-33 and 1:35 respectively (Legrand, 1989: 3-5) lead to the conclusion that if the two parts of the christological introduction of Lk 1:32-35 that is, Lk 1:32-33 and 1:35, are substantially synonymous and have analogical contents, they differ very much by the language in which they are couched.[But the presence of a two stage christology here has been seriously questioned; Strauss, 1995: 92]. Verses 32-33 reflect a Judeo-Christian language by their contents, which is made up of references to Old Testament texts, and their style, which is strongly Semitic. While this points to a Judeo-Christian background for Lk 1:32-33, the style of verse 35 suggests a Hellenistic background. The most important parallel to Lk 1:35 is Rom 1:3-4 (Strauss: 1995: 91-92). If the perspective of verse 35 is specifically christological, that of verses 32-33 is rather messianic. It is true that etymologically the two terms are synonymous since "messiah" says in Hebrew (*meshiah*) what "Christ" says on the basis of Greek (*Christos* = anointed). But concrete theological usage has diverged to the extent that "christology" has come to express Jesus' identity in terms of theological attributes (here holiness, divine sonship and relation with the Holy Spirit), whereas messianism has kept its original Old Testament reference to an expectation of concrete salvation and a programme of liberation of oppressed people or country.

This is exactly the image presented by Lk 1:32-33 where one has perceived "a politico-nationalistic tonality" (Berger, 1973-1974: 29). This is right. The statement does indeed retain the earthly and national implications of the original promise (Strauss, 1995: 89). The present-day Christian reader often makes an unconscious transposition of the text and assumes that words like "throne" and "kingdom," "David" and "house of Jacob" are mere "themes" that have to be taken as symbols of "spiritual" realities and have lost any political value and nationalistic reference to Israel that they might have had originally. Is this transposition legitimate? Are we entitled to assume that a Christian context is incompatible with any reference to Israel? Or does Luke's theology really imply that messianic hopes have to be absorbed and lose their consistence when put in contact with christological faith? (so Schürmann, 1969: 48). Though verse 35 exceeds traditional Jewish expectations, it does not leave the context of the Davidic promises. Rather, the close contextual link between verses 32-33 and 35 indicates that Jesus' divine sonship serves as proof that he is indeed the heir to the throne (Strauss, 1995: 93-94).

The christology of Lk 1:32-33 has been attributed to the same Judeo-Christian milieu as the Magnificat and the Benedictus, which represent a Christian faith that throbs with all the political awareness of classical Old Testament and Judaic messianism. It reflects a faith that identifies with the anguish and expectations of Israel engaged as it is in a concrete history, in the midst of various political, sociological and religious crises. This Judeo-Christian faith could not express its attachment to Jesus the Messiah without reference to the burning issues of the day (Legrand: 1989: 7-11).

A careful analysis of Lk 1:32-35 (Legrand, 1989: 12-18) leads to the conclusion that by putting together the messianic formula of the Judeo-Christian church (Lk 1:32-33) and the christological confession of the Hellenistic Christians (Lk 1:35), Luke did not intend to oppose them or to have one replacing the other. He combined them and intended them to be taken in a dialectic relation as he wanted the two sections of the church at that time to relate to each other in dialogue (Legrand, 1989: 19).

Verse 34: Mary said to the angel,
         "How can this be, since I am a virgin?"

In view of her engagement to Joseph, Mary's question may come as a surprise. The question seems odd, but the preceding oracle itself has been odd in several ways. If the child is to be born in the course of the coming marriage with Joseph, why then did Gabriel not mention him? Why did he make the announcement to Mary rather than to Joseph, who is, after all, the descendant of David? And why to a woman who is engaged but not yet married? The Old Testament does mention annunciations to women, to Hagar in Gen 16:11 and Samson's mother in Judg 13:3, but there is no precedent for an annunciation to an unwed virgin. In so far as there is no precedent, Mary is more like Abraham [a parallel has been drawn between Mary's faith in Lk 1:26-38 and the faith of Abraham in Rom 4], even though no explicit reference is made to Abraham anywhere in this pericope. It is not that the promise of verses 30-33 is strange. What is strange is that it should be made to Mary (Coleridge, 1993: 61).

Excursus: The Virginal Conception

Questions about Mary's words in Lk 1:34 and the virginal conception in Luke in general have been the subject of extensive scholarly research mainly because of several ambiguities in the text. Luke never explicitly states that Mary will conceive as a virgin. The only suggestion of a virginal conception is found in Mary's questioning response in Lk 1:34. The seeming unsuitability of these words from the mouth of a woman engaged to be married has led to a controversy about whether Mary here expressed a vow of perpetual virginity or whether she was simply expressing confusion over how she could conceive a child prior to her actual marriage. The interpretation that favors a vow of perpetual virginity has been popular among a great number of Catholic exegetes, at least until recently. But one seldom hears this view expressed in more recent scholarship, and many scholars consider the idea of a vow of perpetual virginity in the first century as an anachronism. As we will see below, the angel's response to Mary's objection does not provide clear guidance in this matter, since this response itself contains a certain measure of ambiguity. The combination of the oddity of Mary's words and the ambiguity of the angel's response seems to put the virginal conception into question (Landry, 1995: 65-66). In light of this realization, it has been suggested that the present Lukan account can be read as not dealing with a virginal conception. "When this account is read in and for itself – without the overtones of the Matthean annunciation to Joseph – every detail of it could be understood of a child to be born to Mary in the usual way" (Fitzmyer, 1973: 55). Mary's question is then understood not as a substantive objection but as a literary device. The question is not necessarily intended to convey the idea of a virginal conception or to express Mary's thoughts at the time in any way, but only gives the angel an opportunity to speak about the character of the child to be born. Besides, Gabriel's reply in Lk 1:35, speaking about the Holy Spirit coming down upon and overshadowing Mary, can be understood in a figurative way as speaking about Jesus' special relation to God, without implying the absence of human paternity.

While agreeing that Mary's question is not a substantive one but a literary device, others dispute the claim that Lk 1:34 can be read as not dealing with a virginal conception. The primary argument is that the parallelism between the conception/birth of John and the conception/birth of Jesus is decisive on this point. It has been pointed out that numerous details of the parallelism between Jesus and John in Lk 1–2 are obviously designed to show that Jesus is greater than John (Brown, 1974: 360-363). Now this build-up of the superiority of Jesus would fail completely if John the Baptist was conceived in an extraordinary way and Jesus in a natural manner. But it would be continued perfectly if Jesus was virginally conceived, since this would be something completely unattested in previous manifestations of God's power (Brown, 1977: 300-301). This argument caused Fitzmyer to change his mind and return to the more traditional position that Luke does indeed present the virginal conception of Jesus (Fitzmyer, 1981: 338).

One possible source of the virginal conception tradition is usually not mentioned in polite company or in polite books: the possibility that Jesus was at the very least conceived or even born out of wedlock. This idea, which causes shock in the pious and glee in the impious, might be passed over in silence if it were not for the fact that the illegitimacy of Jesus has been proposed as a viable thesis by a few recent scholars. Some Christians might object to any consideration of this theory as an insult to Christian faith. Other Christians might object, in return, that Christian faith proclaims the shocking scandal of the utter "emptying" (cf. Phil 2:7) of the Son of God into our mortal flesh, even to the depths of condemnation as a criminal, mockery and torture, and finally death on a cross. In light of all the horrors that Jesus experienced in his passion and death, illegitimacy could be considered a minor aspect of the "emptying" (*kenosis*). More to the point, though, the method adopted by the quest for the historical Jesus demands that a scholar prescinds from, but does not deny, what is held by faith. If some researchers seriously propose that Jesus' birth was illegitimate, the proposal must be examined seriously. Actually, the charge of illegitimacy is not new. In *Against Celsus* (about A.D. 248), Origen reports that Celsus had heard, from a Jew, a story about Jesus' illegitimacy (Meier, 1991: 222-229).

A new interpretation of Mary's question in Lk 1:34 has recently been proposed (Schaberg, 1987). It addresses the long debated question of why a betrothed woman would object to the announcement that she will become pregnant. Since she has already entered the first stage of marriage, why does Mary not assume that the conception will occur when she is taken to Joseph's home – the "home-taking" – and begins to have relations with him? It is suggested that Mary's objection does not at all question the physical impossibility of a virgin giving birth; rather it questions the possibility of the son of God being born illegitimately to a lowly, humiliated woman who has been made pregnant by a man who is not her husband. Seizing upon the ambiguity of the language of Mary's question, Schaberg moves away from the sense usually understood by interpreters here of the question connoting "How *can* this be, since I have not had sexual relations with any man?" instead translating this phrase: "How *will* this be, since I do not have sexual relations with *my husband?*" The translation "how will this be" is preferable because "it does not prepare the reader to think immediately of an event that is considered physically impossible" (Schaberg, 1987: 84). The translation of *andra* as "husband" is preferable because the reader is thus "alerted to the possibility that the conception will be by someone other than Mary's husband" (Ibid: 85).

Irrespective of whether the proposed translation is acceptable or not, the strength of this proposal is that it takes on the question of *the narrative logic of Mary's question* in a straightforward way. In the present proposal it is clear that the character of Mary has a good reason for asking the question in Lk 1:34. Mary assumes that the pregnancy will occur instantly, but she knows that she will not begin to have intercourse with her husband for quite some time. Therefore, she assumes that the angel is speaking of some other man and asks, "How will this be, since I do not have sexual relations with my husband?" In this way the question does indeed make some sense in the narrative.

The question as to why a betrothed virgin like Mary would object to the idea that she will become pregnant is one that is actually circumvented by many scholars. Rejecting a "psychological" solution – that is, one that attempts to discern what Mary was thinking when she asked the question – they opt for a "literary" solution, namely, that Luke has Mary ask the question for no reason other than to give the angel further opportunity to speak of the child's identity (Brown, 1977: 308; Davis III, 1982: 221-222). "The statement is only meant as an introduction to verse 35" (Schweizer, 1984: 29). To this it is objected that these authors deliberately avoid "psychological" solutions because they assume that all such solutions concern the psychology of the *historical* Mary, which they consider unattainable on the basis of Luke's text. However, it must be pointed out that, although the psychology of the historical Mary is not a concern for the reader, reconstructing the *psychology of the characters who appear in the narrative* is often an essential part of the reading. "The literary versus the psychological are in this case false alternatives. The literary solution here *is* the psychological solution...Let me repeat: I am not speaking of the psychology of the historical Mary, but of the psychology of Mary, a character in the narrative" (Schaberg, 1987: 87-88).

Another reason why the search for the narrative logic of Mary's question is at times considered irrelevant is that the "objecting question" is part of the *form* of the annunciation narrative and occurs in Luke's text for that reason. But this is rejected on the ground that "the question is an essential part of the form *and* of the story line" (Schaberg, 1987: 87). In other words, it is denied that the use of formal patterns would have allowed or obliged authors to include material in their narratives that disrupts the narrative logic of the story. It is a fundamental assumption of literary criticism that even when formal patterns can be discovered, the story should make sense as a story to the reader, and the reader should make sense of the story insofar as this is possible (Landry, 1995: 70). The theory being considered makes sense of Mary's question as an intelligible question addressed by one character to another in terms of the logic of the story. The question that remains is whether the theory presented above makes the *best possible* literary sense out of the narrative.

Is there any support for the theory that the narrative logic of the passage suggests that Mary is impregnated by a man other than her husband? It is claimed that this theory finds support in both the Visitation (Lk 1:39-45) and the Magnificat (Lk 1:46-55).

Firstly, it is noted that Mary went to visit Elizabeth "with haste," a phrase which, linguistically, sometimes has overtones not of eagerness but of terror, alarm, fright, and anxiety. It is suggested that "with haste" (*meta spoudēs*) "may be a clue... that points toward a situation of violence and/or fear in connection with Mary's pregnancy, or at least the idea that she is depicted as reacting with inner disturbance to her pregnancy" (Schaberg,

1987: 90). The implication is, of course, that Mary is frightened because the pregnancy was brought about by seduction or by a man other than her husband (Landry, 1995: 71). Secondly, an elaborate argument is constructed for the idea that the Magnificat supports an illegitimate conception, since it contains several alleged allusions to the law concerning the seduction or rape of a betrothed virgin in Deut 22:23-27, and because it presents Mary as someone who has been humiliated. It must be admitted that the general tone of the Magnificat as a song of personal and social liberation, combined with the curious use of *tapeinōsis* in Lk 1:48, does seem to support the thesis and provide the strongest evidence for an illegitimate conception. Certainly the Magnificat seems truly appropriate only in the mouth of a character who has experienced injustice and justice, oppression and vindication. The appropriateness of the hymn is seen in the hypothesis that Mary had been violated and made pregnant, but that she had been vindicated by God, causing her child to be recognized as God's son and Messiah. Particularly trenchant is Mary's use of *tapeinōsis* in Lk 1:48 where she states that God "has regarded the low estate (*tapeinōsin*) of his handmaiden" (RSV; NRSV: "the lowliness of his servant"). It is argued that this term usually means not "low estate" or "humble station," but "humiliation" (Schaberg, 1987: 97). It is pointed out that theological explanations about Mary's humility and humbleness are unconvincing. The idea that she is "humiliated" because she is a virgin is also unconvincing. It is true that virginity was not valued generally, but in Mary's case, that of a betrothed girl, the circumstances were different. It was certainly nothing to be ashamed of, but rather showed that her father had raised her correctly and afforded her the proper protection. The hypothesis under discussion contends that Mary's "humiliation" stems from the fact that she has been raped or seduced by a man other than her betrothed.

As to the contention that the step parallelism of the birth stories requires that Jesus' birth be superior to John's, and thus that an even greater miracle be present at the conception of Jesus than at the conception of John, it is argued that the principle is correct, but that Brown's application of it is not. "What is 'greater' in the case of Jesus is not the miraculous manner of conception, but God's overcoming of the deeper humiliation" (Schaberg, 1987: 102-103). Here ends this aspect of Schaberg's discussion of the infancy narratives.

Some *critical observations* may be called for. In the silences of the infancy narratives of Matthew and Luke, Schaberg discovers a basis for her claim that these were originally "not about a miraculous conception" but an "illegitimate conception." Schaberg adduces good evidence that Matthew may have acknowledged the tradition. But Luke writes of an illegitimate conception "with much less directness than Matthew" (Schaberg, 1987: 86). Interpreting his narrative is even more a matter of reading silences. Reading silences is as much dangerous as difficult (Dietrich, 1989: 208). In fact, Schaberg's study is highly speculative. There is no doubt that her interpretation is possible, but the question remains *whether the texts demand such an interpretation* (below we will present a more acceptable interpretation). One problem concerns the intentions of Matthew and Luke. If these two evangelists intended to pass on the illegitimacy tradition, as Schaberg holds, why is it almost entirely masked over, especially by Luke? Furthermore, why is it that there is no evidence that any early Christian read the New Testament infancy narratives in the way Schaberg proposes? The absence of early Christian evidence that the narratives were ever read in the way Schaberg proposes is indeed most problematic (Anderson, 1989: 239). As for the Lukan account, one wonders why, given Luke's emphasis on the inclusion of social outcasts, he would not have highlighted rather than covered up the supposed scandalous origins of Jesus as the ultimate example of the overcoming of all social boundaries in Jesus. Schaberg claims that within the patriarchal structure and mindset in which the gospels were written, the illegitimate conception of Jesus was a scandal so deep that it simply had to be repressed (Schaberg, 1987: 196). But how is this tradition any more scandalous than a crucified Messiah? (Reid, 1990: 364-365).

This leads us to another weakness of the theory proposed. It manifests an almost total unawareness of the fact that the story in the gospels is taking place in a *distinctive cultural area*, that is, the first century, Eastern Mediterranean. In the scenarios Schaberg describes we find individualistic, psychologically oriented agents, much like Americans. There is no definition of that cultural form called "paternity"; no definition of Mediterranean marriage in general and the marriage pattern of major groups in the area; hence no way to duly grasp the significance of illegitimacy in that time and place.

Schaberg has to "admit that the fact that we cannot prove that any early Christians read the Infancy Narratives of Matthew and Luke in the way I have proposed their author intended is a major objection against my interpretation. Could these authors have failed so completely in their efforts to communicate the tradition to their early readers? Could the early Christians have failed so completely to understand an important aspect of their narratives? How could such failure be explained?" (Schaberg, 1987: 193). Perhaps there was no failure, but simply a form of thinking deviant and odd from a U.S. and Northern European perspective: since Jesus was raised from the dead he must have been of divine birth. While there is perhaps no direct dependency, the Qu'ran, so redolent of Luke here, offers another example of the sort of Semitic, Eastern Mediterranean form of reasoning present in the gospel accounts: that Jesus, who did not die and who will come again, was born of God's spirit by the Virgin Mary (*Sura* 3 and 19 tells us why and how; Malina, 1988:118-119).

So it seems that Schaberg's theory does not make the best possible literary sense out of the narrative. Our goal here is to use the principles of literary criticism and a construct of an ancient Eastern Mediterranean reader to make as much sense of the annunciation account as possible (Landry, 1995: 72-75).

(1) A first question about the narrative logic of the annunciation to Mary is this: What is the meaning of Mary's question itself? What precisely is she saying in Lk 1:34? When the reader first confronts Mary's question and ponders its logic in the narrative, the reader is likely to conclude that Mary is objecting to the announcement of the birth on the basis of her virginity (contra Schaberg). There are several reasons for this.

First, when Mary's character is introduced in Lk 1:27, the narrator tells us *twice* that she is a virgin (*parthenos*). The double use, one could even say emphasis, of Mary as *parthenos* (Lk 1:27 and 34) is the most impressive piece of evidence for the influence of Isa 7:14 in this section since it does reflect the term found in Isa 7:14LXX. However, by itself, it could also reflect merely the adoption of traditional material without serving to emphasize specifically the fulfillment of Isa 7:14. After all, if the traditional material had it that Mary was a *parthenos*, what other term would Luke use? (Bock, 1987: 61). This can be emphasized because it is intrusive commentary by the narrator. The fact that the narrator finds it important to give us this information, and especially to *repeat* this information, can only mean that it is important for the understanding of the story. Readers would remember it when trying to figure out the logic of Lk 1:34. Just as the narrator had prepared the reader to understand Zechariah's objection in Lk 1:18 by indicating the couple's advanced age in Lk 1:17, so also does the narrator prepare the reader for Mary's objection in Lk 1:34 by indicating her status in Lk 1:27. The parallels between the annunciation stories are crucial (Brown, 1974: 361-362).

Moreover, there are several reasons for believing that Mary *as a literary character* objects to the announcement of birth because she considers this a physical impossibility. This is something that Schaberg wants to avoid: she translates Lk 1:34 in such a way that the reader is not "prejudiced" to think immediately of an event that is physically impossible. What she does not consider is that there may be literary reasons for the reader to think just this. A first reason is that this annunciation seems to parallel very closely the one given to Zechariah in Lk 1:5-25, where Zechariah had objected on the basis of physical impossibility: he and his wife were "advanced in years" – that is, Elizabeth was beyond childbearing age (Landry, 1995: 72-73).

Maybe this is the right place to more accurately compare the annunciations to Zechariah and to Mary. One thing is clear: Mary needs to know more if the comparison with Zechariah's unbelief and Mary's belief is to work convincingly. For the strategy to succeed, the narrator must bring them to different decisions on the basis of the same knowledge. There can be no privileging of one character over the other. In a number of ways, Gabriel's speeches to Zechariah and Mary are similar. Both characters are told what is to happen (a son will be born to them); both are told who this son will be (precursor and messiah), and therefore why this is to happen; neither is told when the birth will be. On this point, Zechariah and Mary are on equal footing.

There is, however, one further point revealed to Zechariah but not to Mary – and that is how this is to happen. In verse 13, Zechariah is told that "your wife Elizabeth will bear you a son." John will be born by divine intervention, but in the normal way nonetheless. In verses 30-33, however, Gabriel says nothing of how the conception and birth will happen and makes no mention of Joseph. This means that at the end of verse 33, Mary knows less than Zechariah, and so does not have the same basis for a decision either to believe or disbelieve. Gabriel must say more if Mary is to come to the same point of knowledge as Zechariah. Because she knows less than Zechariah, hers is the voice not of doubt but of puzzlement. To say that, however, leaves unanswered the question of why the narrator chooses to insert Mary's question rather than have Gabriel continue the oracle uninterrupted.

The insertion of the question at verse 34 wins two advantages for the narrator. First, it insinuates into the narrative a sense of collaboration between Gabriel and Mary in the unfolding of revelation – which contrasts with the sense of confrontation between Gabriel and Zechariah in the first episode. Secondly, it serves as a technique of emphasis, with Mary focusing on what seems to be the insurmountable obstacle to the divine initiative, so that the proclamation of verse 35 will be all the more powerful. This is like the rhetoric of divine glorification in Old Testament narrative, where the difficulty of a proposed divine action is emphasized so that its successful performance will redound all the more to God's glory. The greater the difficulty, the greater the glory for God. In that sense here, Mary focusing on her own virginity is a way of focusing on God; and again the self-effacing narrator prefers to have one of the characters do the focusing.

From a consideration of the question as narrative strategy we turn now to a comparison with the question of Zechariah at the level of *form* and *meaning*. There is no agreement among the critics as to whether the two questions are identical, similar or totally unlike. Brown states that Zechariah's question "is not noticeably different from the objection Mary will pose in Lk 1:34" (Brown, 1977: 280). Others, however, see the difference as crucial. For example, Legrand states that "the two questions are less parallel than it appears" (Legrand, 1981: 78; compare Meynet, 1979: 154). And Meynet remarks that "Mary and Zechariah pose a question (Lk 1:18 and 34): in both cases the question is followed by its motivation introduced by 'for' or 'since'; but whereas Zechariah demands proof, Mary only asks about the 'how'" (Meynet, 1990: 143). But even if it is crucial, the difference is not immediately evident.

The first and most obvious difference between the two questions is their *form*. Where Zechariah asks, "by what shall I know this?" (literal translation), and goes on to mention his and Elizabeth's age, Mary asks, "how will this be?" (literal translation), and goes on to mention her virginity. For all their similarity, the difference between the two questions is more than superficial:

(1) Mary does not focus immediately upon herself, but upon "this," understood as heaven's initiative. This is in contrast with Zechariah who began with stressing his own need to know.

(2) The question asks not *whether*, but *how* – which presumes that what the angel has said will happen, with *estai* understood best and most simply as a future: what is promised will happen, and the question is how it will happen in the circumstances.

(3) Mary questions her own credentials (she is a virgin, literally, "I do not know man") rather than the messenger's credentials. She states a lack in herself rather than imply any lack on heaven's part.

(4) Rather than demanding to see, Mary simply states her inability to see. Hers is a statement of powerlessness rather than an attempt to seize a knowledge which might give her the initiative.

(5) Zechariah's question implied a failure of memory, whereas Mary's implies the memory that all other annunciations have been made to *married* people. Gabriel's oracle presumes a knowledge of Scripture on Mary's part. The narrator will amplify the sense of Mary's knowledge of the Scripture in the Magnificat.

We are now in a position to decide whether the two questions – and by further implication the two episodes – are parallel or not. A study of the differences between verses 18 and 34 suggests that Mary's question is not the dramatic equivalent to Zechariah's question in the first episode. Her question is not a moment of decision in the way that Zechariah's is. She is on the way to a decision that she will voice in verse 38, and part of her journey to that point is a puzzlement that is not the same as doubt. The different narrative function of the two questions means that the first two episodes, for all that they are superficially similar, are not really parallel (Coleridge, 1993: 62-65).

We return now to the discussion of the reasons for believing that Mary *as a literary character* objects to the announcement of birth because she considers this a physical impossibility.

A first reason is that – notwithstanding the differences – this annunciation parallels the one given to Zechariah in Lk 1:5-25, where Zechariah had objected on the basis of physical impossibility: he and his wife were advanced in years – that is, Elizabeth was beyond childbearing age.

Second, the angel compares Mary's situation to that of Elizabeth in Lk 1:36, "And now, your relative Elizabeth has also conceived a son; and this is the sixth month for her who was said to be barren." It seems likely that the angel would mention the pregnancy of Elizabeth only if there was some parallel between her pregnancy and Mary's, namely, that both would be considered physically impossible.

Third, there are the words of the angel in Lk 1:37. Following Mary's question, the angel explains to her how she will become pregnant and then concludes with the phrase: "For nothing will be impossible with God." Again it seems likely that the angel would only have used this phrase if he were speaking of something that is physically impossible, that is, a virginal conception. Certainly there is nothing "impossible" about a rape or seduction, nor is there anything "impossible" about God's vindicating a woman who has been raped or seduced.

(2) A second question about the narrative logic of the passage is this: Why would Mary as a character in the narrative make a statement like this? Even if she is a virgin, why would Mary object to the annunciation on that basis? Why should she not just assume that she would conceive when she is taken to Joseph's home and begins to have relations with him? After considering the various alternatives, it seems clear that an ancient reader would conclude that as a betrothed virgin, Mary objects because she assumes that the angel is telling her that she will become pregnant *almost immediately*, before she could possibly have sexual relations legally with her husband. With respect to the timing of Mary's pregnancy, there seem to be several alternatives. But the most important point in this regard is that if Mary objects to the angel's announcement because she assumes that this pregnancy will begin almost immediately, before she could possibly have sexual relations legally with her husband, she turns out to be right. "If we read Mary's question as one of surprise that she will conceive in the immediate future, rather than in a relatively distant future when she and Joseph will complete the home-taking, the continuation of the narrative indicates that her question is meant as the expression of a correct intuition. The pregnancy apparently is thought to take place in the interval between the annunciation to her and her visit to Elizabeth [since Mary is already pregnant when Elizabeth greets her]" (Schaberg, 1987: 88). Thus, when Mary questions the angel's announcement, she probably understands that this pregnancy will occur almost immediately and she objects almost certainly on the basis of her virginity, in effect saying, "How can I become pregnant now, since I will not have relations with my husband for some time?" In the context of the story Mary is to be understood as expecting an immediate fulfillment of the angel's oracle – as does happen in other call narratives, where the charismatic leader is invested with his charismatic power from the moment he is called (Soares Prabhu, 1977: 274-275). The length of

time before Mary would be taken to Joseph's home and would begin to have relations with him could have been as much as a year (Brown: 1977: 123). Mary clearly sees that, if she was to conceive by Joseph, then the angel would have waited until after the home-taking to present her with this annunciation. This is the most plausible explanation. Why would the angel appear to Mary and say, "You will conceive six to eight months from now"? Annunciations occur after or shortly before the beginning of the pregnancy they announce. Mary realizes this, as her question clearly shows.

(3) A third question about the narrative logic of the annunciation to Mary concerns the logic of the angel's response to Mary. Our answer to this question is that the angel's words make sense only if he is explaining how Mary can conceive in spite of the fact that she is a virgin. There are two parts to this argument.

First, a reading of the angel's response must be able to explain why the angel does not punish Mary for voicing an objection as he punished Zechariah. The reader is probably expecting the angel to rebuke and punish Mary for her doubting question. This is precisely what happened to Zechariah – he doubted the angel's promise of a son and was punished by being made mute. The second annunciation has paralleled the first so closely thus far that the reader probably expects the same reaction. However, the angel· does not punish Mary. He gives her an explanation of her situation and offers some proof for his reliability. In terms of the story's logic, there must be a reason that Zechariah is punished and Mary is not. The only possible reason is that Mary is told she will conceive as a virgin. Zechariah can fairly be punished because there is a precedent for his situation. This had happened before in the Old Testament. Abraham and Sarah also had a child when they were "advanced in years," and Zechariah should have remembered this (see above). On the other hand, there is no Old Testament precedent for a virginal conception. Thus if Mary objects to this, she cannot be faulted in the same way that Zechariah is and it is not surprising that she is not punished as he is. Conversely, if Mary's objection does not concern the unprecedented divine act of a virginal conception, then the question would remain as to why she is not punished or rebuked like Zechariah. The uniqueness of a virginal conception would give her an excuse, but without it she has no excuse and would seemingly be the beneficiary of an unfair double standard.

Second, the angel's words must be understood in such a way that they constitute a real response to Mary's question. It is evident that the answer of the angel to Mary's question creates certain problems for Schaberg. If it is not a response telling Mary how she will become pregnant in spite of her virginity (an idea that Schaberg's interpretation excludes), then what is the purpose of the angel's words? The angel's statements must be seen as almost completely non-responsive to Mary in Schaberg's interpretation.

On the other hand, if the angel is explaining to Mary how she can become pregnant despite her virginity, then his words about divine agency – vague as they are – make a considerable amount of sense. This is also true of the angel's reference to Elizabeth and the reassurance that nothing is impossible for God. These also make sense and serve as a response to Mary only if the angel is talking about a virginal conception.

(4) A fourth point about the narrative logic of the annunciation to Mary concerns her final response to the angel's words in Lk 1:38. The point here is that Mary's response in Lk 1:38 makes sense only if the episode concerns a virginal conception. It seems clear that when Mary says, "Here am I, the servant of the Lord; let it be with me according to your word," what she is doing is consenting to her situation. However, it is impossible to consent to rape or seduction. This element of consent makes it practically impossible for the reader of the Gospel of Luke alone to understand that this pregnancy is illegitimate and perhaps the result of violence done to Mary.

(5) Finally, there are issues of narrative logic that continue beyond the annunciation scene itself. The point is that subsequent scenes in the birth narrative make more sense if one understands Lk 1:26-38 as implying a virginal conception. After the annunciation, Mary proceeds "with haste" to Elizabeth's side out of eagerness, not fear or anxiety. Elizabeth provides confirmation that Mary has become pregnant prior to the home-taking and, significantly, congratulates her for her faith. Elizabeth's words of congratulation make sense only in light of a virginal conception, not in light of a rape or seduction. "It is to the virginal conception rather than to a natural conception that Elizabeth refers when she says to Mary: 'Fortunate is she who believed that the Lord's words to her would find fulfillment' (1:45). No belief would really be required if Mary was to conceive as any other young girl would conceive" (Brown, 1977: 301).

Concluding, we may say that *from a literary perspective*, Schaberg's interpretation may be preferable to that of Brown and Fitzmyer, because she focuses on the dynamics of the narrative rather than Luke's theological purposes and insists that her reading makes sense in terms of the story's logic. However, there are problems with Schaberg's reading. Her translation of Mary's question in Lk 1:34 is unlikely, and she has great difficulties dealing with both the angel's response in Lk 1:35-37 and Mary's final acquiescence in Lk 1:38. We have attempted to show that it is possible to preserve the narrative logic in another way. Luke mentions the fact that Mary is a virgin twice in his introduction of her character precisely because this will become important for the reader's understanding of the plot. When Mary questions the angel's announcement, she understands that this pregnancy will occur immediately and she objects on the basis of her virginity, in effect saying, "How can I become pregnant now, since I will not have relations with my husband for some time?" The angel's response naturally answers Mary's question, explaining to her how she will become pregnant even though she is a virgin, that is, by God's agency. Mary accepts her fate, showing that she believes that the promise made to her will be fulfilled and in fact confirms this belief by aligning herself with other women who have been so blessed, calling herself God's "handmaid," as did Hannah in 1 Sam 1. In the next scene Elizabeth congratulates Mary for believing that there would be a fulfillment of what was spoken to her from the Lord, and Mary goes on to celebrate her extraordinary pregnancy in a long speech. Nothing in the text precludes understanding it in this way (Landry, 1995: 78-79).

In conclusion, we would like to state clearly that the above discussion deals with a *literary* question, namely, whether Luke (and Matthew) wanted to affirm the virginal conception of Jesus. This should be distinguished from the *historical* question of whether the virginal conception actually took place. While we tend to answer the first question in the affirmative, there does not seem to be a truly satisfactory explanation of how early Christians happened upon the idea of a virginal conception (there are no clear extra-biblical parallels) — unless, of course, that is what really took place — which would be an answer to the second question — the totality of *scientifically controllable* evidence leaves an unresolved question (Brown, 1973: 21-68, especially 61-68). Maybe it should also be noted here that the emphasis of past interpretations of the virgin-birth has been the source of the development of excessive mariologies which has had both positive *and negative* effects on women's spirituality, self-understanding, and political empowerment. Luke, on the other hand, in his infancy narrative carefully establishes the foundation of his portrayal of Mary as model disciple (Gallares, 1995: 277-278).

Verse 35: The angel said to her,
> "The Holy Spirit will come upon you,
> and the power of the Most High will overshadow you;
> therefore the child to be born will be holy;
> he will be called Son of God."

If the oracle of Lk 1:30-33 was in some ways strange, the oracle of Lk 1:35 is quite extraordinary. Gabriel moves beyond all precedent to tell Mary that she will conceive the Davidic messiah by direct divine intervention. Because Mary needs to know more in order to decide, Gabriel tells her more; because she has not questioned his authority or reliability, Gabriel says nothing about himself (the narrator calls him simply "the angel"); because hers is the voice not of doubt but of puzzlement, Gabriel responds more graciously, less imperiously than in Lk 1:19-20.

For the second time, Gabriel mentions the Holy Spirit. The first time was in Lk 1:15, where it was said of John that "even before his birth he will be filled with the Holy Spirit." But now there is a difference. In the case of John, the Holy Spirit would help him to fulfill his allotted task, but in the case of Jesus the action of the Holy Spirit is presented more radically. The Holy Spirit will fill John once he is conceived, but Jesus will be conceived by the action of the Spirit. In the case of John, the Spirit *assists*; in the case of Jesus, the Spirit *enables* (Legrand, 1981: 79).

This might suggest that the focus of the narrative falls on Jesus, but that is not how the narrator has it. The parallelism of verse 35 focuses firmly upon heaven (Holy Spirit; the power of the Most High) and Mary (you; you). As throughout the episode, the movement is from God to Mary, with the downward thrust from heaven to earth captured by the threefold *epi-* (*epeleusetai, epi, episkiasei*), leaving a sense of Mary at this point as wholly passive (Coleridge, 1993: 66-67).

Luke's highly nuanced usage of *pneuma*, "Spirit," and *dunamis*, "power," supports the contention that he has crafted the parallel statements in verse 35 to accommodate the traditional account of the Spirit's creative role in the birth of Jesus with his own prophetic understanding of the Spirit. Consistent with his usage elsewhere, in verse 35 Luke associates "power" with the "Spirit" of the tradition because he has in mind a broad range of activities. The divine intervention alluded to in verse 35 is the source of Mary's pregnancy and her inspired proclamation in Lk 1:46-55.

The connection between the promise of the Spirit's presence in verse 35 and Mary's utterance in verses 46-55 can hardly be questioned. All three of the canticles attributed to men or women are proclaimed under the influence of the Spirit's activity (Zechariah – the Benedictus; Mary – the Magnificat; Simeon – the Nunc Dimittis), and the only major adult character who is not brought into direct relationship with the Spirit, Anna, does not utter an oracle. Furthermore, references to the appellation "holy" link verse 35 with the Magnificat (Lk 1:49).

Luke attributes the miraculous birth of Jesus to the activity of the Spirit because this accurately reflected early Christian tradition and it suited his structural scheme of paralleling John with Jesus. However, Luke sought to minimize the contrast between the creative role of the Spirit in the tradition and his own prophetic understanding of the Spirit. He accomplished this task by modifying the tradition, which associated the Spirit with biological conception in an explicit manner (see Mt 1:20). Luke's principal alteration involved the insertion of a reference to "power" paralleling "Spirit" into the narrative. Consistent with his usage elsewhere, this association of "power" with "Spirit" enabled Luke to relate the activity of the Spirit to Mary's prophetic proclamation in the Magnificat and, in a less direct way, to the miraculous birth (Menzies, 1991: 126-128).

But Jews who viewed the Spirit as the Spirit of prophecy did not for that reason eliminate the connection between Spirit and miraculous power. Luke received his view of the Spirit as Spirit of prophecy from Christian circles already all but universally committed to the view that the Spirit was experienced as the Spirit of prophecy, the power of preaching, *and* as miraculous power of, e.g., healing and exorcism. Luke has not significantly departed from this, and associates the Spirit with such power in Lk 1:35 as well as in 4:14; 4:18-19; 24:29; Acts 1:8 and 10:38 (Turner, 1991: 152). In Lk 1:35 the Spirit intervenes in order to mark the radical newness of the role of Jesus in the realization of salvation and to mark the uniqueness of his relationship to God (Mainville, 1990: 200).

The first occurrence of the title "Son of God" in Luke is related to the other, "Son of the Most High" (Lk 1:32). The title "Son of God" had a long history in the ancient Near East and could imply many things. Egyptian pharaohs were called "sons of God" because the sun-god Re was regarded as their father. In the Hellenistic and Roman worlds it was used of rulers. In the same worlds it was often applied to mythical heroes, *thaumatourgoi* (often called *theioi andres*, "divine men"), and famous historical persons (such as Plato, Pythagoras, Apollonius of Tyana, etc.). In such a context the use of this title implied divine favor, divine adoption, and even divine power, being conferred often at the time of enthronement.

As used of Jesus in the New Testament, it has been said to reflect this Hellenistic or Roman background. But one has also to consider the Old Testament and Jewish background of the title. In the Old Testament, "son(s) of God" is used with diverse nuances. It is a mythological title given to angels (Gen 6:2; Job 1:6; 2:1; Ps 29:1; Dan 3:25); a title of predilection for Israel in a collective sense (Ex 4:22; Deut 14:1; Isa 1:2; Wisd 18:13); a title of adoption for a Davidic king (2 Sam 7:14; Ps 2:7), for judges ([for angels?] Ps 82:6), or for the upright individual Jew (Sir 4:10; Wisd 2:18). The singular occurs mostly in post-exilic passages. What should be noted here is that the full title is never found in the Old Testament predicated directly of a future, expected messiah. The title is not synonymous with messiah, even when used of a king. Ps 2 speaks of Yahweh and "his anointed" and refers to the latter as "my Son," but that is at best a royal psalm, addressed to some historic king at his enthronement and not clearly "messianic" in the future sense.

In Palestinian Judaism of the late pre-Christian centuries the title is used at times. The titles "Son of God" and "Son of the Most High" occur in an Aramaic text with phraseology very similar to Lk 1:32, 35. Here, however, they are not predicated of anyone called "messiah" in the text; they may refer to the son of some Jewish king or ruler. Hence there is nothing in the Old Testament or Palestinian Judaism tradition that we know of to show that "Son of God" had a messianic nuance. Yet, even if that cannot be shown, the data show at least that the title "Son of God" was as much at home in Palestinian Judaism as in the contemporary Hellenistic world of the eastern Mediterranean. The chances are that the use of it in both areas has to be respected in the discussion of the origin of the New Testament title (Fitzmyer, 1981: 205-207). Verse 35 interprets in a Christian sense the Davidic messianism of the Jews (Bovon, 1991: 78).

Verses 36-37: (36) And now,
            your relative Elizabeth in her old age
            has also conceived a son;
            and this is the sixth month
            for her who was said to be barren.
        (37) For nothing will be impossible with God."

"And now" refers to the sign, while in verse 31 the same expression referred to the promise (Bovon, 1991: 78). The narrator's switch from Jesus to the pregnant Elizabeth serves the very practical purpose of linking the episode with the first (Lk 1:5-25) and the third (Lk 1:39-56). Yet there is more to the literary scheme than this, since the real shift of focus is not from Jesus to Elizabeth, but from Jesus via Elizabeth to God whose power Gabriel proclaims in the climactic verse 37. Elizabeth is not introduced for her own sake nor in her own right; nothing, for example, is said of the circumstances of Elizabeth's pregnancy. It is not the personal story of Zechariah or Elizabeth which interests the narrator or Gabriel at this point, but rather Elizabeth as sign of God's power. Despite her concealment, she becomes a public witness to the power of God to do what by any ordinary reckoning seems impossible. As an echo of the Old Testament, Elizabeth witnesses to God's power revealed through the biblical story; as a woman of the *present time*, she witnesses God's power not solely as a thing of the *past*; and as a kinswoman of Mary, she witnesses the divine power as mysterious, but not distant. Gabriel's proclamation of the power of God in verses 36-37 is heaven's answer to Mary's statement of her own powerlessness in verse 34. The power of God empowers the powerless; and the hidden Elizabeth is made a sign of that (Coleridge, 1993: 68).

If Elizabeth is a sign, then she is a sign about whom Mary *hears* but whom she does not *see*. Mary must therefore take Gabriel's word on it, accepting the messenger's reliability and authority in a way that was beyond Zechariah. The sign proclaimed to Mary is very different from the sign requested by Zechariah: while he requested a sign that might confer certain knowledge, she is told of a sign which demands faith.

Mary must make the leap from the known to the unknown, since a conception in old age by a normal means cannot be thought of in the same way as a virginal conception by an unmarried woman. On the one hand, we have the belated fulfillment of a lifelong desire, which means the removal of social stigma. On the other hand, we have the totally unheard of approach of God to a woman who has not sought the pregnancy nor even dreamed of its possibility. A knowledge of the biblical witness might well have assured Mary that old and barren women do conceive by God's power, but there was nothing in Scripture which might have encouraged her to make the leap to faith in a virginal conception of the Davidic messiah. [This presumes that Isa 7:14 was not understood at the time as referring to the manner of the child's conception (Brown, 1977: 145-149).] Where Zechariah has been asked to believe that God will do again what he has done before, Mary is asked to believe that God will do what he has never done before. She is given no more than Zechariah, but she is asked to believe a good deal more (Coleridge, 1993: 69).

That nothing is impossible with God is a topos of the Old Testament. See especially Gen 18:14, "Is anything too wonderful for the Lord?" (See also Job 10:13LXX; 42:2; in the New Testament, Lk 18:27 and parallels; Mk 14:36). Verse 37 reads literally: "because any word will not be impossible with God," reminding us of the rather literal translation of Gen 18:14, "Does any word coming from God remain without effect?" The term "word" (*rhēma*, reflecting the Hebrew *dabar*) here, as in Acts 10:37, designates a promised event rather than a simple word. The use of the future here is part of a theology of hope: God will soon realize this impossible thing (Bovon, 1991: 78-79; Bock, 1994: 126).

In Lk 1:35, Gabriel made a climactic revelation of the identity of Jesus: "the child to be born will be holy; he will be called son of God." But then, in one of the sudden switches of focus that punctuate the infancy narrative, Luke turns immediately away from Jesus to God, with Gabriel announcing to Mary the pregnancy of Elizabeth and moving to the climatic statement of verse 37: "For nothing will be impossible with God." The shift is from Jesus' identity to God's power (Coleridge, 1992: 137).

Verse 38: Then Mary said, "Here am I, the servant of the Lord;
           let it be with me according to your word."
           Then the angel departed from her.

In describing herself as the Lord's servant (see also Lk 1:48), Mary recognizes her submission to God's purpose, but also her role in the service of that purpose. Moreover, she claims a place in God's household, so to speak. She who has been given no family heritage by the narrator now affirms her place in God's family. She has been given no status indications except for God's favor and election, and it is to this that she holds at the end of this scene. That is, Mary's words carry with them a fundamental definition of her personhood; indeed, in this socio-historical context, her words relativize and actually jeopardize her status as Joseph's betrothed. For her, partnership with God transcends the claims (and social position) of family (see also Lk 8:19-21; 9:57-62; 12:51-53; 14:25-26; 18:28-30). In the Greco-Roman world and the world of mishnaic literature, the status of a slave was determined by the status of the householder. The status of the head of the family was extended to all who shared with him a relationship of kinship (Martin, 1990: 1-49). When Mary asserts her position as the servant of the Lord, we recognize that she derives her status from him, and so Luke is now initiating his representation of a community of God's people whose fundamental social experience is grounded in their relationship to God. In his characterization of Mary, Luke has begun to undercut the conventional competitive maneuvering for positions of status prevalent in the first-century Mediterranean world. Mary, who seemed to measure low on any status scale – age, family, heritage, gender, and so one – turns out to be the one favored by God and the one who finds her status and identity ultimately in her obedience to God and participation in his salvafic will (Green, 1992: 367-368).

Mary's response in verse 38 is the only appropriate answer for the faithful. Her question "How can this be?" has now become the word of obedient faith. "Let it be!" Her question has served the reader well in allowing for a series of responses, in fact, a three-part answer in verses 35-37. Aside from this last glimpse of obedience, little disclosure of Mary's character or thoughts has been given. She is not only the handmaid of the Lord in bearing the infant, but she recedes in the narrative as well so that the identity and dominion of the Son of God and the son of David may be presented (Tiede, 1988: 51). Mary is also a "Servant of Yahweh" (cf. Isa 49:3; 50:4,10; 52:13). She is the woman of faith whose "yes" is unequivocal (see also Lk 1:48 and Acts 2:18; Johnson, 1991: 38). Mary's word of acceptance is threefold. It is a word about God, about his messenger, and about herself. It is an acceptance of Gabriel's claim of divine omnipotence in verse 37; it is an acceptance of the messenger's reliability and authority; and it is an acceptance of her own status as servant of the omnipotent God. In this threefold aspect, it is a fundamental statement about the contours of faith, and hence a key moment in the narrative (Coleridge, 1993: 69-70).

Mary's response is paradoxical in the way it blends the active and the passive. On the one hand, the narrator has presented her throughout the episode as wholly passive before the divine initiative – and never more so than now. Yet her question in verse 34 made her an active collaborator in the unfolding of the revelation; and now even more, her response makes her sound like a collaborator in the unfolding of the divine plan (Coleridge, 1993: 70). The fiat of Mary is less passive than it seems; implicitly it contains all the exertions of a servant (Legrand, 1981: 82). Moreover, by stressing Mary's acceptance of God's "word" in Lk 1:38, Luke has begun to associate her with those in Israel who were "poor ones" (*anawim*) in the sense of being totally dependent upon God for support. Luke will develop that theme beautifully in the Magnificat (Brown, 1977: 328).

The departure of the angel is an ordinary feature of angelic appearances, since such a heavenly presence has to be temporary (Judg 6:21; Acts 12:10). However, there is also a special Lukan pattern whereby departures terminate the scenes of the Lukan infancy narrative (Lk 1:23, 56; 2:20; Brown, 1977: 292).

In conclusion, we may say that for all their asymmetries, the first two episodes (Lk 1:5-25 and 26-38) work together to form the groundwork of the Lukan narrative, establishing the rudiments of the narrative's vision of both the divine visitation and human recognition of it. In a real sense, the readers now know the "what" of the entire Lukan narrative: God will intervene eschatologically, that is, finally and decisively, through a divine messiah whose reign will last forever. But they also know a good deal more about the "how" than they did at the end of the first episode. They know that the messiah will be Davidic, that his name will be Jesus, that Mary will be his mother, and that John will be a key figure in preparing for his coming. Moreover, the readers know that faith is demanded by God's promise and that the signs of fulfillment demand right interpretation (Coleridge, 1993: 73-74).

3. The Visitation (Lk 1:39-56)

After the important episodes of Lk 1:5-25 and 26-38, the narrative of Lk 1:39-56 seems almost an intermezzo – a moment in which readers and characters may catch their breath before launching into the stories of fulfillment which follow. It has been called "a supplementary unit" (LaVerdiere, 1980: 22), or an "epilogue" (Brown, 1977: 252). Yet from the narrative viewpoint, for all that it may seem an intermezzo, supplement or epilogue, the episode has more narrative weight than descriptions of that kind imply.

The first two episodes of Luke's well-told story are now brought together as the two expectant mothers meet (Tiede, 1988: 51).The narrative function of the episode is to stage a meeting of faith and interpretation, and it does so in a way that shows how faith in the promise and interpretation of the signs are intimately related – as intimately related as promise and fulfillment in the action of God (Coleridge, 1993: 75),

An important element of the episode is the completion of the profile of faith, the rudiments of which were given in the first two episodes. Some would see the link between Lk 1:26-38 and 39-56 as so close that they would read Lk 1:26-56 as a narrative unit (Meynet, 1985: 39-72). Now the narrator turns to the grounds and effects of faith. For the first time in the infancy narrative, the initiative passes to a human character, and more precisely to a believer. Faith therefore appears for the first time as the engine of the plot: it makes the story and helps stir the act of interpretation which the episode will recount. This means that "the stress on cognition rather than action" (Aletti, 1988: 37) is complete in an episode wholly concerned with the explicitation of faith and interpretation as the response required by God's promise and its fulfillment (Coleridge, 1993: 76).

a. The Visitation (Lk 1:39-45)

Verses 39-40: (39) In those days
              Mary set out and went with haste
              to a Judean town in the hill country,
        (40) where she entered the house of Zechariah
              and greeted Elizabeth.

Verse 38 had left the focus on Mary, and this remains so in verse 39 as the narrator has her journeying to Judah. In verses 26-38, Mary was the unmoving focus of the narrative; but now she is the one who moves, her movement being stressed by the first word of the episode (in the Greek text), "rising" (*anastasa*, NRSV: "set out"), which is the first of three verbs of motion used to describe her ("set out, went, entered"). Not only are we told in verse 39 that Mary goes to the "hill country," "to a Judean town," "(into) the house of Zechariah," but also that she returns "to her home" in verse 56 (Coleridge, 1993: 76).

Only here do we learn that the home of Zechariah was not in Jerusalem. As a priest from what could not have been more than a village, Zechariah would not have been a member of the central religious establishment (Malina-Rohrbaugh, 1992: 291).

The narrator says nothing of why Mary goes. Various attempts have been made to minutely examine Mary's psychology at this point (for example, she goes lest the neighbors in Nazareth come to know about her pregnancy), but the text offers no basis for speculation of this kind. On grounds other than the strictly psychological, it is possible that Mary goes on her journey: (1) in obedience to Gabriel; (2) to verify the extraordinary declaration of Gabriel: she needs to see for herself, etc. Yet there are problems with all of these proposals. Gabriel does not issue a command. Nor is there any suggestion that Mary doubts what Gabriel has said of Elizabeth (Coleridge, 1993: 76-77). But it could be said that Gabriel had given her a sign, and that a sign is given to be *seen* (Bock, 1994: 133). It is, however, also possible that the narrator shrouds Mary's motivation in silence in order to focus not upon Mary personally, but rather upon her as servant of the divine plan (Coleridge, 1993: 77).

In verse 36 the narrator mentions that the two women are blood-relatives in order to provide a motive for the journey. [From a narrative point of view, the question is not whether Elizabeth and Mary were in fact blood-relatives. Whether they were or not, the narrative question is why the narrator chooses to include that information (whether factual or not) in the narrative at verse 36]. The question, then, is not why Mary goes, but why the narrator wants the two women to meet (Coleridge, 1993: 77-78).

The exchange of greetings in the Palestinian culture assumed and represented by Luke was both highly stylized and full of significance (see, e.g., Ex 18:7, "Moses went out to meet his father-in-law; he bowed down and kissed him; each asked after the other's welfare, and they went into the tent"). Luke places great emphasis on Mary's greeting; even though we cannot specify its content, he mentions it three times (Lk 1:40,41,44). Its primary significance seems to be on its results – that is, on the response of Elizabeth's unborn child to it, mentioned twice (Lk 1:41,44). Unlike Moses, who goes out to welcome his father-in-law and extends first greetings, Elizabeth is clearly the superior, by normal canons at least. She is a daughter of Aaron, the wife of a priest, the elder of these two women. What is more, had she not received divine affirmation in the blessing of a child? What is surprising, then, is Elizabeth's greeting to Mary. Prompted by the child in her womb, filled with the Holy Spirit, she places herself in the servant's role, bestowing honor on her guest whom she now recognizes as "the mother of my Lord," "blessed... among women." Suddenly the tables have turned, with the result that we have from Elizabeth a second testimony to the favored status of Mary first proclaimed by Gabriel (Lk 1:28,30).

Verses 41-42a: (41)   When Elizabeth heard Mary's greeting,
                the child leaped in her womb.
                And Elizabeth was filled with the Holy Spirit
        (42a) and exclaimed with a loud cry,

Mary's greeting at the end of verse 40 stirs the action. The text suggests that in the response of faith what is *heard* matters more for the narrative than what is *seen*. Though Gabriel gave the pregnant Elizabeth to Mary as a sign, it is now Mary who becomes a sign for Elizabeth, but paradoxically she is a sign that is *heard* rather than *seen*.

The three references to Mary's greeting stress its importance. In verse 40 the narrator reports that Mary "greeted Elizabeth"; in verse 41 that the child leaped when Elizabeth "heard Mary's greeting"; and in verse 44 Elizabeth reports the same thing, referring to "the sound of your greeting." There is no doubt about its importance. What is strange, then, is that the narrator says nothing of its content (Coleridge, 1993: 80). Scholars point out that "the oriental greeting is an extended affair" (Marshall, 1978: 80), that it was "a ceremonial act whose significance lay in the

content of the message" (Ellis, 1966: 76), and that "it is improbable that in her salutation Mary speaks to Elizabeth of the
angelic visit" (Plummer, 1901: 28). The narrator, however, does
not give any such hint. The impression is rather that as soon as
Mary begins her greeting, John leaps in the womb and Elizabeth erupts into speech: it seems neither "an extended affair"
nor "a ceremonial act." The narrative significance of Mary's
greeting lies not in its *content*, which is never reported, but in
its *effect*, which is reported at length.

Its effect is to reinforce the sense of Mary as prime mover
in the narrative. First of all, she has freely decided to make the
journey into the Judean hills: in that sense she is the trigger.
Secondly, once she arrives, it is her greeting that stirs John and
Elizabeth. The first effect of Mary's greeting – and hence the
first act of interpretation of the sign – is John's leap, reported
by the narrator in verse 41 and interpreted later by Elizabeth in
verse 44. Under the influence of the Holy Spirit, she is able to
interpret both signs: the coming of Mary and the leap of John.
The function of the leap is not immediately clear. It is usually
presumed that John leaps joyfully at the presence of the messiah whom Mary carries now in her womb. Yet the narrator has
said nothing of the conception of Jesus. What we know is that
Mary has put her faith in heaven's promise. The other possibility, therefore, is that it is not the presence of Jesus, but the
presence of *Mary the believer* which stirs John in the womb; and
there are reasons to believe so (Coleridge, 1993: 80-81).

First, Mary is the focus of the episode in a way Jesus is not:
she is the one praised by Elizabeth and she is the one who in
turn praises God. The narrative is careful also to associate the
reactions of Elizabeth and John, to the point where it can be
claimed of verse 44 that Elizabeth explains how she knew that
Mary was the mother of the messiah by the joyous movements
of her unborn child (Marshall, 1978: 81), thus establishing a
causal link between John's leap and Elizabeth's inspired knowledge. If, therefore, Elizabeth's reaction is a joyful acclamation of
Mary as mother of the messiah and as woman of faith, then it

would seem more likely that this is also the meaning of John's leap. She may acclaim Mary in verse 43 as "the mother of my Lord," but this is subordinate to the climactic acclamation in verse 45 of Mary as "she who believed" (Coleridge, 1993: 81). Given the way in which the narrative associates the reactions of Elizabeth and John, it is likely that John, like his mother, leaps before Mary, not Jesus (Coleridge, 1992: 137).

Furthermore, in the Third Gospel, the credentials of Jesus are validated not by John but by God. It would seem, then, that John, like Elizabeth, acclaims not Jesus but Mary.

The narrator introduces the Holy Spirit at a point where the action is set for the first time among human characters, and he does so for two reasons. First, the Holy Spirit is the conventional indication that what follows is to be prophetic speech, and therefore in this context designates the character of what Elizabeth is about to say; and secondly, the mention of the Holy Spirit ensures that, although the action is now between human beings, it does not become wholly earth-bound. The initiative has passed to human characters, but heaven still plays its part (Coleridge, 1993: 83).

Lk 1:41 states that upon meeting Mary, Elizabeth was "filled with the Holy Spirit" and pronounced an inspired blessing upon her and the child she was to bear. In Lk 1:41 and 67 we have two instances of "invasive prophetic speech," that is, of prophetic speech conceived of as immediately inspired by the Spirit (Turner, 1992: 74-75). The phrase "filled with the Holy Spirit" occurs again in Lk 1:67 with reference to Zechariah. On the one hand, the Holy Spirit's role in Luke is related to divine empowerment to speak. On the other hand, this enabling presence of the Spirit makes of women and men persons who are able to understand and proclaim the divine purpose, especially its fulfillment in God's intervention in the coming of Jesus. And they do so with profound images of divine deliverance rooted in the covenantal graciousness of God (Green, 1995: 42). The close association between the activity of the Spirit and prophecy is made explicit in the introductory formula: "Zechariah was

filled with the Holy Spirit and spoke this prophecy" Lk 1:67).
This usage of "spoke this prophecy" parallels that of "exclaimed
with a loud cry" in Lk 1:42. Thus in Lk 1:41 and 67 the Spirit
acts as the Spirit of prophecy, inspiring prophetic speech. Luke
highlights the Spirit's role in the prophetic activity of Elizabeth
and Zechariah (Menzies, 1991: 120).

Verses 42b-45: (42b) "Blessed are you among women,
                        and blessed is the fruit of your womb.
                (43)   And why has this happened to me,
                        that the mother of my Lord comes to me?
                (44)   For as soon as I heard the sound of your greet-
                            ing,
                        the child in my womb leaped for joy.
                (45)   And blessed is she who believed
                        that there would be a fulfillment
                        of what was spoken to her by the Lord."

Elizabeth's first words are reminiscent of the greeting and praise
given to a superior in recognition of her or his advanced status
and of the fact that God had blessed this person. Elizabeth's
language here differs, though, from that in Lk 1:45, where she
acknowledges the superiority of her young relative, a status due
to her superior reception of God's beneficence. Consequently,
Elizabeth's question (Lk 1:43) is not surprising. As grateful as
she may be for God's favor on her behalf and as sure as she is
that her disgrace has been overcome (Lk 1:25), she still recognizes the superior role of her young relative. After all, she is the
mother of "my Lord." Elizabeth's second pronouncement of blessing
recognizes Mary as the recipient of divine fortune because of
her faith. The contrast with Zechariah – a male, an elder, a
priest – could scarcely be more stark; he did not believe (Lk
1:20) but she did (Green, 1992: 469-470).

This *status reversal*, foregrounding in unexpected ways the
role of Mary in the developing narrative, receives implicit support in later material. Thus, in Lk 2:5 Joseph is related to Mary
(and not vice versa); in Lk 2:16 Mary is named before Joseph;
in Lk 2:33-34 Simeon, having blessed "them," addresses Mary;
and in Lk 2:48 Mary speaks for herself and Joseph. Moreover,

in the gathering of the disciples in Acts 1:14, Mary is specifically named along with the eleven. In Mary's response in the Magnificat, following the normal form of a psalm of praise, Lk 1:48 grounds Mary's praise in God's prior act: He has looked with favor on the "lowliness" (*tapeinōsis*) of his servant. "Lowliness" may refer to the humiliation of the oppressed people of God (e.g., Deut 26:7; 1 Sam 9:16; 1 Macc 3:51) and, given the other parallels between Mary and Israel in the hymn, Mary's low estate might then be taken as representative of her people's. *Tapeinōsis* also belongs to the language of the "poor" in the Third Gospel, a domain associated especially with a negative social valuation of a person based on such criteria as gender, age, purity, economics, and so on. Hence, Mary's characterization of herself as lowly is not only metaphorical and representational, but is based on her actual social position in Luke's narrative. Her favorable status is a consequence of God's surprising and gracious initiative (Green, 1992: 470-471).

In verses 19-20, Gabriel had given heaven's straightforward assessment of Zechariah's doubt. But in verses 26-38, the heavenly messenger says nothing in response to Mary's expression of faith. He leaves without saying a word in a way that leaves heaven silent in the face of Mary's faith. But the assessment of her faith comes now as Elizabeth and John move to centre stage. In verses 42b-45, then, we have the narrative's dramatic equivalent to verses 19-20. There Gabriel expressed disapproval of Zechariah's doubt; now John and Elizabeth acclaim Mary's faith (Dupont, 1980: 323), as again the narrator leaves evaluation to his characters (Coleridge, 1993: 84).

Elizabeth "exclaimed with a loud voice." The expression is frequently used to describe an inspired utterance (see Mk 9:24; Jn 7:28,37; Rom 8:15; 9:27; Gal 4:6; Stein, 1992: 90). She starts with two forms of the passive participle "blessed" which refer to the action of God towards Mary and Jesus, since these participles are "divine passives" (Bovon, 1991: 87). God is once more hidden behind the divine passive, but is implied as prime mover. He comes to the foreground only in the last word of the speech where

Elizabeth speaks of "a fulfillment of what was spoken to her by the Lord." What was implicit at the start becomes explicit at the end. God may not be the observable focus of the speech, but he is its ground (Coleridge, 1993: 84-85).

Because of the elliptical style of the narration, we cannot be sure of whether or not Mary is pregnant when she goes to visit Elizabeth. True, Elizabeth refers to Mary as "the mother of my Lord" in verse 43, but this could as easily refer to what *will* happen as to what *has* happened (Coleridge, 1992: 137).

The human interest of this encounter between two kins-women under highly unusual circumstances is not lost, and all of the details about "months" and "womb" and "fruit" bring the story down to earth, within a woman's experience of maternity. Nevertheless, the content of these pronouncements is primarily theological, while psychological clues are sparse as to how Mary or Elizabeth may have felt or perceived these events (Tiede, 1988: 53).

Mary, though the focus of the speech, is never named as Mary. She is "blessed among women," in verse 42; "the mother of my Lord" in verse 43; and "she who believed" in verse 45. In each case she is designated in a way that links her to the plan of God. It is not Mary in her own right who appears in the speech, but Mary in relation to God's plan.

The speech itself moves from attention to what God has done for Mary in verse 42 ("blessed") to a focus in verse 45 upon what Mary herself has done ("believed"). Yet it is pre-cisely at the point where the emphasis falls upon what Mary has done that God is named explicitly in the narrative ("by the Lord"). It is also at that point that, in referring to Mary, the speech moves from the second person ("you, your womb, your greeting") to the third person ("blessed is she who believed"). Elizabeth turns from addressing Mary directly to addressing a wider audience (including the readers) to whom she speaks about Mary and to whom she holds Mary up as a model of faith in the divine promise (Coleridge, 1993: 85).

Like Mary, Jesus is never named as Jesus like he was by

Gabriel in verse 31. Instead he is "blessed" and "the fruit of your womb" in verse 42, and "my Lord" in verse 43. In verse 42, he is named in a way that relates him to God (as the source of blessing) and to Mary (as his mother). The case of verse 43 is more complex because for the first time the title "lord" (*kurios*) is used unmistakably for Jesus. Elsewhere it has been used of God (Lk 1:6,9,11, 15,16,17,25,28,32,38), and it will be used of God again in Lk 1:45. Its application to Jesus here implies an unusual and radical relationship of Jesus to God, but the question is what kind of relationship? (George, 1978: 245-251). The messianic Ps 110:1LXX reads, "The Lord said to my lord," with "lord" used to refer to both God and the Davidic messiah. Elizabeth's speech echoes the psalm with its reference to Jesus as "my lord," and to God in verse 45 as "lord." In verse 43, therefore, Jesus is named in a way which relates him to God (as Davidic messiah) and to Elizabeth (as *her* lord) (Coleridge, 1993: 85-86).

A classic Lukan device is using dialogue to reveal the fuller dimension of what the narrative has already revealed. Here the "joy" of John's leap picks up the note of eschatological "joy" (*agalliasis*) promised by the angel to greet John's birth (Lk 1:14). John, in turn, will announce the eschatological "coming of the Lord" (Lk 3:4-17; Johnson, 1991: 41).

The pronouncement of verse 45 is the ultimate benediction on Mary. Verse 42b had already spoken of the unsurpassable blessing of this pregnancy, but Mary's profound and simple trust of the word of the Lord is the greater mark of her being blessed by God. This is clearly confirmed by what we read later in the Gospel: "... 'Blessed is the womb that bore you and the breasts that nursed you!' But he said, 'Blessed rather are those who hear the word of God and obey it!'" (Lk 11:27-28; Tiede, 1988: 54).

b. The Magnificat (Lk 1:46-55)

Introduction. The songs now embedded in Luke's infancy narrative may be some of the earliest expressions we have from the Jesus movement. The Magnificat (Lk 1:46-55), the Benedictus

(Lk 1:68-79), and the Nunc Dimittis (Lk 2:29-32) are clearly separable from their literary context as poetic psalms that interrupt the flow of the stories (Horsley, 1989: 107). Many scholars have maintained that the Magnificat reflects Luke's accent on poverty (Horn, 1983: 137ff.). A recent study contends that the Magnificat reflects various dimensions of suffering (Scheffler, 1993: 48).

The Magnificat is integrated into Mary's visit to Elizabeth, as is clear from the final comment (Lk 1:56). Within this episode it actually forms part of the dialogue between Mary and Elizabeth, but since it dominates this dialogue (constituting ten of the eighteen verses), it can be demarcated as a single unit. Being written in poetic form, it also contrasts with the prose of the narrative in which it is embedded. Still, the Magnificat and the other canticles fit the narrative of Lk 1–2 as a whole and play a vital part, not in moving the story forward, but in expressing Luke's understanding of the significance of Jesus and his place in the history of God's redemptive activity in Israel (Franklin, 1994: 355).

The previous episode presented Mary as a notably solitary figure in her dialogue with Gabriel. At that point, the dramatization of faith was solely between the heavenly messenger and the human character. But once the narrator turns to the dramatization of faith's effects, as he does in this episode, the narration becomes less solitary and more social, with the circle expanding first to include Elizabeth and John. In the Magnificat, the circle expands still further to include "all generations" as the hymn expounds more fully the social implications of faith (Coleridge, 1993: 88).

46 a And Mary said,
   b "My soul magnifies the Lord,
47   and my spirit rejoices in God my Savior,
48 a for he has looked with favor on the lowliness of his
      servant.
   b Surely, from now on all generations will call me blessed;
49 a for the Mighty One has done great things for me,

b and holy is his name.

50 His mercy is for those who fear him from generation to generation.

51 a He has shown strength with his arm;

b he has scattered the proud in the thoughts of their hearts.

52 a He has brought down the powerful from their thrones,

b and lifted up the lowly;

53 a he has filled the hungry with good things,

b and has sent the rich away empty.

54 He has helped his servant Israel, in remembrance of his mercy,

55 a according to the promise he made to our ancestors,

b to Abraham and to his descendants forever."

As far as the *content* is concerned, the motifs to be distinguished in the Magnificat (especially verses 51-55) extend beyond the immediate situation of the episode. "Like an aria in an opera" (Tannehill, 1974: 265) the Magnificat is slotted parenthetically into the Lukan narrative.

From a *text-critical* point of view, the reading "And Elizabeth said" (Lk 1:46) instead of "And Mary said" is the only variant relevant to our purpose. Apart from the overwhelming textual evidence for the reading "Mary," it can be argued that, because of the prominent role he wanted Mary to play in the Gospel, Luke probably took the original hymn and put it into the mouth of Mary (Schürmann, 1969: 72-73; Marshall, 1978: 78; for arguments supporting the opposite view, see Danker, 1988: 42).

As far as the *origin* of the Magnificat is concerned, the only point of agreement among the different theories is that it did not originate with Luke. The songs in the infancy narrative appear to have been inserted later (probably by Luke) for, according to many scholars, they fit somewhat loosely into the context – which would not have been the case had Luke been the sole author (Grigsby, 1984: 160-163).

As far as the *actual origin* of the Magnificat is concerned, it should be noted, first of all, that this poem is a compilation of

Old Testament motifs. There is not a single verse that is not reminiscent of Old Testament verses or phrases (Brown, 1977: 358-359). As a whole it shows strong resemblances with Hannah's song (1 Sam 2:1-10). But it is not so much the words in common with Hannah's song which make the latter clear as Luke's primary model for the Magnificat; rather it is the structure, both of the sentences and of the whole (Goulder, 1989: 226). In both Hannah's song and the Magnificat the conception of a child is seen as bringing salvation to the individual speaker, on a par with the salvation that God gives to the poor and the needy. As in Hannah's song, this salvation is highlighted by the rejection of the rich and the mighty (Scheffler, 1993: 48-50).

The argument that the Magnificat arose in a *Jewish Christian community* and not in purely Jewish circles seems convincing (Brown, 1977: 350; Horn, 1983: 168). According to Brown it originated among a group of Jewish *Anawim* (Poor Ones) who had been converted to Christianity. Originally *Anawim* referred only to economic poverty, but through the rejection of the rich as ungodly it became a religious term, a synonym for "pious," also referring to the lowly, the sick, the downtrodden, widows and orphans (Brown, 1977: 351). In the first century, because of the economic situation, there was a new focus on the economic aspect, also among Jewish Christian *Anawim*. [We should remember here that the emerging consenus of specialists is that Christianity never was a religion composed exclusively of the urban poor or the working proletariat (Norris, 1979: 12)]. "Luke borrowed canticles composed by Jewish Christian Anawim... because he felt kinship to those ideals and to that group" (Brown, 1977: 352). By placing the Magnificat on the lips of Mary, Luke wished to bring out the prominence of the first disciple of Jesus and the embodiment of the Jewish *Anawim* (Bemile, 1986: 77).

Sociologically considered, a Hebrew original for the Magnificat (and the other hymns of the infancy narrative) is intrinsically very likely. The recent scholarly analysis of the language and form of the Magnificat in comparison with contemporary Palestinian Jewish hymns can take us a step further into the milieu

from which it originated. Although the Magnificat fits generally
into the traditional form of declarative psalms of praise (Farris,
1985: 84), it does not fall more precisely into any particular
type of psalm, and some scholars have had reason to abandon
the view that the Magnificat can strictly be subjected to any
one of the existing psalm types (Bemile, 1986: 71). The authors
of the late-Second Temple psalms such as those in Sirach, the
Qumran *Hodayoth*, and Judith 16 still appear to follow particular traditional patterns of Hebrew psalm composition. Ben Sira
and the Qumran authors were clearly well educated and, literarily,
highly productive "sages" or "scribes." A comparison of their
well-formed psalms with the songs in Lk 1–2 suggests that the
latter were produced by less educated people. It would appear
that, in comparison with other, near-contemporary psalms, with
which they share many features of language and theme, the
songs in Lk 1–2 were produced and used in a less learned, more
popular milieu (Horsley, 1989: 108-109). This supports the view
that the Magnificat and the other Lukan hymns originated with
the early Jesus movement in Galilee.

Finally, because these songs speak joyously of a salvation
that has already happened, that is already a reality for which
God is to be praised, a search has been made for some obvious
event of salvation to which they were a response. However, the
suggestions made, such as the victory of the Maccabean revolt
(Winter, 1954: 328-347; Ford, 1984: 20) or the crucifixion and
resurrection of Jesus (Brown, 1977: 363), are less than satisfactory.

A likely explanation of the origin of the Magnificat would
be that it was composed in a community that believed that the
messiah of David's line had already come (Farris, 1985: 94). So,
the Magnificat may represent the *voice of the early Jesus movement* in Galilee. Our interest is fundamentally in the meaning
of the Magnificat to the concrete groups of people who used it.
In this connection, given its probable popular Palestinian Jewish origins, it is all the more significant that it was preserved
and utilized by a Greek writer called Luke. The song must have

been of considerable importance to some communities in the "Jesus movement" to have been translated from Hebrew into Greek prior to Luke (Grigsby, 1984: 165), or, less probably, by Luke himself. And Luke himself must have deemed it either of such importance that it should be preserved for its own sake or eminently suitable to express the significance of Jesus' birth (Horsley, 1989: 109-110). As such the Magnificat fits well in the infancy narrative which, in its entirety, intends to express the significance of Jesus' birth and mission.

Simply paying attention to the language and style of the Magnificat should be sufficient to indicate that *this song portrays intense conflict*. Strong verbs of action dominate both strophes, verses 46-50 and 51-55. Indeed in the Greek text those verbs usually stand first in their respective lines, and both the conjunctions and the articles were eliminated, thus giving greater prominence to the action verbs (Tannehill, 1974: 273). In the second strophe, verses 51-55, the parallelism of poetic lines changes from synonymous and synthetic to antithetic, articulating sharp contrasts and conflict.

The language and style accord with the subject of the song: God's revolutionary overthrow of the established governing authorities ("the mighty from their thrones") on behalf of Israel. The words and phrases used throughout the Magnificat are taken from and vividly recall the whole tradition of victory songs and hymns of praise celebrating God's victorious liberation of the people of Israel from their oppressive enemies.

The dependence on and allusions to the Song of Hannah in 1 Sam 2:1-10 and to God's paradigmatic "mighty acts" of deliverance of Israel from bondage in Egypt are particularly striking, but there are a number of parallels and reminiscences to other Old Testament hymns of praise as well (Brown, 1977: 358-360). The closest parallels in style and in praise of or appeal to God for liberation from enemies are found significantly in Jewish hymns from the period of intense conflict with and resistance to Hellenistic and Roman imperialism, such as those in Judith, 1 Maccabees, the Psalms and the War Scroll from Qumran, and the apocalypses of 2 Baruch and 4 Ezra. By paying attention to the ways in which the Magnificat echoes the rich biblical traditions that celebrate God's liberation or the ways it parallels contemporary hymns, we can more adequately discern the meaning of Mary's song of salvation (Horsley, 1989: 110-111).

The objective of God's salvation in the Magnificat is clearly the liberation of the people of Israel, as stated explicitly in verse 54. The designation of Israel as "servant" parallels the contemporary psalms of deliverance, the one being an appeal to God to send the anointed king as agent of the people's liberation and restoration (Pss Sol 12:7; 17:21). In biblical, particularly psalmic, language, moreover, the term "the poor/humble/lowly" in verse 52 is a clear reference to the people of Israel, usually in the condition of domination, oppression, and affliction (Deut 26:7; Ps 136:23, including the contexts). It has been argued on the basis of the use of *Anawim* in certain Psalms that "the lowly" here refers to those who possess a certain spiritual humility, even to the community of humble righteous ones within Jewish society, some of whom must now have converted to Christianity and produced this hymn (Brown, 1977: 352-355). But most passages concerning "the lowly" refer to concrete socioeconomic and political conditions, not primarily spiritual humility, and the term often refers to the people generally, not to some community or remnant within the overall society (Horsley, 1989: 111). The "poor" represent not only the economically impoverished but all those who are marginal or excluded from human fellowship, the outcast. This theme is a major one in the Gospel (see Lk 4:18; 6:20; 7:22; 14:13,21; 16:20,22; Johnson, 1991: 79). The lowly and the poor are also, according to traditional expression, the politically powerless (Danker, 1988: 106).

God accomplishes the liberation of his people by "scattering the proud" and "putting down the mighty from their thrones" (Lk 1:51-52). "The proud" are indeed spiritually arrogant. But more concretely they are the enemies of God, either alien or domestic rulers, as can be seen in the tradition of songs praising

God's redemption (Pss 18:27; 89:10). Thus "on the day of the Lord," in which the warrior-champion of Israel will deliver the people from domination, God will decisively humble the proud and exalted (Isa 2:11-12; 13:11). Perhaps the most striking parallel to the Magnificat in this respect is a near-contemporary messianic psalm in which both the illegitimate and oppressive rulers (the Hasmoneans) and foreign conquerors (the Romans) are called "proud" (Ps Sol 17:8,15,26; see also Ps Sol 2:1-2,25,28-31).

But if God "scatters the proud" and "topples the mighty from their thrones," this is clearly a *political liberation* of the people from concrete political enemies (and not simply some vague and indefinite "salvific intervention in Israel's history"). The new liberation for which God is praised in the Magnificat is surely no less specific and concrete than the previous great historical acts of deliverance to which it alludes, the redemption from bondage in Egypt, the rescue from the Canaanite kings, and the defense against the Philistines – and Mary leads the hymn of praise to God, the savior of the people, as had Miriam, Deborah, and David of old (Ex 15; Judg 5; Ps 18 = 2 Sam 22) (Horsley, 1989: 111-112).

In addition to constituting a liberation of the people from arrogant rulers, the deliverance praised in the Magnificat is also a *social revolution*, the termination of the seemingly endless class conflict with the deliverance of the lowly and the provision of food for the hungry. As noted, "lowliness/lowly" refers to those who have suffered exploitation, oppression and affliction by the wealthy and powerful ruling groups. The class conflict in which the arrogant, sinful rulers perpetuated systematic injustice for the poor is regularly portrayed in precisely the terms used in the Magnificat (e.g., Sir 10:7,12-13). God's concern for, and the defense or liberation of, the lowly from arrogant rulers is a prominent theme, particularly in prophetic oracles and stories as well as in the tradition of hymnic celebration of God's deliverance in which the Magnificat stands (e.g., Ps 18:27; Isa 2:11-12; Ps Sol 17:26,46; and cf. wisdom teaching such as Sir 109:14-

17). It may not be accidental that the descriptions of the arrogance of the oppressive rulers alternates between alien nations or imperial rulers and the rulers of Jewish society itself. In the very structure of the imperial situation, imperial regimes ruled through local aristocracies and client-kings, and the latter were dependent on the imperial regime for the maintenance of their privileged position at the head of their own people. Thus liberation of the people from the arrogant rulers would have meant the toppling of both local and alien rulers from their thrones. In order to assert the only true, divine rule, God had to put down pretentious human rulers. But the revolution described in the Magnificat is not simply "political." It is social as well; for the poor, marginal peasantry, heretofore exploited to the point that they went hungry themselves in order to render up the tribute and taxation demanded by their local and imperial rulers, are being "filled with good things." A new social order of justice and plenty is at hand (Horsley, 1989: 113). In other words, "The kingdom of God has come near" (Lk 10:9,11).

The social revolutionary message of the Magnificat is often blunted by current scholarly interpretation of the toppling of the rulers and the exaltation of the lowly in terms of "eschatological reversal." But there is nothing in the Lukan context to suggest that God's redemptive actions here are eschatological. And in the Magnificat itself, God's overthrow of the rulers and exaltation of the lowly is portrayed in much the same way as the typical historical actions of God in near-contemporary poetry such as Sir 10:14 and the War Scroll from Qumran ("You have raised the fallen by your strength, and have cut down the high and mighty" [1QM 14:10-11]). Like the blessings Jesus proclaims for the poor and the hungry, so the salvation expressed in hymnic form in the Magnificat involves concrete socio-economic transformations. Mary's song praises God for effecting dramatic social and economic changes (Horsley, 1989: 113-114).

The Magnificat gives vigorous expression to the frustrations and expectations arising from an oppressed situation. The community of the poor in which this hymn took shape has experienced the insensitive conceit of the rich and the proud (Lk 1:51) and the oppression of the mighty (Lk 1:52); they know what it is to be underprivileged, "of low degree" (Lk 1:52) and to have to go hungry (Lk 1:53). The have shared the humiliation of the country, Israel (Lk 1:54). The promises made to the patriarchs (Lk 1:54-55) are no empty words for them, nor even mere symbols of "spiritual" graces: they express the anguished longing for liberation. Faith in the covenant implied for them, exactly as for the ancient Israelites, salvation from outside and inside enemies, fearless security and the reign of righteousness and justice (see Lk 1:74-75; Legrand, 1989: 7-8).

The reversal described here between the proud and the mighty, on the one hand, and those of low degree, on the other, can also be seen in terms of honor-shame. The usual categories of what is of worth are being turned upside down. The theme of reversal of fortunes is a common one in both the literature of the Near East and the Old Testament. Note also the term "rich." In agrarian societies, the terms "rich" and "poor" are more than economic or political, though economics and politics are included. To be rich in the New Testament is to be able to defend one's honor, one's position. To be poor is to be vulnerable, open to attack and loss (Malina-Rohrbaugh, 1992: 291).

Verses 46-47:   (46) And Mary said,
                "My soul magnifies the Lord.
                (47) and my spirit rejoices in God my Savior,

Though verses 46-49 relate ostensibly to Mary's personal situation there are various suggestions that more is involved. There is certainly a point in seeing Mary's words in a wider frame of reference than that of her personal triumph. Her role in the Magnificat is unique; but nevertheless she stands among the people as one of those whom the messiah comes to save (Seccombe, 1982: 74-75).

The poem begins with two lines in synonymous parallelism that establish the celebrative character of the song. The primary actor of the song, God, is praised by the recipient of God's action. Commentators are agreed that "my soul" and the paralleled "my spirit" do not refer here to entities within the human personality but are simply periphrastic ways of saying "I." The text reminds us of several Old Testament passages. "Then my soul shall rejoice in the Lord, exulting in his deliverance" (Ps 35:9). "My heart exults in the Lord, my strength is exalted in my God" (1 Sam 1:1-2; Hannah's song). "I shall find gladness in the Lord; I shall rejoice in God my Savior" (Hab 3:18). Although Habakkuk is the most exact parallel to verse 47, the vocabulary of the Magnificat has been influenced by many other Old Testament passages. "Magnify" and "rejoice" appear together in Ps 19:5LXX; 40:16; 70:4. The parallel between "soul" and "spirit" is found in Isa 26:9; Job 12:10; Dan 3:39,86. The last parallel, coming as it does in the Song of the Three Children, is especially noteworthy. To the two verses as a whole, Ps 35:9 and, to a lesser degree, 1 Sam 2:1, are parallel. (Farris, 1985: 118,186). It is without a doubt correct to say that "It [the couplet] looks like a quotation, but it is not. It is freshly minted" (Jones, 1968: 21).

The reference to God as "my Savior," which echoes Habakkuk's hymn, was uttered by a spokesperson of Jewish Christians, a member of the early Jesus movement, who believed that Habakkuk's longing for salvation had seen fulfillment. Luke, who esteems Mary as the first Christian disciple, has placed the hymn on her lips and thus given her the role of spokesperson of the Anawim. He had an excellent antecedent for this in the Old Testament portrait of Hannah the mother of Samuel. We shall see that the Mary/Hannah parallelism continues in Lk 2 when Mary brings Jesus to the temple, even as Hannah brought Samuel to the tabernacle of Shiloh. Another good antecedent was Judith, "blessed among women," who also sang a song of the oppressed and weak people (Judith 13:18; 16:11; Brown, 1977: 357,360).

In describing God as her "Savior," Mary is not just pointing to her individual blessing as mother of the messiah, nor is she expressing a notion of personal salvation (all Luke's references to Jesus as "Savior" have in view the nation – Lk 2:11; Acts 5:31; 13:23). Rather, Mary is identifying herself with the people that God has pledged to save through his messiah (Seccombe, 1981: 75).

"The Lord... God my Savior" is identified more precisely as "the mighty one" in verse 49. This is clearly the divine warrior, the champion of Israel who saves the people from their enemy oppressors, as in Zeph 3:17. "He has shown strength with his arm" (Lk 1:51) is similarly a reference to the divine warrior, who, in Ps 89:13, 10, has "a mighty arm," with which he "scattered his enemies." The "great things" done by the mighty one refers to events of liberation, as in Deut 10:21 and Ps 105, and "holy is his name" similarly refers to God's redemption of and provision of land and food for his people, as in Ps 111, which is echoed also in the Benedictus (Lk 1:68). The hymn thus focuses on praise of God as the champion of the people and evokes a long and deep memory of God's great acts of deliverance such as the exodus from Egypt and the prophetic promises of renewed redemption (Horsley, 1989: 111). It has even been argued that the Exodus provides the main background for the salvation language of the Magnificat (Vogels, 1975: 279-296).

The verb "magnify" here means to "declare great" rather than to make great, as in Ps 69:30, "I will praise the name of God with a song; I will magnify him with thanksgiving." Mary celebrates the "greatness" of the Lord God and is filled with praise for God's beneficent and liberating deeds.

Verse 48: for he has looked with favor on the lowliness of his servant.
            Surely, from now on all generations will call me blessed.

At this point, in accordance with the pattern of declarative psalms, the reason for praise is given. Many scholars consider this verse an interpolation by Luke to adapt the hymn to its present context (Farris, 185: 114; Brown, 1977: 356-357; York, 1991: 48). By alluding to the words of two Old Testament mothers, Hannah (verse 48a) and Leah (verse 48b), the hymn makes clear that the speaker praises God for the gift of a son. By describing herself as the Lord's "servant," Mary acknowledges her submission to God's purpose and her role in assisting that purpose, and also claims a place in God's household. That is, her response is one of absolute identification with God and his aims so that partnership in the purpose of God transcends even the claims of family (see Lk 8:19-21; 9:57-62; 12:51-53; 14:25-26; 18:28-30; Green, 1995: 36).

The "servant" here is a particular individual in contrast to the "servant" of verse 54, which is Israel. Mary is not, however, simply speaking as an individual. Because God has looked on her "lowliness," the "lowly" are exalted (verse 52). That Mary speaks for the people is also shown by the change from first-person singular self-references in the first part of the hymn (verses 48-49) to the first-person plural of the conclusion "our ancestors" (verse 55). The "I" who speaks in the hymn is both a particular individual, Mary, and the representative of God's people (Farris, 1985: 118). The word *tapeinōsis*, translated here "lowliness," is in the Old Testament often descriptive of persecution or oppression from which God delivers his people, e.g., Deut 26:7; Ps 136:23. In 1 Sam 1:11 (the Hannah story), which is almost certainly the background for the usage here, *tapeinōsis* translates a Hebrew word which is related to the concept of the *Anawim*. Hannah was one of the "poor ones" because of her barrenness, but *tapeinōsis* can refer to low estate in a much wider sense (Brown, 1977: 336).

The second half of the verse represents a parenthetical glimpse into the future. Mary is to be called "blessed" by all future generations. The Old Testament background of the verse is clearly the word of Leah (Gen 30:13). The verse contains, therefore, two clear references to Old Testament mothers, Leah and Hannah. Its inclusion seems to tie the hymn to its context and makes Mary the speaking "I" of the hymn (Farris, 1985: 21,25,119).

Verse 49a: For the Mighty One has done great things for me,

Another, somewhat more general motive for praise is given (Marshall, 1978: 83). The Lord can be magnified, declared great, because he has done "great things" (Ernst, 1977: 81). This motive clause also anticipates the remainder of the hymn. The "great

things" are the "mighty acts of God." Ps 111:2,9 may have inspired much of the wording of verse 49, but Deut 10:21, where
the mighty acts of God are those connected with the Exodus,
closely parallels verse 49a. In the Magnificat the mighty acts
are specified in verses 51ff. (Jones, 1968: 23). *Dunatoi*, "the mighty
ones," are usually human in the Old Testament, but the word
is occasionally used of God, as the divine warrior who rescues
his people (Ps 24:8; 45:2(3); Zeph 3:17; Brown, 1977: 337; Bock,
1994: 151).

Verses 49b-50: 49b: and holy is his name.
                 50: His mercy is for those who fear him,
                     from generation to generation.

Verse 49b belongs with verse 50 rather than with verse 49a
(Farris, 1985: 120). Lk 1:50 forms a transition in that Mary
turns from a consideration of God's specific action for her (Lk
1:47-49) to a consideration of God's actions for his people (Lk
1:51-53). Such transitions from the individual (first-person singular) to the community (third-person plural) are common in
the Psalms (e.g., Pss 9; 30; 66; 68; 72; 117; 137; Nolland, 1989:
71; Bock, 1994: 153). Moreover, verses 49b and 50 are also
linked to verses 54 and 55 by the use of "mercy" (*eleos*). Furthermore, both passages relate God's mercy to past and future
generations. Two general statements are made about God's nature: he is holy and he is merciful. Descriptive psalms of praise
characteristically praise both God's majesty and his goodness
(Westermann, 1966: 131). In this couplet the Magnificat con-
forms to that pattern.

The background of verse 49b is Ps 111:9: "He sent redemption
to his people; he has commanded his covenant forever, holy
and awesome is his name," a verse to which the Benedictus
also alludes (Lk 1:68). God is to be held holy because he does
great and fearful things for his people. There is a certain resemblance between this statement and the first petition of the Lord's
prayer. The Old Testament background of verse 50 is clearly Ps
103:17: "But the steadfast love of the Lord is from everlasting
to everlasting on those who fear him..." The allusion to this

psalm is the only justification for the traditional versification of the hymn. Without that Old Testament background it might seem preferable to attach "those who fear him" to the next verse, viz., "to those who fear him he has shown strength with his arm; he has scattered the proud in the thoughts of their hearts."

Verse 51: He has shown strength with his arm;
he has scattered the proud in the thoughts of their hearts.

Verse 51 begins a series of three couplets in antithetical parallelism in each of which God shows his mercy to his people but punishes his people's enemies. In the traditional division of the verses, verse 51a lacks a recipient of God's mercy to balance the "proud" of verse 51b. Taking "those who fear him" with verse 51a supplies that lack. It would also improve the parallelism of verses 49b and 50 for there is nothing in the former verse which corresponds to "those who fear him." A glance at a Hebrew reconstruction of the text shows that the balance of the word mass, so important in Hebrew poetry, would also be improved by taking these words with what follows (Winter, 1954: 346). Even if this division of the verses is not accepted, it is clear that "those who fear him" are the ones for whom God acts in verse 51 (Brown, 1977: 337). "Those who fear him" are those who acknowledge God's sovereignty (de Cantanzero, 1963: 166ff.). That God acts graciously to those who fear him is not a new idea. It appears, for example, frequently in the Psalms (Ps 25:11; 34:9; 85:9; 103:11,13,17), and at several points in the Psalms of Solomon (Ps Sol 2:33; 13:12; 15:13).

In verse 51 the hymn changes its focus from *what God is* to *what he has done*. The aorist verbs look back at the birth of Jesus, but also express vividly the sure consequences of that coming.

Behind the first half of this verse lie Ps 89:10, "You crushed Rahab like a carcass; you scattered your enemies with your mighty arm," and Ps 118:15-16, "The right hand of the Lord does valiantly; the right hand of the Lord is exalted; the right hand of the Lord does valiantly." The reference to the "arm" of the Lord shows that the Exodus paradigm is still in the forefront. The fact that such language passed into liturgical descriptions of the Exodus no doubt ensured its transmission in relation to the theme of salvation. In Isaiah, and to a lesser extent, Ezekiel, it is used to describe the new Exodus (Seccombe, 1981: 77-78). The divine warrior language of verse 51a reminds one of the title "mighty one" in verse 49. Furthermore, both verses use the same verb *epoiēsen*, literally "made." In effect, this verse rephrases verse 49a (Tannehill, 1974: 272). By doing so, verse 51 links the more general statements of God's activity with the more personal ones in the first part of the hymn.

The expression "shown," or literally "made," strength is not a native Greek one (Brown, 1977: 337). The "arm" of God is a symbol of his power (Ernst, 1977: 86) and is frequently connected with the Exodus events (Marshall, 1978: 83). The images of divine power offered in verses 51-54a are images of a God who is prepared to immerse himself in the socio-economic world of the human being: the divine power which inscribes itself in human flesh also inscribes itself in the flesh of human society (Coleridge, 1993: 92).

The second half of the verse introduces a new theme, that God acts not only *for* those who depend on him, but also *against* those who refuse to do so (Tannehill, 1974: 275). The "proud" are those who are self-sufficient; they look down on the humble (verse 52) but not up to God. In effect, they are the opposite of those who fear him (verse 50). Pride is the characteristic of the enemies of God's people. Ps Sol 17 attributes this fault four times to the enemy (Ps Sol 17:6,13,23,41; Jones, 1968: 25). The location of this particular form of pride is the heart, the center of reasoning power (Brown, 1977: 337; see Obad 3:3-4: "...Your proud heart has deceived you... You say in your heart, 'Who will bring me down to the ground?'"). The strong language of verse 51 points toward the very forceful, carefully constructed climax of the poem found in verses 52-53 (York, 1991: 50).

Verses 52-53:   (52) He has brought down the powerful from their
                       thrones,
                       and lifted up the lowly;
                 (53) he has filled the hungry with good things,
                       and sent the rich away empty.

Verses 52-53 form a unit of thought. They make use of the
common classical Old Testament motif of the reversal of fortunes. Their unity is indicated by a clear chiastic structure
(Tannehill, 1974: 267). If the work that God does against the
wicked can be designated as A, and the work for his people by
B, the structure of the four lines is: ABBA. The quatrain as a
whole is paralleled by 1 Sam 2:7-8 (Hannah's song), but its
individual members more closely resemble various other texts.

The reversal of social position will occur in the final exercise of God's power. Who is described? The lowly (*tapeinous*)
stand in contrast to the powerful (*dunastas*), a term that refers
to rulers (Gen 50:4). That rulers are removed from their thrones
makes the nuance of *tapeinous* clear. The powerful are governing rulers. The lowly are those oppressed by these rulers (Bock,
1994: 156).

The reversal presented in verses 51-53 is almost universally
described as *eschatological* reversal. Such an identification, however, does not solve the problem of the function of these verses
in the narrative as a whole. Whatever one claims for the
eschatological nature of the reversals in these verses must also
take into consideration the relationship of these verses to that
part of the Magnificat in which Mary states, "from now on all
generations will call me blessed" (Lk 1:48). Regardless of one's
decision about the authenticity of verse 48b, it projects an extended period of time before the Last Day (Esler, 1987: 64).
The suggestion that God's action toward Mary is an eschatological
event signaling the beginning of the end still may be appropriate for the Gospel as a whole if one does not demand that the
"end" be imminent (Schottroff, 1978: 305-306). If by eschatology
one is referring to the *broader concept of the break-up of the existing order*, then it is possible to understand God's acts towards

Mary as eschatological and to see the reversals of verses 51-53 as indicative of the new order that has already been inaugurated. While Luke never rules out the apocalyptic notions of a new age, it is clear that, in the person of Jesus, the future has broken into the present. It is therefore appropriate that the reversal found in the Magnificat should be linked to God's actions toward "his servant." In her the new order has begun (York, 1991: 54-55).

The eschatological reversal announced in verses 52-53 makes no sense unless the Old Testament understanding of poverty as a state of unjust oppression continues in the New Testament. God must redress injustice and can only do this by bringing down the oppressor (the rich) and lifting up the oppressed (the poor; Soares-Prabhu, 1991: 160). The first line declares that God has pulled the rulers down from their thrones. The language of this half verse is reminiscent of Job 12:19, "He leads priests away stripped, and overthrows the mighty," and Sir 10:14, "The Lord overthrows the thrones of rulers and enthrones the lowly in their place." "The powerful" (*dunastai*) could be any kind of ruler from the minor official to the emperor, but the fact that they are to be put down from their *thrones* suggests that the Magnificat is thinking less of the petty harassment of the people and more of those who hold ultimate sway keeping them a subject and oppressed people (Seccombe, 1982: 79).

At this point we have touched upon a matter which has keenly interested biblical scholars for many years. Who are "the lowly" or, more simply, "the poor?" There is voluminous literature on the poor, both in the Bible as a whole and, more specifically, in the Gospel of Luke. To discuss the problem in depth would certainly demand an entire volume (Seccombe, 1982: 21-69; Mealand, 1980: 103-104).

The problem that must chiefly concern us here is, quite specifically, who are the "poor" *in the Magnificat?* In the first place it is obvious that they are the opposite of the "proud" (verse 51), the "mighty" (verse 52a), and the "rich" (verse 53a; see above). They are "those who fear God" (verse 50), the "hungry" (verse 53b), and ultimately, Israel (verse 54). Most importantly, they are those for whom God has acted (verses 51ff.).

The complex of ideas associated with the "poor" in the Magnificat finds its antecedent in the Psalms, where several Hebrew words are used to describe the poor and afflicted and these, in turn, are rendered by several Greek words in the Septuagint. These words cluster together in such a way, however, that one is justified in treating them together. According to the Psalms, God delivers a "poor" and "humble" people, but humbles the arrogant (Ps 18:27). He saves the poor man (here *ptōchos*, like in the first beatitude, etc.) and his angel camps around those who fear him (Ps 34:6-7). The nation of Israel can be called the "poor" (Ps 72:2; 149:4). Above all, the poor are those whom God saves (Ps 34:18; Ps 35:10 [*ptōchon*]; cf. Prov 3:34).

There seem to be three closely related elements in the language used about the "poor": attitude, situation, and national identity. The poor are not only the destitute, they are those who depend utterly on Yahweh. They are, however, also very often those who live in real affliction and so cry to Yahweh because of their need. They are also the recipients of salvation; God sees their weakness and delivers them from it. Finally, the word can be a self-designation for Israel.

The hungry and rich are not further groups, but an alternative characterization of the lowly and the powerful. Salvation means the satisfaction of the needs of the hungry and the destruction of the oppressors (Seccombe, 1981: 79). The poverty and hunger of the oppressed in the Magnificat may also have been spiritual, but we should not forget the physical realities faced by the early Christians. The first followers of Jesus were Galileans; and Galilee, victimized by absentee ownership of estates (see Lk 20:9), was the spawning ground of first-century revolts against a repressive occupation and taxation it engendered (Acts 5:37; Brown, 1977: 363).

None of these aspects of the word are irrelevant to the Magnificat. The word *tapeinōsis* derives its strength and power from the many layers of meaning given to it by ancient biblical

use. Those of low estate certainly share the ultimate dependence on Yahweh characteristic of the Old Testament poor.
Their situation has been one of need and perhaps is so still. But
here we have a significant development: rescue of the poor,
which is characteristic of God, has definitively been achieved.
Those who sing the hymn may be the poor and afflicted but
they are already the *saved poor*. They are also Israel (Seccombe,
1982: 91ff.), but they are the Israel whom God has helped. By
reference to the companion hymn, the Benedictus, we know
the nature of that help: God has visited and redeemed his people
by sending the messiah of David's line, Jesus. By doing so God
has achieved the final, definitive deliverance of his people (Johnson,
1977: 127-158). But the word *tapeinous* ought not to attract all
attention. It is marvelously appropriate here not only because
its use calls forth a particularly rich array of Old Testament
associations but because it has obvious opposites, the proud and
the rich. This suits the intention of this section of the hymn
which states clearly that God has reversed the orders of society.
That God reverses the orders of society, pulling down those
who are high and raising up the lowly, is a sign of his righteousness and sovereignty (Farris, 1985: 121-123).

Verse 54: He has helped his servant Israel,
          in remembrance of his mercy,

The verse summarizes the "great things" for which God is praised:
he has "helped his servant Israel." Israel is called servant as at
Isa 41:8; 44:1, etc. What has been done for Mary has consequences for Israel. All three hymns of Luke's infancy narrative
emphasize that God has done something for "Israel." "He has
helped his servant Israel" (Lk 1:54). The God of Israel has "looked
favorably on his people and redeemed them" (Lk 1:68). The
present salvation is "for glory to your people Israel" (Lk 2:32).
The Jewish Christians, to whom the composition of these hymns
probably ought to be attributed, here identify themselves with
Israel.

  The second line recalls Ps 98:3, "He has remembered his

steadfast love and faithfulness to the house of Israel." In acting the way it is described God calls to mind his covenant relationship with Israel (C.F. Evans, 1990: 176). When his people in Egypt cried because of their bondage God remembered his covenant with Abraham, Isaac and Jacob (Ex 2:23-25). Thus, in the last verses of the Magnificat, even more obviously than at the beginning, attention is on salvation understood in terms of the paradigms of Exodus and the new Exodus (Seccombe, 1982: 77). We must be careful not to interpret the eschatological reversal solely in a spiritualized form, so that the context of the national hope is lost (Lk 1:54-55; Bock, 1994: 157).

Verse 55: according to the promise he made to our ancestors,
    to Abraham and his descendants forever."

At this point one comes across an assertion which is repeated with even greater emphasis in the Benedictus (Lk 1:72-73), and implied by the Nunc Dimittis (Lk 2:30-31): the present salvation is the fulfillment of ancient promise. It is the culmination of saving history. Like Lk 1:72 the language appears to be colored by the memory of Micah 7:20, "You will show faithfulness to Jacob and unswerving loyalty to Abraham, as you have sworn to our ancestors from the days of old." But it may well be that only a Christian author would weave together these Old Testament expressions into such a decisive affirmation (Jones, 1968: 28).

The promise was "to our ancestors, to Abraham and his descendants forever." The figure of Abraham reappears in the Benedictus (Lk 1:73). Indeed, Father Abraham appears twenty-two times in Luke-Acts as a whole. God's promise to the fathers, from Abraham onward, is a theme that runs through the whole of Luke's two-volume work (Dahl, 1966: 151). He appears as the recipient par excellence of the promise that now finds fulfillment.

The hymn ends with the word "forever." Such a formula very frequently ends a psalm and it should not be attached too closely to any preceding part of speech. The formula has two functions: it states that the present salvation is not ephemeral but will last for all time and it marks the end of the psalm (Farris, 1985: 124-126). "Forever" translates *eis ton aiōna*, literally, "into the age." It refers to the messianic age of deliverance. Since what is found in that age will continue forever (Plummer, 1901: 34), one can speak idiomatically of God, remembering his mercy forever, of his constancy extending to the end (Bock, 1994: 16).

Verse 56: And Mary remained with her about three months and then returned to her home.

This verse is an editorial notice. Luke favors "about" with numbers (Lk 3:23; 9:14,28; Acts 1:15), and the verb "to return" (*hupostrephein*, thirty-three times in Luke-Acts as contrasted with four times in the rest of the New Testament) is his word. The notice removes Mary from the scene (see Lk 1:23,38) at the latest possible time in Elizabeth's pregnancy to allow the birth of John to be narrated as a separate incident (C.F. Evans, 1990: 177).

Conclusion. The episode of the visitation has completed the profile of faith begun in the earlier episodes. Faith has appeared for the first time as the engine of the plot as Mary, after her word of faith in verse 38, takes the initiative and goes to visit Elizabeth, even though what Gabriel had said to her could not be construed as invitation or command. Once Mary arrives, her greeting serves as the immediate trigger of the action that follows. The initiative therefore passes from God to Mary. In the Magnificat, understood as the birth of human memory, the narrator depicts Mary revealing, as the ground of her faith, a right reading of past signs. Where Zechariah's doubt entailed a failure of memory, Mary comes to faith because she is able to look backwards and trace a path through Scripture in a way that accords with the understanding of Scripture as promise found first in Gabriel's speech in verses 13-17. In that sense, the Magnificat looks back to her word of faith in verse 38 and reveals its hermeneutical ground. It also has Mary name her faith as Abrahamic, identifying her with the seed of Abraham and contrasting her with Zechariah, who used the words of Abraham but did not share his faith. If the Magnificat lays bare the ground of faith, it also dramatizes praise of God as faith's first fruit (Coleridge, 1993: 97-98). An episode that has added such substance to the narration of the human response to God's action must be judged more than an intermezzo, supplement or epilogue. In the sweep of the infancy narrative, the episode has brought the readers to the threshold of the stories of fulfillment, knowing that God's visitation, insofar as it is promise, demands faith, and knowing too what faith involves – where it comes from and what it brings to birth. The readers also know that God's visitation, insofar as it is fulfillment, demands a right interpretation of ambiguous signs. As the shape of God's visitation shifts from promise to fulfillment, the question for the readers is what signs fulfillment of the promise might bring, and whether or not the characters will succeed in reading them aright (Coleridge, 1993: 99).

The whole section of Lk 1:24-56 presupposes a situation inside a house; at the same time, it contains numerous references to the political and social fate of the whole people of Israel and its future (Gabriel's speech, Elizabeth's words to Mary, Mary's Magnificat). The two women's sisterhood and their fate are interwoven with each other and with the *fate of the people* as the exaltation of the debased. The *degradation of women* and the *degradation of the people* belong together. The text is about people's degradation at the time when the Gospel was composed and when its oral and written sources came into being; it is about the Jewish people during the Pax Romana. The Magnificat and the other hymns need to be read from a social-historical perspective. The people's return to God, their political liberation and their social justice go together. Mary's degradation is not described in the Magnificat, but it is seen as part of the people's degradation. Just as the people's liberation calls for the people to turn back to God, the liberation of debased women is connected with women's *liberating actions*. Such

actions are the core of the gynocentric narrative of Elizabeth
and Mary. The two women prophetically herald God's world
revolution, God's option for the poor, which begins as an option for Mary and for women; she is "blessed *among women*"
(Lk 1:42), all generations to come shall call her blessed (Lk
1:48). The exaltation of debased Mary begins the liberaton of
the people, begins the actualization of the option for women
and the poor. Mary's experience of oppression is not specifically mentioned; it is part of women's experience of degradation, for example, that of childless women, and that which a
politically oppressed or predominantly hungry people endure.
Mary is one of such women, one of such people. She heralds
the world revolution and gives liberation a name: Jesus (Lk
1:31; Schottroff, 1995: 192-195).

4. The Birth of John the Baptist (Lk 1:57-80)

Introduction. Lk 1:57-80 is both an end and a beginning.
On the one hand, it brings the narrative to a point of rest,
completing the story of John the Baptist begun in Lk 1:5-25.
Much of what was promised in Lk 1:5-25 is fulfilled: the promised son is born, his birth is greeted with joy, he is named John,
Zechariah is released from his silence. After the seclusion of Lk
1:26-38 and 39-56, the scene is again set in the public arena.
In Lk 1:5-25, it was "the people" at prayer; now it is the crowd
of "neighbors and relatives" that is present. The narrative reassumes
its public dimension. Moreover, there are points of similarity
with the previous episode. All of this suggests that this episode
looks back to what preceded and concludes the first phase of
the infancy narrative.

At the same time, there are clear differences between this
episode and both the opening scene (Lk 1:5-25) and the immediately preceding episode (Lk 1:39-56). Lk 1:5-25 was situated
for the most part in the Jerusalem temple and then briefly in
the house of Zechariah. Lk 1:57-80, however, is situated for the
most part in the house of Zechariah, then briefly in the Judean

hills, and finally in the desert. The differences suggest that Lk 1:57-80 is as much a beginning as an end, that it does not only look back to what has been, but also looks ahead to what is coming. It would seem then that we are at a point of transition – a point where the narrator concludes the first phase of the infancy narrative in order to begin the second (Coleridge, 1993: 100-101).

Mary has returned to Nazareth, but the narrator and the reader stay with Elizabeth, to whom the focus shifts and who, for a brief moment, becomes the focus of the narrative.

a. The Birth of John (Lk 1:57-66)

Verse 57: Now the time came for Elizabeth to give birth, and she bore a son.

Literally, the verse begins with the words, "And to Elizabeth," which suggests that she is more recipient than agent. Literally the verse begins, "And to Elizabeth was fulfilled (*eplesthe*) the time," in which "was fulfilled" could simply denote the completion of the time of pregnancy; but in the Lukan narrative, which makes so much of fulfillment, the overtone is unmistakable (Fitzmyer, 1981: 373). The solemn expression (also found in Lk 1:23; 2:6,21,22) may have overtones of the fulfillment of God's promise (Schweizer, 1984: 38).

In verse 57b, Elizabeth becomes the subject. At this point, the initiative passes entirely to Elizabeth, and it will remain with her until the end of verse 60. She who remained in the background through most of Lk 1:5-25 and who turned all attention away from herself to Mary in Lk 1:39-56, now briefly comes to the center stage and, as believer, will initiate the action in this episode before she disappears from the narrative altogether (Coleridge, 1993: 102).

Verse 58: Her neighbors and relatives heard
that the Lord had shown his great mercy to her,
and they rejoiced with her.

The narrator does not focus on the figure of the newborn child, even though he is destined to play so decisive a role in the unfolding of the divine plan. It is peculiar too that the narrator delays the report of Elizabeth's reaction to the birth. He also decides to delay the report of Zechariah's reaction, of which nothing is said until verse 64. The delay serves to continue the total backgrounding of Zechariah, which began in verse 24. In these first two verses of this episode, John, Elizabeth and Zechariah are all left out of consideration in different ways and the focus is on the crowd of "neighbors and relatives" who are very much in evidence in verse 58 and will remain so through much of the episode (Coleridge, 1993: 103).

The crowd's reaction is reported without delay; and it confirms the truth of what Gabriel said in verse 14b: "and many will rejoice at his birth." Their reaction is essentially theocentric, as they recognize God as subject and his action as manifestation of his mercy, with *eleos* echoing both verse 25 and the Magnificat, and anticipating the Benedictus. At this point, the crowd reads the signs well. Their interpretation stems from a knowledge of what God has done in the past: Scripture testifies that God can give children to old and sterile women. Later in the episode they will bear the word of God's action into the wider circle of the Judean hill country (Coleridge, 1993: 104).

These people play a double role in the scene. They are supportive in the narrator's summary (Lk 1:58) and antagonistic in the scene proper (Lk 1:61; Kozar, 1990: 217). Moreover, they validate the events, as required in honor-shame societies. As talk spread (Lk 1:65), especially about the lifting of the curse, the new information would have served everyone in the hill country as a guide for interaction with Zechariah and his family as well as for reassessing opinions of them. Among non-literate peoples (only two to four percent could read or write in agrarian societies), communication is basicaly by word of mouth. Where reputation (honor status) is concerned, gossip informed the community about (and validated) ongoing gains and losses and thereby provided a guide to proper social interaction. Its effects could be both positive (confirm honor, spread reputation, shape and guide public interaction) and negative (undermine others), though overall it tended to maintain the status quo by highlighting deviation (Malina-Rohrbaugh, 1992: 292, 308).

Verses 59-61: (59) On the eighth day they came to circumcise the child,
and they were going to call him Zechariah after his father.
(60) But his mother said, "No; he is to be called John."
(61) They said to her, "None of your relatives has this name."

Lk 1:57-59 establishes the background of the scene for the reader. At verse 59 the narrator moves ahead in story time to the incident that bears the narrative weight of the episode. Indeed, with the arrival of the day on which the child is to be circumcised and named (Lk 1:59a), the scene proper begins (Kozar, 1990: 217-218). According to the instructions found in Gen 17:9-14, the child is circumcised on the eighth day (Danker, 1988: 46). There is evidence for the practice of naming a child after a grandfather (1 Macc 2:1-2), but in view of the extraordinary circumstances, attention is here focused on the father (Danker, 1988: 46). Though the origins of circumcision are obscure, it is clear that it was widely practiced in the societies of the ancient Near East. The significance of the practice varied, since its meaning depended on social context. Although there may be some *religious* significance to the practice of infant circumcision (a sign of covenant relations, but see Jer 9:25), a number of the *social* implications of the practice can be seen in Luke's Gospel. There can be little doubt of the early association of circumcision with the acceptance of a child by the father as his own. Acceptance by the father that a child was his own may also account for the association of circumcision with naming; see Lk 1:59 and 2:21. Finally, community participation in the rite sealed with public recognition a father's acknowledgement that he had assumed paternal responsibility (Malina-Rohrbaugh, 1992: 292-293).

Although circumcision is mentioned first and the naming is

an addendum to circumcision, the naming is the narrator's real concern, and the circumcision is never mentioned again after verse 59. As in Lk 1:5-25, we have a Jewish rite mentioned, but never narrated; and the effect is the same as in the first episode. It has been suggested that the association of naming and circumcision is the result of Hellenistic influence (Ellis, 1966: 75; Marshall, 1978: 88; Ernst, 1977: 9). From a narrative point of view, however, the key question is not the historical one, but the question of why the narrator chooses to associate circumcision and naming, whatever the historical facts may have been. It stands in the narrative as an image of the way in which the divine action now unfolding surpasses (without rejecting) the world of Judaism, symbolized here as earlier by one of its rites. This is why the narrator chooses to associate the naming with the circumcision, even though the more usual Jewish practice seems to have been to name the child at birth (Coleridge, 1993: 105; Danker, 1988: 46).

The "neighbors and relatives" had already begun to call (meaning suggested by the imperfect tense) the child after his father, on the assumption that custom would prevail and that there was no decision to be made in the matter. Elizabeth's brusque rejoinder to the crowd – the strong formulation *ouchi alla* implying more than a polite difference of opinion with the crowd – provokes the action that is the episode's real concern. The obvious surprise is that Elizabeth usurps the place of Zechariah, the one that the reader expects to utter these words – in fact, in Lk 1:13, addressing Zechariah, Gabriel had said, "you will name him John." But this is the very point of the present narrative. Elizabeth, the woman who correctly sees the Lord's hand in her pregnancy, the reliable vehicle who informs the reader that Mary will be "mother" and confidently explains the dual reason that Mary is blessed, is the character who fittingly calls the child "John" (Kozar, 1990: 218).

Elizabeth's rejoinder prompts the question of how she has come to the knowledge that her words imply, since in previous episodes there was no indication that Elizabeth knew of Gabriel's instruction concerning the child's name. The narrator chooses not to tell the reader how Elizabeth knows; and the effect of this is to leave the "how" of the divine action concealed. The will of heaven has been communicated to Elizabeth somehow; but the narrator leaves the details undisclosed in order to build into the episode for the first time the paradoxical combination of revelation and concealment that marks the presentation of God's action in Lk 1:57-80 (Coleridge, 1993: 107-108). To ask the question of how Elizabeth received the knowledge implied in her rejoinder is to fail to understand Luke's narrative, which was not meant to bear such scrutiny (Fitzmyer, 1981: 381; Danker, 1988: 46).

Verses 62-64: (62) Then they began motioning to his father
to find out what name he wanted to give him.
(63) He asked for a writing tablet and wrote,
"His name is John."
And all of them were amazed.
(64) Immediately his mouth was opened and his tongue freed,
and he began to speak, praising God.

By having the crowd turn to Zechariah, the narrator strengthens the sense that for the neighbors and relatives the naming of the child is a matter for human decision (see the optative *theloi*), and for human decision along the lines prescribed by convention. Clearly the crowd expects the dumbstruck patriarch to defend convention and reject the strange whimsicality of his wife. The sense is that Zechariah is the one in control. They appeal to him as the ultimate source of authority (C.F. Evans, 1990: 180). But then the narrator has Zechariah re-enter the narrative by making a gesture which signals his powerlessness in the face of the divine action; because he cannot speak, he requests a "writing tablet." His gesture of taking charge (as the *crowd* might see it) is in fact (as the *readers* know) a gesture signaling that heaven has the upper hand. At this point of the narrative, it is a question of who is in control (Coleridge, 1993: 108).

Somewhat puzzlingly, the narrator has the crowd make signs to Zechariah when they turn to him. Although there is no suggestion in Lk 1:22 that Zechariah has also been afflicted with deafness, in the popular mind muteness and deafness would be inseparably connected (see Mk 7:32, 37; 9:25). Luke registers normal cultural reactions and he records that the relatives made signs to the father (Danker, 1988: 46). But underlying this and other attempts at interpretation found in the commentaries is a speculation that is not grounded in the narrative itself, e.g., that Zechariah was deaf as well as dumb. The answer to the question as to why the crowd makes signs to Zechariah must lie elsewhere. It is first worth noting that "they began motioning" in verse 62 is a different compound of the same verb used of Zechariah in verse 22, "he kept motioning." The verbal link suggests that there is a link between the signing of Zechariah to the people earlier and the signing of the crowd to him now. But what kind of link? Since it is the crowd that seems the narrative's real concern at this point, it is therefore by attending to the crowd rather than to Zechariah that an answer may be found to the question of why the narrator has the crowd make signs to Zechariah (Coleridge, 1993: 109).

What is clear is that they are seeking to overturn what they take to be Elizabeth's decision to call the child John. In this, they are unwittingly seeking to thwart the divine plan declared by Gabriel in verse 13, "you will name him John," and in the attempt, they turn to Zechariah who in his own way has sought to thwart the divine plan in the first episode (Lk 1:5-25). As a result, Zechariah was struck silent in a way which forced him to use signs to communicate (*dianeuōn*) to the people. Now as they seek to enlist Zechariah's support in their unwitting attempt to thwart the divine plan, the narrator has the crowd use Zechariah's language of signs (*eneneuon*). They are like him because, though they seek to thwart the divine plan, they end up collaborating with it – again unwittingly. This is because in turning to Zechariah they draw him back into the narrative for the first time since verse 23, and not in a way that will thwart the divine plan, but rather in a way that will accept and acclaim the divine plan as Zechariah breaks into praise (verse 64).

When Zechariah's written answer comes in verse 63, it comes not as a report of a decision he has made, but as a declaration of a state of affairs which transcends Zechariah's own power of choice: "His name is John." Gabriel's prophecy is fulfilled; and the declaration stands in the narrative as a symbol of Zechariah's acceptance of God's plan. It is also the birth of proclamation, as the future "he is to be called John" [he will be called John] of verse 60 gives way to the present "is." His announcement signals that he has read correctly the signs of God's action and that he reads the larger promise differently in the light of the fulfillment he witnessed. Zechariah has come to the understanding and acceptance of the divine plan at which he balked in the first episode; and this understanding and acceptance become the ground for public proclamation, however terse and cryptic it may be in its first moment. Zechariah is miraculously released from the punishment for his previous disbelief, as the angel had predicted (Lk 1:20). This is stressed by the word "immediately" (*parachrēma*, a favorite Lukan word which appears here for the first time; C.F. Evans, 1990: 180; Fabricius, 1985:62-66).

Elizabeth and the readers know that this is a proclamation of the divine plan; but since no explanation is given as to why the child is to be called John, the crowd does not know. The readers but not the crowd know that in seeming to confirm Elizabeth's decision, Zechariah in fact confirms the decision of God, and that he does so freely, with no hint of heavenly manipulation or compulsion of any kind. The first thing Zechariah did after receiving his speech again was "praising God" (Fitzmyer, 1981: 382). The best the crowd can manage is an amazement from which none is exempt as "all" makes clear (Coleridge, 1993: 110-111).

Verses 65-66: (65) Fear came over all their neighbors,
and all these things were talked about
throughout the entire hill country of Judea.

(66) All who heard them pondered them and said,
"What then will this child become?"
For, indeed, the hand of the Lord was with him.

In a concluding summary (Lk 1:65-66), the narrator first notes that the emotion of fear – already experienced by Zechariah (Lk 1:12) and Mary (Lk 1:30) – now touches the crowd (Lk 1:65a). Then, description of the crowd's reaction returns the reader's attention not to Zechariah, who has just recovered his speech (Lk 1:64), but to his son (Kozar, 1990: 219). In verses 65-66 the narrator interpolates a longer and more nuanced report of the crowd's reaction between the report of Zechariah's praise of God in verse 64b and the Benedictus (Lk 1:67-79). From the amazement provoked by Zechariah's declaration in verse 63, the crowd moves now to fear in the wake of his praise of God in verse 64. Here, as before fear is the standard human response to the irruption of the numinous. The crowd has come to a sense that God is stirring in unusual ways in the events that they have witnessed. They recognized God's hand in enabling Elizabeth to give birth; and that recognition moved them to joy (verse 58). Now they recognize God's hand in enabling Zechariah to speak; and that recognition moves them to fear (verse 65). It is Zechariah's return to speech which suggests to the crowd that there may be more to this divine intervention than the undoing of the past in the life of a childless couple. Sterile women have given birth before by God's grace; but something new is afoot here. In verse 66, fear gives birth to a question which looks wonderingly to the future, understanding that God is shaping something, but asking what this might be (Coleridge, 1993: 112-113). Thus, verses 65-66 supply the crucial clues to understand what follows, with the three decisive clues given in verse 66: (1) "All who heard them pondered them"[RSV: laid them up in their hearts] is almost a directive that all who rightly understand will join in such faithful consideration. Right understanding is a matter of the heart. (2) The question, "What then will this child become?," is thus a question of faith and wonder, inviting Zechariah's interpretive canticle (Lk 1:67-79). (3) Luke's parting remark, "For, indeed, the hand of the Lord was with him," does not attribute this verdict to any of the characters in the story. It is an uncharacteristically direct comment by the narrator to supplement and confirm the readiness of the people to receive this child of divine promise (Tiede, 1988: 59). Let's move now to a more detailed analysis of these two verses.

The fear, that is, numinous awe in the presence of divine activity (Marshall, 1978: 89), comes upon "all the neighbors," which leaves the readers wondering what happened to the "relatives" who in verse 58 were part of the crowd, and whose presence was insinuated again in verse 61 with the mention of "your relatives." They are not mentioned here because in verses 65-66 the perspective is spatial, where earlier in verses 58-63 it was more familial, which is why the "relatives" were added to the neighbors. In verse 65, the light falls first on the neighbors and then broadens to include the whole hill country of Judah. The narrator has the word of God's stirring spread beyond the narrow circles of the first three episodes (Lk 1:5-25, 26-38, 39-56; Coleridge, 1993: 113). Designation of the affected people as "all who heard" (Lk 1:66) confirms the power of the word, for the larger group is constituted by hearing (Kozar, 1990: 219). Luke wants to call attention to the magnitude of the events (the child's unexpected name and the father's regaining speech), as he also shows by inserting the Benedictus (Brown, 1977: 370).

Those who hear the news in the Judean hills store the memory of it "in their hearts" (NRSV: "pondered them"). This again heightens the importance of the events (Stein, 1992: 98). It gives an apocalyptic tone to the narrative (Hendrickx, 1984a: 89,103-104; Danker, 1988: 47). They hear of the signs but they have no way of interpreting them rightly: for that they must wait. This is the first of the infancy narrative's three references to a character or characters storing in their heart words and/or events that for the time being remain puzzling (it will be said of Mary in Lk 2:19 and again in 2:51). In verse 66 it implies at least three things: (1) words are heard that the crowd fails to understand; (2) the words have mysterious and portentous implications for the future of the one spoken about; (3) the act of storing in the heart implies not only incomprehension, but also an openness to clarification in the future, a preparedness to live with unclarity in the hope that there will come a time when the puzzling signs will disclose their true meaning. It remains to be seen whether or not it has the same meaning and effect in each of the infancy's three instances (Coleridge, 1993: 114).

The question, "What then will this child become?" looks to the distant future when John will begin his public ministry (Lk 3:1-20). The use of the neuter "what," rather than "who," suggests that the *role* of the child is at stake (Brown, 1977: 370). The news has spread in space from Zechariah's house to the entire hill-country; and now those who hear the news look from the present moment to a mysterious future. And, just as joy gave way first to bafflement and then amazement, so now amazement gives way to fear and finally to a less anguished sense that great things may be in store (Coleridge, 1993: 114). In the present sequence of the story, Zechariah answers the question, "What then will this child become?," in the Benedictus (Brown, 1977: 376).

The expression "[the] hand of the Lord" is only found in Luke-Acts in the New Testament (Acts 11:21; 13:11). The expression is not common in the Septuagint. "Hand of the Lord" is an anthropomorphism for the active presence of the power of God (Isa 41:20; 66:14; compare "his arm" in Lk 1:51; Nolland, 1989: 80).

b. The Benedictus (Lk 1:67-79)

Introduction. The Benedictus is composed of *two quite distinct sections*. From verse 67 to 75 the finite verbs are aorists (past tense) and the hymn is a praise hymn (*beraka*) to God. From verse 76 the tense shifts to the future and Zechariah addresses the infant John directly. This section has been described as a "birth ode" (*genathliakon*). Because of this change in style, many have argued that these two sections have different origins, and various source theories have been proposed. Three views predominate: (1) The hymn is a composition of two original hymns, the first of Jewish origin (verses 68-75), and the second of Christian or Baptist origin (verses 76-79). (2) The hymn is an original unity (a Jewish or Jewish-Christian messianic psalm) to which Luke (or another Christian) has added the mention of John's activity in verses 76-77. (3) The hymn is a unity (including verses 76-77) that has undergone Lukan redaction (Farris, 1985: 15-30,128-133). Whether or not these two sections are of different origin, in its present Lukan context the hymn forms a unified composition and may be shown to play an integral part in Luke's narrative development.

Several themes introduced already by Luke are picked up and developed in the hymn; others, which will become important in the subsequent narrative, are introduced for the first time (Strauss, 1995: 97-98). An examination of five of these themes, namely, (1) the actions of God, (2) the agent of the promised deliverance is the coming Davidic king, (3) the focus on the Abrahamic covenant, (4) John, the forerunner, and (5) Jesus as the "dawn from on high" (*anatolē*), illuminate the theological and christological importance of the hymn for Luke (Strauss, 1995: 98-108).

Like Lk 1:13-17 and the Magnificat, the Benedictus is composed as a biblical tapestry, "a cento-like composition" (Fitzmyer, 1981: 376), weaving together quotation, reference and echo from the Law, the Prophets and the Psalms, as can easily be seen from a concise presentation of the array of Old Testament texts found in it (Brown, 1977: 386-389). The whole of Scripture converges in the canticle, which begins as praise and ends as prophecy.

Insofar as it gathers up all Scripture into a cry of praise and, in doing so, *looks to the past*, the Benedictus reveals the ground of Zechariah's faith as the Magnificat did of Mary's: faith requires the understanding of Scripture implied in verses 13-17 and verses 46-55, a right reading of the past.

Insofar as it gathers up the whole of Scripture into a prophecy of John's ministry and, in doing so, *looks to the future*, the

Benedictus declares how Scripture (understood as promise in its entirety) is coming to fulfillment in the events unfolding now and in the future events they portend.

The Benedictus is, above all, prophetic interpretation – an interpretation of God's action now and in the future, an interpretation dependent upon a particular reading of Scripture, arising from faith and the extraordinary knowledge conferred by the Holy Spirit, and offered not by Zechariah to the neighbors but by the narrator to the reader (Coleridge, 1993: 118-119).

As with the Magnificat, perhaps our principal difficulties in attempting to hear the Benedictus and its message are to strip away the Christian christological concepts and concerns that were read into it at a later time but that are simply not in the biblical text, and to cut through the peculiar modern assumption that biblical literature and its message are somehow primarily "religious," and not politico-economic as well.

The song here placed in the mouth of Zechariah is literarily completely separable from its narrative context. According to some scholars, one could move from Lk 1:66 to 1:80 without noticing that anything is missing. The song, moreover, is not primarily focused on the significance of John the Baptist. Only verses 76-77, usually viewed as a Lukan insertion by those who recognize the rest of the song as a pre-Lukan "Jewish (Christian)" hymn, connect it with its narrative context, and finally, as it were, answer the question all were asking, "What then will this child become?" (Lk 1:66).

The Benedictus was originally a song about God's liberation of his people from subjection to their Roman and domestic rulers so that, as God fulfills his covenant to Abraham, they can serve God by maintaining covenantal justice among the people. So, the song celebrates God's salvation of the people in a comprehensive sense, the socio-political dimension being inseparable from the religious (Horsley, 1989: 114-115, 118-119).

Funtions of the Benedictus. The Benedictus has usually been regarded as a hymn expressing praise to God, and a number of features of the text support its form-critical designation as a declarative psalm of praise (Farris, 1985: 76-85). Zechariah the worshipper rejoices in God's saving act. But closer analysis indicates a further function. The unit is addressed not only to God but also to human beings. Along with praise, proclamation is expressed. Praise and proclamation easily co-exist. The hymnic style of the Benedictus is not so pronounced as to exclude other functions (Gloer, 1984: 132).

The Benedictus has two introductions. The first (Lk 1:64) establishes a hymnic function. The second introduction at verse 67, immediately prior to the hymn, points toward a proclamatory function by its use of quite different introductory verbs – "he spoke this prophecy/he prophesied", and "he was filled." If Luke had wished to emphasize the expression of praise, he could have employed his favorite verb of praise *aineō*, "to praise." Instead he uses two verbs of proclamation.

"He prophesied" is an important choice. "To prophesy" is not used in any of its five other Lukan occurrences to designate hymnic or cultic activity directed towards God (Lk 22:64; Acts 2:17,18; 19:6; 21:9). Human audiences, rather than God, are the addressees of this verb. Luke's usage of the cognate noun "prophet" confirms this observation; the address of a "prophet" is not directed to God or Christ but to human beings. Prophets exhort and strengthen, interpret the scriptures, predict the future and guide the community (Ellis, 1970: 55-67). The Benedictus exemplifies several of these functions (Carter, 1988: 243).

The other introductory verb in verse 67 reinforces this presentation. "He was filled" (*eplēsthē*) is a distinctive Lukan verb (twenty-two of its twenty-four New Testament usages occur in Luke-Acts) and is not employed elsewhere by Luke to express praise and worship. Significantly, the word appears predominantly in Luke in association with the Holy Spirit (Lk 1:15,41,67; Acts 2:4; 4:8,31; 9:17; 13:52), which conveys the power of preaching (Delling, 1968: 130). Since "he was filled" occurs in Lk 1:68 in relation to the Spirit, it belongs to this primary grouping. It is a verb which Luke uses to denote proclamation, and to style Zechariah as a preacher. In addition to noting these verbs of proclamation, it is worth repeating the fact that the vocabulary of Zechariah's proclamation has much in common with the vocabulary in the speeches of Acts (Benoit, 1957: 189). One has observed eighteen similarities between the Benedictus and the speech of Acts 3:12-26 (Gryglewicz, 1974-1975: 265-273). Zechariah's proclamation thus employs a significant amount of language in common with Luke's other preachers – Peter, Stephen, and Paul (Carter, 1988: 243-244).

67   Then his father Zechariah was filled with the Holy Spirit and spoke this prophecy:

68 a "Blessed be the Lord God of Israel,

68 b for he has looked favorably on his people and redeemed them.

69   He has raised up a mighty savior for us in the house of his servant David,

70   as he spoke through the mouth of his holy prophets from of old,

71   that we would be saved from our enemies
      and from the hand of all who hate us.

72   Thus he has shown the mercy promised to our ancestors,
      and has remembered his holy covenant,

73   the oath he swore to our ancestor Abraham
      to grant us that we,

74   being rescued from the hands of our enemies,
      might serve him without fear,

75   in holiness and righteousness
      before him all our days.

76   And you, child,
      will be called the prophet of the Most High;
      for you will go before the Lord
      to prepare his ways,

77   to give knowledge of salvation to his people
      by the forgiveness of their sins.

78   By the tender mercy of our God,
      the dawn from on high will break upon us,

79   to give light to those who sit in darkness
        and in the shadow of death,
        to guide our feet into the way of peace."

Verse 67: Then the father Zechariah was filled with the Holy Spirit
          and spoke this prophecy:

Zechariah proves to be one of the prophets (Lk 1:67-79), as he is said to be "filled with the Holy Spirit" (Lk 1:67). Again, a direct characterization of a human character, this time by the narrator, provides indirect characterization of the Spirit, since Luke explicitly connects "filled with the Holy Spirit" and "prophecy" (Fitzmyer, 1981: 382; Johnson, 1991: 45). The close association between the Spirit and prophecy is made very explicit. The usage of "he spoke this prophecy" parallels that of "exclaimed with a loud cry" in Lk 1:42. Thus in Lk 1:42 and 1:67 the Spirit acts as a spirit of prophecy, inspiring prophetic speech. Luke highlights the Spirit's role in the prophetic activity of Elizabeth and Zechariah, as well as John (Menzies, 1991: 120). Zechariah's Spirit-inspired song (verses 68-79) proclaims God's faithfulness to Israel; God will remember the *covenant* with Israel, and the *oath* sworn to Abraham (verses 72-73, forming the center of the Benedictus). John's role as a prophet and forerunner is stipulated (verses 76-77; cf. Lk 3:1-6). Zechariah's prophecy concerning God's faithfulness to Israel is explicitly said to be inspired by the Spirit. This gives it an extra degree of narrative authority: here the human character is guaranteed to be a reliable commentator. The Spirit thus functions as the guarantor of Zechariah's statement that God is faithful (Shepherd, 1994: 118-119).

Verse 68a: "Blessed be the Lord God of Israel,

The opening words of the Benedictus almost quote Pss 41:13(14); 72:18; 106:48, "Blessed be the Lord, the God of Israel," the well-known formula from the Psalter. It is also found in 1 Kgs 1:48, where it is used by David at the enthronement of his son Solomon. As an opening formula, it resembles the beginning of the Hymn of Return in the Qumran War Scroll: "Blessed be the God of Israel, who preserves mercy for his covenant and periods of salvation for his people" (1QM 14:4; Fitzmyer, 1981: 382). Verses 68-69 have also been related to the fifteenth invocation of the synagogue prayer called the Eighteen Benedictions (Manns, 1992: 162-166).

Verse 68b: for he has looked favorably on his people
         and redeemed them.

"Looking with favor" is an expression used elsewhere in Luke to point to God's gracious coming (*episkeptomai* ["to visit"] – Lk 1:68,78; 7:16; *episkopē* ["visitation"] – Lk 19:44), repeatedly within narrative settings, emphasizing the redemptive ministry of Jesus (Green, 1995: 38). Literally, the text reads "he has visited his people," an expression that in the Septuagint often denotes God's gracious visitation of his people, bringing them deliverance of various sorts, such as the imminent exodus from bondage in Egypt (Ex 4:31), sufficient crops and food following a devastating famine (Ruth 1:6), and what is clearly politico-economic care or rescue of the people with the memory of the exodus in mind (Pss 80:14; 106:4; Horsley, 1989: 115). Yahweh's visitation is associated with "salvation" or "deliverance" in Ps 106:4, whereas here it is specifically related to his raising of "the horn of salvation" (Lk 1:69; NRSV: "a mighty savior"). The same verb ("to visit") will be used in Lk 1:78; 7:16 to refer to the coming of some personal instrument of salvation (Fitzmyer, 1981: 383).

That God "redeemed them," literally, "made redemption," echoes Ps 111:9, "He sent redemption to his people; he has commanded his covenant forever." There is nothing that forces us to interpret this in a purely spiritual sense. In Ps 111:9 it stands parallel to the socio-political "he commanded his covenant," and such mighty works of God as provision of food and land. The phrase refers to God's ransom or release of his people, apparently from their enemies, judging from the immediate context (Horsley, 1989: 115).

Verse 69: He has raised up a mighty savior for us
         in the house of his servant David,

The expression "a horn of salvation" (NRSV: "mighty savior")
alludes to Ps 18:2(3), "The Lord is my rock... my shield, and
the horn of my salvation..." (= 2 Sam 2:3). There may also be
an allusion to 1 Sam 2:10, where Hannah sings of Yahweh raising on high "the horn of his Anointed One" (NRSV: "the power
of his anointed"). The figure is derived from an animal's horn,
especially that of wild buffalo or oxen, which symbolizes strength
and power (Deut 33:17). The lifting up of the horns in the Old
Testament refers to the animal's tossing of its horns in a display
of might (Ps 148:14). In any case, "horn of salvation" has been
understood by many as a title for an agent of God's salvation in
David's house, i.e., in a loose sense a messianic title (Fitzmyer,
1981: 383).

It is a bold political statement. It is difficult not to find
christological significance in "the horn of salvation." But the
term does not *necessarily* refer to a Davidic king, much less *the*
messiah. The phrase may allude to the saving power of God, as
in Ps 18:2(3). But one could say that it is at least messianic in
the minimal sense of referring to some divinely chosen figure in
Hannah's song (1 Sam 2:10).

The statement of Lk 1:69 obviously makes explicit that this
horn of salvation is "raised up... in the house of his servant
David," thus recalling memories of the vigorous leadership David
provided in establishing the independence of Israel and evoking
whatever hopes may have focused on new Davidic leadership.
But the image in the Benedictus seems to be more of relief
than of royal triumph (Horsley, 1989: 115-116).

Verse 70: as he spoke through the mouth of his holy prophets from of
         old,

Because verse 70 is the only subordinate clause in this part of
the canticle and because the word-order (in Greek) is close to
that of Acts 3:21, this verse is regarded by some scholars as a
Lukan insertion into the traditional hymn of praise. It would

thus be stressing the Lukan theme of promise and fulfillment (Fitzmyer, 1981: 384).

The prophetic interpretation of the divine visitation begins by looking backwards. We observed the same phenomenon in the oracles of Gabriel and in verses 51-55 of the Magnificat, so that by now the pattern is well established: look to the past in order to understand what God is doing now and what he will do in the future. Right remembering is essential. Zechariah moves back through time from what God is doing now through the prophetic transmission of the Abrahamic promise to the Abrahamic promise itself, which here, as in the Magnificat, is understood as the origin of the divine visitation.

Where Gabriel in verses 32-33 had spoken of the Davidic messiah in terms of royal power and government, Zechariah in verses 68-75 speaks of the Davidic messiah in terms of military power and victory, with the image of "a horn of salvation" used to describe the mode of divine visitation. The military over-tones of the title are echoed in verse 71. Zechariah also extols the mercy of God (verse 72); but the concrete manifestation of mercy is understood here as military success guaranteeing Israel a peace that will allow undistracted and enduring service of God. In raising up a Davidic messiah capable of bringing victory of this kind and therefore lasting peace, God has shown his fidelity to the Abrahamic promise transmitted by the prophets (Coleridge, 1993: 119-120).

Verse 71: that we would be saved from our enemies
        and from the hand of all who hate us.

The language of salvation in verse 71 may echo the Deutero-Isaian description of the Servant of the Lord who is to serve for "salvation to the ends of the earth" (Brown, 1977: 385). The wording of the verse echoes Ps 18:17 (18), "He delivered me from my strong enemy, and from those who hate me...," and Ps 106:10, "So he saved them from the hand of the foe, and delivered them from the hand of the enemy." Lk 1:71 (and 74) would appear to specify that the people's salvation is more particularly and concretely from their political enemies. In Ps 18:17 and Ps 106:10, the enemies are concrete, domestic or alien, political foes – in the latter case, the Egyptians; as in those close parallels, so in the Benedictus itself. "Our enemies/all who hate us," however far-ranging the broader connotations may be, refers to particular political enemies. To specify them as Israel's national enemies may be somewhat misleading, or perhaps rather an imposition of modern assumptions about international politics. The concrete enemies meant in the Benedictus would have been clear from the historical context in which the song was sung. And in first-century Palestine, "enemies" could have meant the heads of the Jewish temple-state as well as the Roman rulers (Horsley, 1989: 117). The term "enemies" certainly need not be understood in the narrowly political sense of Roman oppression. To a peasant, enemies are all those who try to get what is rightfully his. They are those who destroy his honor, take his land, undermine his family, and threaten his women. It would have made little difference to peasants whether the ones doing this were Romans, the Jerusalem establishment, or dangerous neighbors (Malina-Rohrbaugh, 1992: 292).

Verses 72-73:   (72) Thus he has shown the mercy promised to our
                        ancestors,
                        and has remembered his holy covenant.
                (73) the oath that he swore to our ancestor Abraham,
                        to grant us

Verses 72-75 also have a politico-religious and not merely a religious reference. The covenant and oath that God swore to Abraham included possession of land and a prosperous independent life of their own for the Israelite people as well as blessings for other people. Nothing in the Benedictus indicates that the biblical precedent is broadened or narrowed, much less deserted. Rather, the Benedictus appears to have the biblical history of the exodus latently in mind (Horsley, 1989: 117). God's mercy is, as often in the Septuagint, God's *hesed* or covenant love. "To remember his holy covenant" is a Semitic expression for "in accordance with", "in fidelity to." Luke repeats the idea of

God showing mercy in Acts 3:25. God's performing mercy means
that he takes decisive action for his own (Bock, 1994: 184).
The expression "holy covenant" begins to appear in the Jewish
literature of the intertestamental period (1 Macc 1:15, 63). The
parallelism with the next line indicates that the *covenant with
Abraham and his seed* is in mind, but at this period the *Mosaic
covenant* with Israel was thought to be in continuity with the
patriarchal covenants. What modern scholarship understands
as two different covenants, that to Abraham and that through
Moses, ancient Jews would have understood as one. The content of the covenant is then specified. It consists not of a two-
sided agreement but of an oath to Abraham (Farris, 1985: 137).
God took an oath (Gen 22:16-18), and later words of God refer
back to that oath (Gen 26:3; Deut 7:8; Brown, 1977: 372).
What was promised in Gen 22:16-18 is interpreted in a broad
sense. It is not the gift of the promised land, but the gift of
deliverance from enemies for the continual service and worship
of God (Fitzmyer, 1981: 385).

Verses 74-75: (74) that we, being rescued from the hands of our
                    enemies,
                    might serve him without fear,
               (75) in holiness and righteousness
                    before him all our days.

At this point the hymn gives the content of the oath (Farris,
1985: 138). The term "serve" (*latreuein*) simply cannot be narrowed to mean cultic "worship." It means to serve in a more
comprehensive way, in the entire way of life of a people. In the
exodus the people of Israel are called to leave Egypt to serve
God. Once they were delivered from Egyptian bondage, they
contracted to serve God in covenantal justice or righteousness.
Verses 74-75 form a close parallel (Horsley, 1989: 117).

Verses 74-75 express the purpose and gift of God's saving
mission in terms of the safety and freedom to worship and to
serve God throughout life without fear. Nothing is indicated
here about "salvation" in another world. The this-worldly social
and political dimensions of divine salvation are understood to

be fundamental to the "redemption" that is being declared to Israel (Tiede, 1988: 62).

"To serve, to worship" (*latreuein*) is a key verb, embracing a twofold meaning – a specific act of worship and obedient living. This service to God may be expressed specifically in worship and prayer (Lk 2:37), or, more generally and frequently, in the whole of life that manifests one's loyalty and commitment of heart. Such commitment was exhibited by Jesus (Lk 4:8) and by Paul (Acts 24:14); this way of living is God's will for his people (Acts 7:7). In this verb Zechariah sets forth as the goal of God's redemptive act a life of service and worship. The two datives "in holiness" and "in righteousness" emphasize the point [the two datives occur together in Wis 9:3 where Solomon recognizes these qualities as being God's expectation of human life, and so asks for wisdom to be sent to enable such living]. In its few septuagintal usages, "holiness," denotes personal piety and righteous obedience. Its two New Testament usages express a quality that is not merely a virtue but is a consequence of the new birth manifested in righteous living. Likewise "righteousness before him" is not isolated rectitude but designates the fulfillment of God's will in an action which is pleasing to him. The psalmic phrase "all our days" indicates the time span throughout which such service is to be rendered. In proclaiming God's saving act, Zechariah amplifies greatly the significance of the events beyond the immediate context (Carter, 1988: 245-246).

In the phrase "[service] in holiness and righteousness," "holiness" (*hosiotēs*) describes the proper attitude in respect to God; "righteousness" (*dikaiosunē*) is conformity with God's precepts, especially as they involve one in relation to others (Wis 9:3). To a Greco-Roman, these two qualities suggest people of the highest excellence (Danker, 1988: 48-49).

Verses 76-77: (76) And you, child, will be called the prophet of the Most High;
for you will go before the Lord to prepare his ways,
(77) to give the knowledge of salvation to his people by the forgiveness of their sins.

Zechariah has made it clear in verse 70 that it is the prophets who have transmitted and interpreted the Abrahamic promise; and he himself has been placed among the prophets by the narrator in verse 67 ("he spoke this prophecy"). Zechariah now addresses his own child in terms that anticipate Lk 7:26. He places John among the prophets, among those who will announce and interpret God's visitation of his people. According to Zechariah, John will announce that the salvation of God will come through the Davidic messiah in the form of forgiveness of sins (Coleridge, 1993: 120-121).

The expression "prophet of the Most High" is not found in the Old Testament but it occurs in the *Testament of Levi* 8:15, used of a new king to arise from Levi. That John "will go before the Lord" is promised in Lk 1:15,17.

The phrase "the knowledge of salvation" is nowhere found in the Old Testament, and seems to be a Lukan creation. As in the Old Testament, "knowledge" here moves beyond a sense of factual knowledge to an experience of what is known, in this case, forgiveness. Similarly the phrase *aphesis hamartiōn* ("forgiveness of sins") is not found in the Old Testament even if the idea of forgiveness is found frequently (Brown, 1977: 373). The phrase does, however, occur in the Qumran texts. This will be the precursor's act of preparation, his interpretation of the Davidic messiah, which is a substantial reinterpretation of what we saw in verses 70-75. The precursor will prepare for the Davidic messiah by alerting the people to the signs of his coming; and the pre-eminent sign will be the forgiveness of sins.

This forgiveness will be the concrete manifestation of the mercy of God, no longer expressed by *eleos* as it was in the Magnificat and in verse 72, but now by the stronger *splagchna eleous*, literally, "the bowels of mercy," but rendered "the tender mercy" by NRSV. *Splagchna* refers literally to vital organs, for example, heart, liver, lungs, which were thought to be the seat of emotion. Metaphorically, it refers to "the heart of mercy" (Coleridge, 1993: 121-122; Menken, 1988:107-114).

The Lukan addition of verses 76-77 fits well into the rest of

the Benedictus. The description of John here more closely parallels that found later in Lk 3:3-4; 7:26 than the one in the
infancy narrative context itself (Lk 1:16-17). But the role of
John here fits the features of God's salvation stated in the rest
of the Benedictus. The child is to have the role of the prophet
preparing "the way of the Lord" (Mal 3:1,23; and Isa 40:3, which
is the "new exodus"). That the experience of salvation consists
in "the forgiveness of sins" does not lessen the socio-political
character or increase the spiritual aspect of the deliverance. The
context has been clearly stated in verses 73-75 as the covenantal service of God in just relations. In the Benedictus the "forgiveness of sins" provides a new beginning for the people in
living covenantal righteousness (Horsley, 1989: 118).

Verses 78-79: (78) By the tender mercy of our God,
     the dawn from on high will break upon us,
    (79) to give light to those who sit in darkness
     and in the shadow of death,
     to guide our feet into the way of peace."

The visitation that this child manifests is already a disclosure of
divine mercy, and the baptism of forgiveness will prove to be
central to the divine strategy of the deliverance of the people.
God's "tender mercy" has been revealed in that this prophet is
authorized with a divine word of forgiveness, not vengeance.
Still, the word of forgiveness is not so much the end of God's
mission as the necessary means, given the human situation.

The second line of verse 78 may be translated "in which
[= God's mercy] the light-filled branch from on high shall visit
us." God's mercy is the point of origin or the source for the
visitation (Danker, 1988: 50). The "dawn" was probably a rich
scriptural allusion to the awesome splendor of divine presence,
now come to save and restore humankind (Mal 4:2). Perhaps
even the rising up of the messianic "shoot of David" (Jer 23:5)
was envisioned. The scriptural images are so rich that it is clear
that Luke continues to engage contemporary scriptural interpretation. Nevertheless, the promise of the dawning of a new
day of light and life and divine compassion is an image of a

new beginning of hope and freedom which has begun but is not yet completed (Tiede, 1988: 64).

Verse 79 touches upon the plight of those who sit in darkness and in the shadow of death, needing light and guidance. Isa 9:1 and 42:7 (compare Ps 107:10) are the probable sources for the first part of this verse. "Darkness" and "death" were frequently linked in lamentations about the hazards and brevity of life (Danker, 1988: 50). The verse offers a clue to the persistence of the divine project without suggesting that the coming of God's kingdom will create immediate utopias. New liberation and direction may be given to the people, as it was to Israel in the exile, even if the full deployment of the "way of peace" and salvation may be slow (Ibidem).

The last word of the Benedictus, *eirēnē*, "peace," is the first occurrence of the word in Luke-Acts. The word occurs fourteen times in the Gospel and seven times in Acts [over against four times in Matthew, once in Mark, and six in John]. From this simple word count, then, one begins to think that Luke is much more interested in associating the word and concept of "peace" with the Jesus experience than are the other evangelists. A discussion of the seven instances in which "peace" occurs in Acts leads to the conclusion that "peace" is used by the author of Acts to describe certain conditions or situations having to do with the Christian event. Acts points significantly, at times, to a cause of peace which we do not find in secular historical studies (Kilgallen, 1989: 56-62). While this second Lukan volume is therefore informative about the peculiar type of peace offered to the world (see especially Acts 10:36; 15:33; 16:36), we must say that it is the antecedent volume, the Gospel of Luke, that more fully brings to the forefront the relationship between peace and the Jesus event.

Interpreting the symbolism of the Benedictus, we realize Luke's claim that Jesus will bring human beings to a highly desired state of peace. Peace itself is not defined, but its meaning is understood clearly enough from the symbols ranked opposite to it. The citations from Isa 9:1 and 42:6-7 suggest, on the one

hand, that this Prince of Peace, who provides light, is an answer to the needs of the Southern Kingdom of Judah (931-587
B.C.), whose Davidic royal descendants have proved incapable
of saving their people. On the other hand, he is that mysterious
person who will be God's agent to bring back the Israelites from
their exile in Babylon (587-538 B.C.) and who will eventually
be considered by future Israel to be the messiah, he who ini-
tiates the final moment of this age and leads Israel into the new
age.

Zechariah's hymn uses forceful, archtypal symbols of that
human experience which all people know so thoroughly. "Darkness
and the shadow of death" are symbols of ignorance about the
way to go to reach happiness and of the disintegration of the
human person that contradicts every aspiration of the human
soul – these symbols succinctly recall the existential plight of
each and every human being, from which no one can save him/
herself. If we take "in darkness and in the shadow of death" as
a hendiadys [the expression of an idea by two nouns connected
by "and" instead of by a noun and an adjective], we may read
it as "the dark shadow of death" or "the shadowy darkness of
death." We are here brought face to face, not with this or that
human event or series of human events, but with human existence itself – an existence which knows its own bitter fatality;
the destruction of its very self is contained in itself, for it neither knows the way to happiness nor can it put off forever the
return to dust.

It is against these powerful, even overwhelming realities,
which are the very fabric of human existence, that Zechariah
sings of the coming of Jesus. It is he who will resolve both of
these destructive realities, ignorance of the way to happiness
and death. The resolution of these human frustrations is said to
lead eventually to peace, for it is through Jesus that one will
find the road that leads to peace. Happiness, though we have
used this word before, is not the word here; the word is "peace,"
a state of existence that results from a saving from archtypal
ignorance and death. More carefully put, Jesus is the one who

will enable us to walk the path of peace. "Path of peace" suggests not only that a road leads to peace, but that peace will characterize the walk along this road.

The resolution of these tragic human characteristics, ignorance and death, is clearly ascribed primarily to God in that it is his free intervention into human existence that will be responsible for replacing the effects of ignorance and death with peace. An essential element of this freeing act is Jesus, whether we speak of his teaching or of his death, or of any other facet of his life for others: he is the light. Thus, we are faced, from the beginning of Luke's Gospel, with the claim that peace is the result of divine intervention, and that that fundamental peace, which is the opposite and the healing of ignorance and death, cannot be said to be owed to human efforts. That is, without God's mercy (Lk 1:78a) and without the "dawn" (Lk 1:78b), we sit, no matter what our progress, in terrible darkness and within the very shadow of death. What is particularly remarkable here is that "peace" is the positive up-lifting, the promised benefit used to counter the terribly upsetting ignorance and fear of death which plagues all humankind; it is, at least in this passage, peace that is the result of salvation from ignorance and death (Kilgallen, 1989: 62-64).

According to Isa 59:10, "the way of peace" is associated with justice. To Greco-Romans, as to Israelites, peace went hand in hand with stability as the choicest benefaction that a head of state could render. When justice is perverted and the rights of other people are violated, there is no peace and people's sins cry out against them (Isa 59:12-15). Only those who turn from transgression will experience God as redeemer (Isa 59:20; see Lk 1:74). Luke's readers will recall this passage when they read his later recital of Jerusalem's failure to recognize the things that make for her peace (Lk 19:42; Danker, 1988: 51)

Conclusion: In sum, the Benedictus is a song about God's liberation of his people from subjection to their Roman and domestic rulers so that, as God fulfills the covenant to Abraham, they can serve God by maintaining covenantal justice among

the people. In order to illustrate how this song could have expressed the concrete experience of Palestinian Jewish followers
of Jesus who were convinced that God had delivered the people
and made present the saving "reign of God," we can compare
the expressions of a contemporary Jewish community from which
we now have abundant sources. Utilizing many of the same phrases
or idioms, though with somewhat different combinations and
emphases, two passages from the Qumran community state a
similar combination of God's visiting and redeeming the people,
saving them from their enemies, raising up a leader, keeping
the covenant with the ancestors, and leading the people in the
covenantal way of life (Horsley, 1989: 118):

> Blessed be the God of Israel
>   who keeps mercy towards His Covenant,
> and the appointed times of salvation
>   with the people he has delivered (1QM 14:4-5).

> Remembering the Covenant of the forefathers,... He vis-
> ited them, and He caused a plant root to spring from
> Israel and Aaron to inherit His Land and to prosper on
> the good things of His earth... And He raised for them
> a Teacher of Righteousness to guide them in the way
> of His heart (CD 1:5-12).

Verse 80: The child grew and became strong in spirit,
            and he was in the wilderness
            until the day he appeared publicly to Israel.

Verse 80 rounds off this episode with a narrative "growth
refrain" (see also Lk 2:40 and 2:52). Luke's narrative refrains
are modeled on those in 1 Sam 2:21 and 26, "And the boy
Samuel grew up in the presence of the Lord... Now the boy
Samuel continued to grow both in stature and in favor with the
Lord and with the people." Luke adapts the form to fit John's
case specifically with the mention of his being "strong in spirit"
and "in the wilderness." Nevertheless, both John and Jesus are
thus presented by Luke in terms which recapitulate the story of

the child Samuel whose wondrous birth and childhood prepared him as the forerunner, prophet, and anointer of David (Tiede, 1988: 64). To become "strong in spirit" means to develop inner resources for the understanding and performance of God's will. According to Lk 1:15, John was to be filled with the Holy Spirit.

Because of the phrase "in the wilderness," it has been suggested that John the Baptist was associated with communities that settled near the Dead Sea. But there are a number of differences between John and the Essenes and members of the community at Qumran. For example, his proclamation does not consist of legal prescriptions, and it is addressed to all who come and not merely to a closed fellowship. One can only speculate whether John had a youthful encounter with Qumran and then struck out on paths of his own (Danker, 1988: 51).

The words "till the day of his manifestation" (NRSV: "until the day he appeared publicly") refer to the beginning of John's public ministry. The expression has a bureaucratic connotation, being used in the Greco-Roman world of administrative assignment. The Greek word *anadeixis* can also have a technical meaning, found in the papyri, of "commissioning" or "installation." This would then be a solemn expression for the public ministry of John (Fitzmyer, 1981: 389). In Luke's work, only Jesus (Lk 10:1) or God (Acts 1:24) is the agent of such demonstration. Hence John does not appear until the word of the Lord comes to him (Lk 3:2; Danker, 1988: 52). The opening of John the Baptist's ministry in Lk 3:2, "the word of God came to John son of Zechariah in the wilderness," is an appropriate continuation of Lk 1:80 (Brown, 1977: 376).

5. The Birth of Jesus (Lk 2:1-20, 21)

Introduction. For a variety of quite natural reasons, this passage is one of the most over-interpreted in the New Testament, making it difficult to sort out what comments are helpful to the reader that wants to understand how Luke constructs his overall story in order to accomplish his goals (Johnson, 1991: 51).

This narrative is a masterpiece deserving acclaim and admiration as well as analysis. Popular dramatizations of the story and scholarly studies have agreed in recognizing the literary clarity, scriptural coloring, socio-political illumination of this episode. Yet appreciation for its brilliance is only increased by treating the story critically within the larger purposes of Luke's literary, scriptural, and theological project.

Like the rest of the stories that surround it, Luke's account of Jesus' birth is evocative, intimating and declaring the infant's identity in rich traditional titles. The scriptural histories of Samuel and David have supplied motifs for Luke's story of Jesus' birth and childhood. Roman traditions of the prodigies, which accompanied the birth and childhood of Caesar Augustus, may also have had a direct effect on Luke's telling of the birth of this Davidic ruler in the time of Caesar Augustus. The story of the birth of this messiah, Savior, and Lord (Lk 2:11), is told against the backdrop of Roman imperial history. It is thus a testimony to the ultimate regency of the God of Israel with the child Jesus as the sign and agent of that gracious rule (Tiede, 1988: 65).

Lk 2:1-20 clearly falls into three main parts: (1) the setting for the birth of Jesus in Bethlehem (Lk 2:1-5); (2) the birth itself (Lk 2:6-7); and (3) the manifestation of the newborn child to the shepherds and the reaction of all who heard of it to the birth and manifestation (Lk 2:8-20). The third part can again be subdivided in: (a) Lk 2:8-14, the manifestation of the child; (b) Lk 2:15-20, the reaction to the manifestation (Fitzmyer, 1981: 392; Stein, 1992: 104).

The connection between Lk 2:1-20 and the episodes of the first phase of the infancy narrative is complex. There are enough discontinuities to have scholars claim that Lk 2 is not only fully intelligible on its own without Lk 1, but every section of it is opposed to any combination with an introductory story (Bultmann, 1972: 294). It is true that the narrative changes key with its setting now in the world of the Roman Empire rather than the world of Judaism, and that Lk 2:1 reads as the beginning rather than the continuation of a narrative. It is also true that the accent falls more upon what has happened than upon what will happen, and that the one character to survive from earlier episodes is Mary, though even she appears differently (Coleridge, 1993: 128-129).

But there are also undeniable links with what has gone on before. The fulfillment of Gabriel's prophecies in Lk 1:30-35 gains momentum; the narrator again has God communicate through an angel; the news of the shepherds prompts amazement in all who hear it and, in the case of Mary, a storing in the heart similar to Lk 1:66. As a whole too the episode is shaped in ways similar to the previous episode. The birth is followed by the announcement of the child's identity; those to whom the announcement is made spread the news; and this in turn prompts amazement in those who hear. Here again we have the Lukan technique of reprise (Coleridge, 1993: 129). But the parallelism here is much looser than in the case of the annunciations (Nolland, 1989: 98).

The *divine visitation* becomes more explicit with the messiah's birth, as Luke proceeds to show that in Jesus the main outlines of the New Age begin to take shape (Danker, 1988: 52). Yet, paradoxically, in a sense the visitation becomes more difficult for humans to recognize, since God visits his people in ways more surprising than ever. The fulfillment of Gabriel's prophecies in Lk 1:30-35 begins, just as in the previous episode the fulfillment of his prophecies in Lk 1:13-20 began; but the shape of fulfillment now is considerably less predictable than it was in the story of John's birth (Coleridge, 1993: 129-130). The prophecy-fulfillment motif is nevertheless unmistakable (Johnson, 1991: 52), although we must admit that in Lk 2:1-20 the narrator presents signs of fulfillment which seem at odds with the meaning of the event, and right interpretation of them is therefore cast as a challenge. This is again an episode in which the narrator is less concerned with *what has happened* and more concerned with *what it means* and how human beings respond to it (Coleridge, 1993: 130).

Verses 1-5: (1) In those days a decree went out from Emperor Augustus
that all the world should be registered.
(2) This was the first registration
and was taken while Quirinius was governor of Syria.
(3) All went to their own towns to be registered.
(4) Joseph also went from the town of Nazareth in
Galilee
to Judea, to the city of David called Bethlehem,
because he was descended from the house and
family of David.
(5) He went to be registered with Mary,
to whom he was engaged and who was expecting a
child.

It may seem arbitrary to read verses 1-5 rather than verses 1-7
as the first section of the episode (Brown, 1977: 410; Ernst,
1977: 99); yet there are narrative reasons for doing so. In the
first five verses, the narrator sets the context for the episode by
reporting the imperial decree and the obedience of Joseph and
Mary in response to it. In verse 6, as elsewhere in the Lukan
narrative, the initial *egeneto*, "it happened" (Aletti, 1988: 137
n. 11), which repeats the *egeneto* found at the beginning of verse
1 (Tremel, 1981: 594), signals a shift – a shift from the realm of
Caesar's sway to the very different realm of God's sway [regard-
ing *egeneto*, see the commentary on Lk 1:8-10]. The authority
of Caesar brings Joseph and Mary to Bethlehem, but the readers know that it is the authority of God that brings the child to
birth. What begins in verse 1 is the narration of Caesar's plan,
but what resumes in verse 6 is the narration of the implementation of God's plan; and this brings with it a change of subject as
the initiative passes from Caesar (and Joseph) to Mary. The
two narrative programmes are related, but quite distinct: hence
the decision to make the break after verse 5 (Coleridge, 1993:
130).

The statements in verses 1-5 serve a double purpose: (1)
They bring together in their own way the two traditions that
Jesus was a Galilean, whose home was Nazareth, and that as
"the son of David" he was, or ought to be, of Bethlehemite
origin. Hence the detailed precision of verse 4. (2) The state-

ments provide the otherwise non-chronological traditions with a fixed point in history, and a notorious one at that, namely the census also mentioned in Acts 5:37 (C.F. Evans, 1990: 189-190).

Verses 1-2: (1) In those days a decree went out from Emperor Augustus that all the world should be registered.
          (2) This was the first registration
               and was taken while Quirinius was governor of Syria.

Luke begins his account with the reason for Joseph and Mary's trip to Bethlehem and Jesus' subsequent birth there. At least part of his purpose is to explain why Jesus, whose family is from Nazareth, nevertheless was born in Bethlehem. The purpose of the trip is the worldwide census decreed by Caesar Augustus requiring all to register in their own cities.

Scholars have long been troubled by Luke's "historical blunder" with respect to the census (Schürmann, 1969: 100-101; Brown, 1977: 547-555; Marshall, 1978: 99-104; Fitzmyer, 1981: 400-405; Nolland, 1989: 94-96,99-102; C.F. Evans, 1990: 193-195). The problem is that Quirinius, as far as is known, governed Syria only during A.D. 6-7, and not at all in 6/5 B.C. Why then does Luke say that Jesus was born during a census that took place while Quirinius was governor of Syria? (Brindle, 1984: 43). Luke mentions the census under Quirinius once more in Acts 5:37 but without precise time indication: "after him Judas the Galilean rose up at the time of the census." But in Acts 5:37, the census is related to a series of events and actions that would eventually lead to open war with the Romans (Jankowski, 1981: 11). Our non-Lukan sources mention neither a "world-wide" census ordered by Augustus nor a census in Palestine during the reign of Herod the Great. "All the world": the Greek word *oikoumenē* means the *orbis terrarum*, the civilized world over which the Roman emperor was lord (Brown, 1977: 395). The term *oikoumenē* can mean "known world" but the context here demands the translation "empire" (Johnson, 1991: 49). There is no evidence that Quirinius was legate of Syria during Herod's lifetime. All attempts to reconcile the Lukan anachronism with what we otherwise know of Roman history have reached a frustrating stalemate – frustrating, because Luke proposes to render an orderly account, and indeed he maintains a chronological interest throughout his writing (Lk 1:3,5; 3:1-2; Acts 11:28; 12:1-3, 18-23; 18:12-17; 24:27-25:1). Without new epigraphical or textual evidence, the deadlock will continue (Creed, 1957: 28-30).

From time to time efforts are undertaken to show that the arguments against Lk 1:1-2 are not valid. It is then pointed out that there were regionally limited as well as general censuses in the reign of Augustus. Under Roman law it was necessary for all, including the wife and the household members, to be enrolled. Since Herod was a client-king, a Roman census could have taken place in his kingdom. And Luke does not necessarily imply that Quirinius was the main governor at the time of the census (Lawrence, 1992: 193-205). These efforts are less than convincing. But some scholars continue to defend Luke's historical accuracy (Marshall, 1978: 100-104; Nolland, 1989: 96-102).

One may also try to solve the problem by proposing an alternative translation: "This census was the first *before that* under the governorship of Quirinius in Syria." It is then claimed that Lk 2:2 fits well both grammatically and historically when taken to mean that the census of the time of Jesus' birth was the census *before* the well-known, later census of Quirinius. This first one was "in the days of Herod the king" (Brindle, 1984: 50, 52).

Recently, some have tried to save at least part of Luke's presentation. It is pointed out that in A.D. 6, Augustus introduced a five-percent inheritance tax that was binding on all Roman citizens except the very poor. It must have required an up-to-date census data to establish who was taxable and thus maximize the income. Quirinius probably decided to carry out this census along with his provincial census in A.D. 6-7. Luke failed to realize that Augustus' edict applied only to Roman citizens. But he did not invent the "decree of Caesar Augustus" out of nothing (Wiseman, 1987: 479-480).

As always in these situations, the primary question for a narrative approach is, why did the narrator choose to include the element, whether historically factual or not? – though if we know that it is not historically factual, the question becomes, why did the narrator choose to include a fictional element into his narrative? In this particular case, however, we cannot be sure of whether or not the census was historically factual or not (Coleridge, 1993: 131). Our concern is not the historical veracity of the statement, but the way the statement functions within the narrative (Sheely, 1992: 103).

From the point of view of narrative logistics, the imperial decree serves to bring Joseph and Mary from Nazareth to Bethlehem for the birth – that the one born may match Jewish expectation that the Davidic messiah be born in Bethlehem. Moreover, as with the introduction in Lk 1:5-7, the report of the census serves to embed the narration of God's visitation: God appears from within the human world (Coleridge, 1993: 131-132). Or, it can more precisely be suggested that the purpose is to show how God speaks in an earthly historical event rather than in a philosophical system explaining the world, or in a myth embodying a universal truth that would be true apart from its mythic presentation (Schweizer, 1984: 48). Where in Lk 1:5-7 it was the world of Jewish politics and religion, now it is the larger and more secular world of the Roman Empire; and this might be read as the narrator's way of pointing to the wider significance of Jesus (Brown, 1977: 414-415; Marshall, 1978: 98).

The juxtaposition of the Roman census (mentioned four times) with the coming of Jesus, together with the giving of titles to Jesus used elsewhere in Luke's world for the emperor (e.g., "Savior" and "Lord" – cf. Lk 2:1,11), emphasizes the opposition of Jesus' arrival to the status quo of the Roman empire (Green, 1995: 34).

The narrator chooses to begin the second phase of the infancy narrative with the story of a human initiative that sets the action in motion. The initiative is an act of human authority from the center of the world that includes the whole world. In both Lk 1:5 and 3:1 the reference to royal authority functions primarily as a chronological marker, but the reference to Augustus in Lk 2:1 does not. Neither Herod in Lk 1:5 nor Tiberius and his minions in Lk 3:1 do anything: they are simply named. But in Lk 2:1 Augustus, without appearing on the stage of the narrative, acts: it is from him that the decree goes forth. The narrator presents him therefore as one who takes the initiative and exercises authority. In verse 2, we see that the imperial power is mediated from Caesar through the governor Quirinius. Not only a source, but also a line of authority is evoked (Coleridge, 1993: 131).

The imperial decree implies two things: first a possession (and therefore control) of those who are counted, "the whole world" (Gueuret, 1983: 108), and secondly a compulsion, with the narrator describing the decree as *dogma*, and reporting that it was met by prompt and universal obedience (Coleridge, 1993: 131-132).

The census is mentioned four times in the space of five verses (Lk 2:1-5). The prosperity and peace for which the Roman Empire is now known was produced through initial conquest and plunder, and maintained through subsequent taxation of a conquered people. And a census such as that mentioned by Luke had as its purpose the preparation of tax rolls. Moreover, the explicit naming of the Emperor Augustus in Lk 2:1 is of interest, for it refers to Octavian, who had been recognized as "the divine savior who has brought peace to the world." The fact that in this very context Jesus is presented as Savior, Lord, the one through whom peace comes to the world (Lk 2:11, 14), can hardly be accidental. Luke thus makes his audience aware at the very outset that the narrative of "the events that have been fulfilled among us" (Lk 1:1) is set squarely in the midst of the political turmoil of the Roman occupation of Palestine. Other data underscores the importance of this aspect of Luke's world. In light of several passages in the Gospel (Lk 7:1-10; 13:1-2; 21:20-24; 23:2-5,38) the Roman political world appears to be more than a mere "backdrop" to Luke's narrative (Green, 1995: 7-8).

What is most noticeable about the identification of the census and about the use of an empire-wide registration to date Jesus' birth is the choice of the landmarks of Roman imperial chronology rather than of Jewish kings. The conception and birth of John the Baptist are linked with the reign of Herod (Lk 1:5), but the narrator of Luke's Gospel does not bracket the birth of Jesus with a mention of Herod the way Matthew's Gospel does. Instead, every effort is made to concentrate on the world outside Judea (Sheely, 1992: 103).

Luke created, probably inadvertently, a proper name by his use of *Augoustos*. It seems that Luke used this title transliterated from Latin (Augustus) to avoid using *Sebastos* at this point in his Gospel, due to the basically sacred connotation that *Sebastos* would have evoked from his Greek audience (venerable Caesar!; Morris, 1992: 142-144).

Highly regarded biblical scholars interpret the appearance of Caesar Augustus in Lk 2:1 as merely a setting for the birth of Jesus. The emperor's decree of a census is correspondingly viewed as a literary device. Neither Caesar Augustus nor the census are important in themselves. At most, the most powerful figure in the world serves as a facilitating agent of God, who by his edict of registration brings about the fact that Jesus is born in the town of David (Fitzmyer, 1981: 393). Besides providing a "chronological framework," the Roman emperor Augustus is "ironically... serving God's plan" in his decree (Brown, 1977: 414-415). Luke thus associates the birth of the messiah with a famous Roman emperor whose lengthy reign was widely regarded as the era of peace (Fitzmyer, 1981: 393-394). Augustus had "pacified the world" and then been widely celebrated as "savior of the whole world." Luke, of course, was not denying the imperial ideals but merely presenting an implicit challenge to the imperial propaganda (Brown, 1977: 415).

One must wonder, however, whether the appearance of Caesar Augustus and his decree is all that innocuous in this story. The contents of the angel's message to the shepherds and the heavenly host's chorus later in the story fly directly in the face. of these "imperial ideals." Jesus is announced not just as "the messiah, the lord," but as "savior" as well (Lk 2:11). Now "messiah" and "lord" may very well be interpreted as kerygmatic titles stemming from the Jewish Christian community of Palestine. However, "savior" is not a major title for Jesus in the New Testament; this is the only application of the term to Jesus in the synoptic Gospels. And in the narrative context it is juxtaposed with Caesar Augustus, who was known far and wide as the "savior" of the world. Moreover, the only time the term is used in an authentic Pauline letter is in a revealed "word of the Lord" in which the return of Christ to earth is portrayed in terms of the triumphal *parousia* of the Roman emperor (the "savior") to a city that joyously celebrates his coming (Phil 3:20).

For two or three generations prior to the victory of Augustus at the battle of Actium (31 B.C.), the cities and peoples of the eastern Mediterranean had experienced virtually continuous political conflict and chaos. With his victory at Actium, Augustus was able to bring peace and order into the world for the first time in anybody's memory. The empire he established was *salvation*, and he himself was the *savior*.

Starting almost immediately and continuing into subsequent generations was an outpouring of gratitude and good will toward Augustus himself as well as to Rome for bringing the peace for which the people had yearned so long. From all corners of the empire came exultant outbursts of praise for the ruler who had brought peace, order, harmony, and prosperity. It appears in every form of literature, such as poetry, history, and philosophy, as well as in inscriptions and official communications. And a genuinely religious feeling is expressed in the explicitly religious language and concepts, some of which are highly familiar from the New Testament and subsequent Christian usage. Prevailing is the praise of the all-powerful, wise, and virtuous ruler Augustus (or his successor) who has brought peace and prosperity to the world in fulfillment of the hopes of humankind.

Therefore, particularly in the cities of the eastern Mediterranean, the imperial savior was honored, indeed worshipped, as divine (Horsley, 1989: 26).

The Roman empire was a religious as well as a political reality. Just as a city-state entailed a civic religion, an Empire-State entailed an empire-worship; and an empire-worship in turn entailed the worship of an emperor. And, in connection with the nativity narrative in Lk 2, the important point is to realize that the key symbols of the sacral imperial politics were that Caesar (Augustus and his successors) was the divine *savior* who had brought *peace* to the world. "Peace" was indeed the key religious-political concept of the Roman emperors.

The *Pax Romana*, of course, was a peace imposed by military might, and the imposition of the *Pax Romana*, of course, meant subjection. Pax Romana was defined by the rulers of the Roman empire without any sentimental or humanistic facade. Peace and security meant the subjugation of and victory over other nations. It meant the suppression of even a mere hint of resistance. "Peace" and "security" were the political-religious words with which this situation was normally summarized. In the middle of the first century A.D., Paul offered a very terse summary of the feelings that Jews and Christians had toward this political and military situation: "For you yourselves know very well that the day of the Lord will come like a thief in the night. When they say, 'There is peace and security,' then sudden destruction wil come upon them, as labor pains come upon a pregnant woman, and there will be no escape!" (1 Thes 5:2-3; Schottroff, 1992: 156-157).

How this peace bore on the Palestinian Jews of Jesus' time is portrayed vividly in an abundant literature, from cryptic allusions in some of the Dead Sea Scrolls, to gruesome visions in apocalyptic literature, to sharp comments in rabbinic debates. The most direct and descriptive statements perhaps come from the historian Flavius Josephus, who participated in the great Jewish War of 66-70 A.D., first as a Jewish general, and then as an adviser to the Roman troops. Although he writes history basically from the Roman point of view, he is also sensitive to what happened to his people, even if from his own aristocratic standpoint.

The stubborn Palestinian Jews were conquered four times in the course of two centuries before they acquiesced in the *Pax Romana* – twice by around the time Jesus was born, once more before Matthew and Luke were written, and once again before those Gospels were widely read. The initial phase of conquest lasted for a generation, from Pompey's initial subjection of the country in 63 B.C. until the Romans' client-king Herod had finally conquered the people with the help of Roman troops in 37 B.C. The slaughter and enslavement were not extreme in the initial conquest by Pompey, but thereafter the Palestinian Jews suffered repeated brutality, partly as the result of Roman attempts to suppress continuing resistance led by rival Hasmonean figures, and partly because of the struggle among powerful Roman leaders for control of the empire. The second Roman conquest, in response to massive popular Jewish rebellions in every major Jewish district of Palestine, occurred right around the time Jesus was supposedly born, that is, at the death of Herod in 4 B.C. The slaughter and enslavement that ensued is noteworthy because it occurred in places in which Jesus and his followers lived or were active, according to gospel traditions. The Roman troops captured and burned the city of Sepphoris, a few miles from Nazareth, and reduced its inhabitants to slavery. The Romans scoured the country for rebels, imprisoned many, and crucified about two thousand (Josephus, *Jewish War*). We know that Sepphoris was being totally rebuilt as the regional capital of Galilee by Herod Antipas during the decades which coincided exactly with Jesus' years in nearby Nazareth (Batey, 1991: 64-7).

The most fully documented Roman conquest of the Jews – and Jewish rebellion – was the great Jewish War of 66-70 A.D., in which Josephus was a principal actor and often an eyewitness. The Romans, having been completely driven out of Palestine by a massive popular revolt, had to organize a major military mobilization to retake the country and were merciless in the reconquest. After a prolonged siege, Jerusalem was taken, the defenders killed or enslaved, and the temple and city destroyed.

The general tension between Roman imperial rule and the Palestinian Jewish people was focused on the tribute that Rome demanded. This is precisely the framing, the heading of the story of Jesus' actual birth in Lk 2:1-20. More important than discussions regarding the chronological discrepancies is the question of what Roman taxation meant for people such as Mary and Joseph, the shepherds, or the readers of this story – along with what the birth of a "savior" may have meant in relation to that taxation. On the level of literary analysis, the observation that it is "paradoxical" that the description of the census (the "elaborate setting" in Lk 2:1-5) is longer than the description of the birth itself (Lk 2:6-7; Brown, 1977: 412, 414) suggests that the census itself was of some significance. It seems more than "a purely literary device" to bring Mary and Joseph, who were residents of Nazareth, to Bethlehem, the city of David, so that Jesus could be born according to messianic expectation (so Fitzmyer, 1981: 393). Far from being "a purely literary device," the census is itself an important component in the overall story. This is confirmed by the importance of the tribute issue toward the end of Luke's Gospel, namely the accusation before Pilate that Jesus is "forbidding us to pay taxes to Caesar" (Lk 23:2, 5), the truth of which depends on how Lk 20:19-26, on paying taxes to Caesar, is understood, especially the expressions "the things that are the emperor's" and "the things that are God's."

In the ancient world, the rulers of imperial societies lived by conquest, and none more aggressively than the dominant Roman aristocracy. Following the initial conquest, in which they plundered temples and palaces for booty and towns and villages for slaves, they then exacted tribute from the conquered people. The tribute was intended as a means of demeaning the subjected people as well as a source of support for the imperial apparatus. From the time of Julius Caesar, the

Palestinian Jewish peasants rendered to Caesar roughly 12.5 percent of their crops annually except in sabbatical years. Rendering tribute to Caesar, of course, did not involve any alleviation of the traditional economic burden of rendering tithes to the high-priestly government of the Jerusalem temple-state, which was also ostensibly a duty owed to God. That the high-priests, who were the principal beneficiaries of the traditional Jewish tithes and offerings owed to the temple and priests, were also responsible for collecting the tribute under the Roman governors in the first century A.D. is a telling illustration of the politico-economic chain of domination under the *Pax Romana*. So, the decree that all must go to their ancestral house or town of origin to be enrolled for taxation in this story reveals the whole system of domination and exploitation (Horsley, 1989: 33-36).

The imperial decree is shown to have two contrasting effects. On the one hand, it ensures that Joseph and Mary are brought to Bethlehem for the birth, with Caesar appearing as one who unwittingly collaborates with God's plan in ensuring that the circumstances of the Davidic messiah's birth are right; but on the other hand, it upsets what might seem to be God's plan, since it ensures that the circumstances of the birth are in other ways decidedly strange. In that sense, Caesar appears as one who (again unwittingly) works against the divine plan (Coleridge, 1993: 132-133).

Verses 3-4: (3) All went to their own towns to be registered.
(4) Joseph also went from the town of Nazareth in Galilee
to Judea, to the city of David called Bethlehem, because he was descended from the house and family of David.

That "all" went to their own towns is a Lukan hyperbole again, like the reference in verse 1 to "the whole world." While for Joseph "his own city" means his ancestral city of Bethlehem, Nazareth is designated as "their own city" in Lk 2:39 in the sense of residence. In Roman censuses there is no clear evi-

dence of the practice of going to an *ancestral* city to be enrolled; the oft-cited examples from Egypt are not the same as
what Luke describes (Brown, 1977: 396).

Luke seems to assume that the census covered Galilee;
but the first Roman census under Quirinius in A.D. 6-7 covered only Judea, where Archelaus had been deposed. Joseph
went from the town of Nazareth where he and Mary lived
(Lk 2:39), a view that contrasts with the implication in Mt
2:11 that they had their house in Bethlehem. How did the
evangelist come to associate presence in the ancestral town,
wherever that may be, with registration for the census, since
it has been established that this was not Roman practice? It
has been proposed that an answer may be found in Lev 25:8-
10, a text dealing with the Jubilee, which ends: "and everyone of you to your own family (*eis tēn patrida autou*)." In Lk
2:3 we read, "all went to their own towns (*eis tēn heautou
polin*)," but in Lk 2:4 we have "from the house and family
(*patrias*) of David." The passage of Lev 25:8-10 may have
encouraged Luke to develop his machinery of census so as to
bring Joseph and Mary from Nazareth to Bethlehem (Kilpatrick,
1989: 264-265).

"The city of David" is normally the designation of Jerusalem, as in 2 Sam 5:7,9. Luke's description of Bethlehem as the
"city of David" is unusual since the town is never so designated
in the Old Testament or in Judaism. Nevertheless, Bethlehem
is closely associated with David in the Old Testament. It was
his birthplace and original home (1 Sam 17:12ff.; 17:58), a place
where he returned for family occasions (1 Sam 20:6, 28-29)
and retained an affection for in his later life (2 Sam 23:15).
Apart from the key prophecy of Micah 5:2 (MT 5:1), little importance is given to the town in the Old Testament or in Second Temple Judaism. Only a few targumic and rabbinic sources
designate Bethlehem as the place of the messiah's origin (Strack-
Billerbeck I, 1965: 82-83). It has been claimed that in Judaism
the appearance of the Davidic shoot is expected in Jerusalem,
but not in Bethlehem (Burger, 1970: 24,136). This, however, is

a somewhat misleading statement. Jewish expectations related to Jerusalem center on the messiah's *activities*, not on his *origin* (Strauss, 1995: 110).

The Greek word *patria*, here translated "family," has the general sense of the family as derived from the father, but it can have the more general meanings of "house" (which in our present verse is the translation of *oikos*) or even "tribe" or "nation" (Acts 3:25). The context suggests that the terms *oikos* and *patria* are used co-referentially, both referring to Joseph's Davidic descent (Strauss, 1995: 109).

Verses 5: He went to be registered with Mary,
　　　　to whom he was engaged
　　　　and who was expecting a child.

It is not clear with which verb "with Mary" is to be connected. Are we to understand that Mary was to be inscribed in the census (this is not an impossibility in Roman practice), or are we to think that she accompanied Joseph so that they would be together when the birth came? On the assumption that a betrothed couple would ordinarily not travel together as is stated in this verse, some readers have wondered whether Mary and Joseph were now legally married? Others have marveled over Mary's journey under the prevailing circumstances. Luke does not bother to answer the overly curious. The reference to Mary being "engaged" recalls Lk 1:27 and reminds the reader that Mary stands in the same relationship to Joseph. The mention of her pregnancy simply accounts for the fact that while they were in Bethlehem she gave birth (cf, Lk 1:57). One can in fact ascribe much of Luke's literary art to his economy of narrative and his resistance to pedantic adornment (Danker, 1988: 55).

Verses 6-7: (6) While they were there,
　　　　　　the time came for her to deliver her child.
　　　　　(7) And she gave birth to her firstborn son,
　　　　　　and wrapped him in bands of cloth,
　　　　　　and laid him in a manger,
　　　　　　because there was no place for them in the inn.

To this point, the narrator has evoked the source and line of a human authority that is universal in scope, which implies possession and demands obedience, and which has contrasting effects as regards the plan of God. At verse 6, however, the narrator moves to resume the narration of the exercise of divine authority, which will show itself to be quite different. By way of analogy to Lk 2:15-20 (see below) one has proposed to divide Lk 2:6-14 into the following: (1) Lk 2:6-7: *dabar* as event: the birth of Jesus; (2) Lk 2:8-12: *dabar* as word: the proclamation of the angel; (3) Lk 2:13-14: *dabar* as doxology: the song of praise of the heavenly host (Wolff, 1981: 23).

The account of the birth of Jesus is strikingly laconic when compared to the apocryphal accounts. Works such as the *Protoevangelium of James* (Bovon, 1987: 165-166), the *Armenian Infancy Gospel*, the *Latin Infancy Gospel*, and the *Arabic Infancy Gospel* are profuse in their accounts of the details of the birth and are remarkable for the miraculous portents which they associate with the event. But still more striking is the way in which the narrator switches suddenly from the birth scene in verse 7 to the shepherds in verse 8. If this is such a climactic moment in the narrative, surely it would have made more sense to focus on the birth more intensely and at greater length; and surely it would have made more sense to have the light shine around the newborn child (as the apocryphals do) than around the shepherds. At the moment where he enters the human scene, the figure of Jesus is passed over in a way which looks to the action of heaven (Coleridge, 1992: 138).

Given how crucial the birth is from many points of view, it is remarkable that it is recounted in so terse a style, as noted by many scholars without tackling the question as to why the narrator might have it this way (Schürmann, 1969: 98; Brown, 1977: 418; Ernst, 1977: 105; Laurentin, 1982: 223; Nolland, 1989: 105). They all state *that* the narration is brief. From narrative-critical viewpoint, the question is *why* the narration is so brief.

While in the apocryphal versions the birth is reported in detail and is accompanied by an array of marvellous signs, here it is narrated in a single verse focusing on the "what" but not the "how." We are not told when the child was born, though verse 8 may hint that it was during the night. Verse 6 implies that Mary and Joseph have been in Bethlehem for some time, but does not specify how long. We are told where the birth does not happen ("in the inn"), but not exactly where it does happen. The mention of the manger in verse 7 seems to suggest that it was in a space reserved for animals, but more than that we are not told. Again the apocryphal accounts are very detailed in their description of the place, with the majority favoring a cave (Coleridge, 1993: 133-134).

Joseph disappears from the narrative at the critical moment. Verse 18 will suggest that there were others present, if not at the birth itself then at least shortly afterwards, but there is no hint of this in verse 7. Joseph vanishes and Mary is presented solely in terms of what she does. Then above and beyond all this, the narrator says nothing of why God may want things this way. If he is as all-powerfull as Gabriel claimed in Lk 1:37, then God might have managed better the birth of the messiah. We are given the strange facts of the birth by the narrator, but no interpretation.

Joseph disappears from the scene and Mary regains the initiative. The focus is on her alone; and she is the subject of the three verbs in verse 7 ("gave birth, wrapped, and laid"). The report of Mary's actions after the birth presents a puzzling combination (Coleridge, 1993: 134-135). Although the expression "firstborn" (*prōtotokos*) is sometimes clearly equivalent to "only born" (*monogenēs*; Ps Sol 13:8 [9]; 18:4), some would take this to mean "first born among many." However, the use of "firstborn" rather than "only born" proves only that Luke had no interest in presenting Jesus as Mary's only son. Actually the designation "firstborn" tells us only that there was no child before Jesus, and that therefore he was to have the privileges and position that Hebrew tradition gives to the firstborn (Ex 13:2; Num 3:12-13; 18:15-16). In light of Lk 1:32, "firstborn" emphasizes that this son has the right of inheritance to the throne of David (see 2 Chron 21:3; Danker, 1988: 55). Luke mentions it here to prepare for the dedication of Jesus as firstborn in Lk 2:22-23. That the designation need not imply the birth of subsequent children is clear from the grave inscription of a Jewish woman named Arsinoe, found near ancient Leontopolis in Egypt and dated to 5 B.C. The Greek text reads: "In the pains of giving birth to a firstborn child, Fate brought me to the end of my life." If she died in giving birth to her firstborn, obviously she had no more children (Brown, 1977: 398).

The report of Mary's actions after the birth presents a puzzling combination. As a pair they seem banal given what the reader knows to be the significance of the event.

"She wrapped him in bands of cloth," literally, "she swaddled him," refers to an ordinary human initiative, meaning that she wrapped strips or bands of cloth around the limbs of the newborn to keep his limbs straight by means of restraint (Johnson, 1991: 50).

To swaddle a baby is a sign of parental care (Wisd 7:4), and the lack of swaddling is seen as neglect in the allegorical description of Jerusalem in Ez 15:4. It is not to be understood as a sign of poverty or of the messiah's low birth (Fitzmyer, 1981: 408; Brown, 1977: 419). From the narrative point of view what matters is that at the point where the narrator moves from the narration of Caesar's sway to the narration of God's sway, we again have a story of a human initiative, and of the most ordinary kind: a woman gives birth and then swaddles the newborn. The readers might have expected God to take the initiative immediately and in more dramatic fashion (Coleridge, 1993: 136).

"[She] laid him in a manger (*phatnē*)." The Greek *phatnē* can mean a "stall" for tying up animals, or a "manger." i.e., a trough for feeding them. A stall might be either outdoors or indoors; the latter is implied in Lk 13:15 where a man can set his animals loose from a *phatnē* and lead them out to give them a drink. A manger might be a movable trough placed on the ground, or a cavity in a low rock shelf. Luke does not give us enough context to decide. The fact that the *phatnē* is contrasted with the *kataluma* or "lodgings" may favor the meaning "stall." However, the picture of wrapping the baby and laying him down better suits a cradle-like manger. The Christmas-crib scenes, popularized by Francis of Assisi, have fixed the image of a manger. No mention is made of animals in Luke's text. Oxen and donkeys have been introduced into this nativity scene from a combination of Luke's reference to the *phatnē* (both stall and manger imply animals) with the lament of God in Isa 1:3LXX, "The ox knows its owner, and the donkey its master's crib [manger], but Israel does not know, my people do not understand" (Brown, 1977: 399; Bovon, 1987: 169).

Mary's second action of placing the child in a manger is even more surprising to the modern reader than wrapping him in swaddling cloths. If the first action seems banal, this second action seems absurd – again given what the readers know to be the identity of the newborn. This is an example of what the Russian formalists (especially Viktor Shklovsky) call "defamiliarization," where there is a disorientating association that leads to a revision of the elements associated. Here it is the association of messiah and manger which is disorienting, and which demands a revision of messianic expectation (Resseguie, 1990: 147-153). To the question, "Why the manger?," the narrator offers one immediate answer: "because there was no place for them in the inn" (Coleridge, 1993: 136).

"There was no place for them in the inn." Peassant houses normally had only one room, though sometimes a guest room would have been attached. The family usually occupied one end of the main room (often raised) and the animals the other. A manger was located in between. The manger would have been the normal place for peasant births, with the women of the house assisting. The fact that Joseph comes to Bethlehem to be enrolled may imply that he had land (hence family) there, since the census or enrollment was for land taxation purposes. If so, he would have been obligated to stay with family, not in a commercial inn. Being a small village only a two-hour walk from Jerusalem, Bethlehem almost certainly had no commercial inns anyway. If close family were not available, mention of Joseph's lineage would have resulted in immediate village recognition that he belonged, and space in a house would have been made available. The fact that there was no "place" for Joseph and Mary in the guest room meant that it was already occupied by someone who socially outranked them (Malina-Rohrbaugh, 1992: 297).

Although the Greek word in Lk 2:7 can sometimes mean "inn," it normally refers to a large furnished room attached to a peasant house and is best translated "guest room." The only other use of this term in the New Testament is in the account of the Last Supper (Mk 14:14; Lk 22:11), where it is translated "upper room." The normal word for a commercial inn is *pandocheion*, which the Third Evangelist uses in Lk 10:34. Actually, *kataluma*, a compound of *kata* + *luein*, "loose," denotes a place where one "lets down" one's harness (or baggage) for the night (cf. Lk 9:12; 19:7). In 2 Sam 7:6LXX, *kataluma* describes the dwelling place of the Divine presence in the desert travels of Israel (Brown, 1977: 400). More important for the Lukan story, Elkanah and Hannah, on their visit to the sanctuary of Shiloh, stay in a *kataluma* (1 Sam 1:18LXX), which may have influenced Luke's expression here. It should be understood as a public caravansary or khan, where groups of travelers would spend the night under one roof (Fitzmyer, 1981: 408). So far a "surface-interpretation" of Lk 2:7.

The details about the swaddling and the manger are repeated later (Lk 2:12, 16) and must be of significance. Most of the popular reflection on verse 7, however, misses Luke's point. Certainly irrelevant are speculations about why there was no room at the lodgings, especially when these speculations lead to homilies about the supposed heartlessness of the unmentioned innkeeper and the hardship of the situation for the impoverished parents (Brown, 1977: 418-419). However, many scholars believe that there is a deeper dimension to Luke's depiction of Jesus' situation and that we are not dealing here with a simple report of fact, but a midrash-like interpretation of the meaning of the fact of Jesus' birth.

The manger appears three times in Lk 2:1-20 (verses 7, 12, 16) and Luke refers to it as a "sign" (Lk 2:12; Baily, 1964: 1-4). What is the manger's symbolism? Several suggestions have been made, one of which relates the symbolism of the Lukan manger to God's complaint in Isa 1:3LXX: "The ox knows its owner, and the donkey its master's crib [manger], but Israel does not know, my people do not understand" (Giblin, 1967: 99-101). Isaiah is comparing the behavior of the people with that of the ox and the donkey. The ox knows to whom it belongs, the donkey knows where to look for its sustenance; but the people of Israel do not know to whom they belong and do not know where to look for their sustenance. Luke would be proclaiming that the Isaian statement is repealed. The shepherds are led to and will find the manger again, and the sign of their finding the child in the manger – indeed, their *finding the child* is part of the sign! – means that with the birth of this child God has finally and decisively reaffirmed his resolve to be the sustenance of his people. And God's people have begun to know the manger of their Lord.

The "inn" or the "lodgings" may have been brought into the picture through Jer 14:8 addressed to the Lord and Savior of Israel: "O hope of Israel its savior in time of trouble, why should you be like a stranger in the land, like a traveler turning aside for the night." Jeremiah is saying that God is aloof from his people, and when he happens to pass through the country, he behaves like a stranger who has no friends or relatives to stay with and therefore stays in an inn. So, to stay in an inn means to behave like a stranger. But Jesus comes to his own. Therefore, the Lord and Savior of Israel no longer stays in an "inn" [Note the word "savior" in Jer 14:8].

The swaddling, far from being a sign of poverty, may be a sign that Israel's messiah is not an outcast among his people, but is properly received and cared for. In Wis 7:3-5, Solomon, son of David and king, affirms: "And when I was born... I was nursed with care in swaddling cloths. For no king has had a different beginning of existence." So, the child born is also a son of David and a king.

Summing up, we may say that the symbolism in all of this is that Jesus is born in the town of David, not in a lodge like a stranger, but in the manger of the Lord, who is the sustainer of his people. Like Solomon, David's most famous son in the past, Jesus is swaddled in token of his regal condition, but also of his human condition (Fitzmyer, 1981: 395).

Verses 8-20: (8)   In that region there were *shepherds* living in the fields,

keeping watch over their flock by night....

(20) The *shepherds* returned,

glorifying and praising God for all they had heard and seen,

as it had been told them.

While not an explicit allusion to Micah 5:4 (there it is the ruler who is the shepherd), the references to the shepherds after the double mention of David in verse 4 may perhaps recall David's role as shepherd (Schürmann, 1969: 108). As already seen above, the third section of Lk 2:1-20, verses 8-20, the manifestation of the newborn child to the shepherds and the reaction of all who heard of the birth and manifestation, can be divided into two, Lk 2:8-14 and 2:15-20, the first of which deals with the manifestation of the child. But it is also clear that for Luke, Lk 2:8-20 is a self-contained unit. Lk 2:8 contains a presentation of the shepherds and Lk 2:20 constitutes a magnificent inclusion (Neirynck, 1960: 42). The passage takes the form of an "apocalypse" (Tremel, 1981: 594).

Verses 8: In that region there were shepherds living in the fields,

keeping watch over their flock by night.

In verse 8, the narrator turns unexpectedly from the newborn child to the shepherds who will play a decisive role from now until the end of Lk 2:1-20. From a narrative point of view, however, the prime question is not why God might choose the shepherds to receive the revelation, but why the narrator turns the reader's attention away from the birth scene when he might easily and more naturally have focused on the reaction of Mary and Joseph. He prefers instead to make both parents and child recede into the background, and to turn to the fields outside Bethlehem. The phrase "keeping watch over their flock by night" is equivalent to "keeping night watch over their flock." The point is not that they received the news during the night, but probably that they were ready for it when it came, presumably at daybreak (Danker, 1988: 56). Verses 1-5 have told of human initiative, and verses 6-7, if they have begun the narration of God's sway, have still focused on human initiative, as if God, having set things in motion in earlier episodes, has now departed from the scene. But in verse 8 the divine initiative is reasserted in unexpected ways.

As in the first two episodes (Lk 1:5-25 and 26-38), heaven triggers the real action of the episode. At the beginning of the episode it may have seemed that it was Caesar who, with the census, was the prime mover of the plot. But in verse 9 it is again an angel who stirs the real action as the heavens open once more. That the news comes from heaven through the angel suggests that, as with the promises made through Gabriel, so now with the birth: the initiative at every turn rests directly with heaven. It is God who has intervened directly to bring the child to birth (Lk 1:35), and it is God who now intervenes directly to announce and interpret the fact of fulfillment (Coleridge, 1993: 137-138).

Having settled this literary question, we can now turn to the question, why – in Luke's view – God might choose the *shepherds* to receive the revelation. Indeed, news of the birth of the messiah is first made known, not to religious or secular rulers of the land, but to lowly inhabitants of the area, busy with other matters. The chord of "the lowly" has already been struck in the Magnificat (Lk 1:52) and foreshadows the use of it in the Gospel proper (Lk 7:22; Fitzmyer, 1981: 408).

To modern romantics the shepherds described by Luke take on the gentleness of their flocks, or are examples of virtue (Kamphaus, 1974: 281), and in recent centuries they have triumphed over the magi as a better Christmas symbol for common folks. But such interests are foreign to Luke's purpose. In fact, far from being regarded as either gentle or noble, in Jesus' time shepherds were often considered as dishonest, outside the Law. A Jewish writing, *Talmud Babylon Sanhedrin* 25b mentions that herdsmen were added by the early rabbis to the list of those ineligible to be judge or witness since frequently they grazed their flocks on other people's lands. Thus, they were among the type of dishonest people who were excluded from court. In any case, the herdsman was despised: "There is no more disreputable occupation than that of a shepherd" (Midrash Ps 23:2). This has led to the suggestion that they represented the sinners whom Jesus came to save (Lk 5:32; 7:34; 15:1; 19:7; Stein, 1992: 108); yet there is no hint of that in Lk 2:8-20 (Brown, 1977: 420).

We noted already above that Caesar's census receives far more narrative space (Lk 2:1-5) than the actual birth of Jesus (Lk 2:6-7). By comparison, the annunciation to and the response by the shepherds are clearly the center of attention (Lk 2:8-20). Moreover, the shepherds are the representatives here of the whole people: they are receiving the "good news," which will provide jubilation for "the whole people" (Lk 2:10). It is conceivable, of course, that the shepherds and the manger can simply be understood as bits of local color in the story. But the fact that the shepherds have such a key role as recipients and proclaimers of the good news of the savior's birth suggests that we should not simply dismiss them as local color.

After the previous narrative in Lk 1, in which the child to be born is clearly interpreted as the son of David who will rule over Israel and as the horn of salvation in the house of God's servant David (Lk 1:32-33,69), the presentation in Lk 2 of Jesus' being born in the town of David among shepherds would suggest the "one shepherd" of Ez 34:23-24. And that allusion might be confirmed by the angels' proclaiming "peace" on earth, since in the next verse in Ezekiel, God promises to make a "covenant of peace." There is no clear indication in the text of Lk 2, however, that such an allusion is present (Horsley, 1989: 102).

But the picture of "despised trades" and of shepherds in particular is highly problematic, particularly with regard to the sources on which it is based. The texts from which the lists are taken are very late, hence not good evidence for the time of Jesus. Equally as important as the dating of evidence should be the social location of evidence. It is unlikely that rabbinic debates on who is ineligible to serve as witnesses in court provide good evidence for whether people were despised or hated "by the people." We would certainly have to take the rabbis' social status and attitudes into account. Thus we do not have here solid direct evidence that shepherds were a specially despised group of people in first-century Palestine (Horsley, 1989: 102-103; C.F. Evans, 1990: 203).

We may have, however, a reflection of the suspicion in which shepherds were held by those in high status or an indication that shepherds had very low social status in certain Jewish areas in the fourth or fifth centuries A.D. And either of these interpretations suggest that the social status of shepherds may have been fairly low in earlier centuries as well. There does not appear to be evidence that shepherds were "despised by the people" at the time of Jesus. It seems clear in a story such as Lk 2:8-20 that they were understood as part of "the whole people." But their status in the society generally was probably very low (Horsley, 1993: 103).

If Bethlehem and other places where there was insufficient rainfall to do extensive cultivation of the soil was "shepherd country," then the shepherds in such areas were the equivalent of the farmers or peasants elsewhere. The shepherds in the story set in Bethlehem represent the *ordinary people*, the peasantry of the area. Crops were cultivated in the area, as we know from the Book of Ruth. But the herding of flocks was probably very important also, given the local ecology. And in a story about

the birth of the messiah from the lineage of David, who himself
had been a shepherd when anointed king, it would naturally be
shepherds who would receive the good news, witness the event,
and proclaim it. Two points belong integrally together in the
story: first, the messiah and savior has been born in the midst
of and indeed as one of the ordinary people; and second, the
shepherds, as the obvious local representatives of those ordinary people, are called to witness and proclaim the good news
of the eventual liberation the child represents (Horsley, 1989:104).

Josephus reports a concrete social phenomenon in
Judea contemporaneous with Jesus' birth that illustrates not only
that shepherds were, in certain areas, an integral part of the
peasantry, but also that other common people looked to shepherds for distinctive leadership, even though they were despised
by those of high status.

> And then there was Athronges, a man whose impor-
> tance derived neither from the renown of his forefa-
> thers, nor from the superiority of his character, nor the
> extent of his means. He was an obscure shepherd, yet
> remarkable for his stature and strength... He also had
> four brothers... Each of them led an armed band, for a
> great throng had assembled around them... Athronges
> held council on what was to be done... He held power
> for a long time, having been designated king (*Antiqui-
> ties* 17.278-281).

As the popular messianic movement in Judea illustrates, the
common people, including shepherds, were ready to become
involved in a movement directed against Roman and Herodian
rule and led by a king from among their midst. This appears to
be precisely what is announced to and by the shepherds in Lk
2:8-20, as well as celebrated in the songs of Lk 1–2, except that
the army is a heavenly one in Lk 2, not one of Judean peasants
as in the movement led by the particularly acclaimed king
Athronges (Horsley, 1989: 104).

The manger in which the child was laid suggests and fits

with the same interpretation, either by itself or understood in connection with Isa 1:3. The contrast between this savior, laid in an animal feeding trough while his parents were traveling an appreciable distance to be registered for their assessment of tribute, and the exalted position of Caesar, who could demand that tribute, is clear. That the child is laid in a manger, then, is declared to be a *sign* for the shepherds that the savior, the messiah and lord, has been born in the city of David (Lk 2:12). A sign in biblical history and literature is not simply an authenticating proof or token of a message or a promised future event, but usually also affects or is directly related to the people addressed in the message. Now it might not seem so to urban and urbane intellectuals, who cultivate more sophisticated, higher levels of meaning, but the simple fact that Jesus is laid in a manger by itself could well be the sign in this case, as the narrative states. The exemplification that bears out the message that a savior and messiah has been born *for them* and *for the whole people* is that the child is right there in the manger in their midst, as one of them. The other figures that the Jewish common people recognized as significant leaders of deliverance for themselves in this period – the popular kings and popular prophets – were apparently from among the people: Athronges, a lowly shepherd; Judas, son of Hezekiah the Galilean bandit chieftain. And such humble origins for the messiah would not have been in contrast to standard expectations, for we are finally realizing that there is precious little evidence that there were any standardized or generally held expectations of "the messiah" at this time in Jewish Palestine, let alone that a regal messiah was the standard expectation (Horsley, 1989: 105).

The sign for the shepherds could thus finally be that the child is laid in the Lord's manger, symbol of God's sustenance of his people, by analogy with the donkey's manger in Isa 1:3. But then, what would God's sustenance of his people be in the context of this story in Lk 2:1-20, as suggested by the allusion to Isa 1:3? Luke and his early readers probably would still have appreciated the covenantal denotations in Isaiah's language: the Lord's sustenance consisted in the great acts of righteousness or redemption, such as the exodus (and Israel's "knowing" should have been keeping covenantal righteousness or justice). The laying of the child in the manger of the Lord would thus have been the sign, that is, the exemplification that related directly to the shepherds, of the coming redemption or "deliverance from the hands of our enemies" (Lk 1:71,73; Horsley, 1993: 105-106).

The preceding considerations suggest that the shepherds of Lk 2 should not be overinterpreted, whether in the older fashion as symbols of some idyllic pastoral life or in the more recent mode as representatives of the despised and ostracized in Jewish society. Shepherds were simply part of the peasantry in ancient Palestinian society. Peasants, almost by definition, were poor, and, especially in relation to their rulers and certain other (but not all) urban dwellers, were lowly in status. Shepherds, while not despised by the people, were apparently some of the lowliest of the lowly. Thus, in addition to shepherds being the obvious recipients of the message of the birth of the messiah/savior in the environs of the "Davidic" city of Bethlehem, for them to receive the message and visit the child dramatically illustrates that the messiah has been born among the lowly ordinary people as the leader of their liberation. What the angel announced and what Mary and Zechariah had sung about in Lk 1 has been inaugurated among the shepherds with the child laid in a manger (Horsley, 1989: 106). In social-science terms, the role that the shepherds play here is an important one of validating events that require public recognition before honor can be ascribed. Hence Luke is careful to record their report to others of what they had seen and heard (Lk 2:17; Malina-Rohrbaugh, 1992: 296).

Verse 9: Then the angel of the Lord stood before them,
        and the glory of the Lord shone around them,
        and they were terrified.

Unlike in Lk 1:19,26, the angel of the Lord remains anonymous, but is reinforced by an angelic host (Lk 2:13), and his utterance is that of God (Lk 2:15; C.F. Evans, 1990: 203). As at times in the Old Testament, what is here announced by "the angel of the Lord" is subsequently attributed to God himself (Lk 2:15; Fitzmyer, 1981: 409).

"The glory of the Lord" is the first appearance in Luke-Acts of the important word *doxa*. In Greek this meant "appearance," "reputation." In the Septuagint it underwent a transformation, and was given a special force as the translation of the Hebrew word *kabod* meaning "weight," "splendor" with reference to Yahweh's self-manifestation and presence in the form of a numinous cloud or God's perceptible presence to his people (Ex 16:10; Num 14:10; so here, "shone around"). It was then constantly associated with Yahweh, and with heavenly beings around him. It was the nearest Hebrew thought got to expressing God's "being" (cf. Acts 7:55), and could be a synonym for God, especially in the form "*the* glory" (C.F. Evans, 1990: 203). In verse 9, the narrator has "the glory of the Lord" shine around the shepherds, with the image of light in darkness (verse 8: "by night") strengthening the sense that the fulfillment of the prophecy of Lk 1:78b-79a has begun. It also underscores the fact that, with the birth of Jesus, the presence of God becomes more overt [in neither of the appearances of Gabriel was he accompanied by the *doxa* of the Lord]. At Christmas, the presence of God is no longer engulfed in Mary's womb, but becomes engulfing: the divine presence engulfs the shepherds (Laurentin, 1982: 228). Surprisingly perhaps, the glory of the Lord surrounds not the newborn child, as in the *Protoevangelium of James*, but the shepherds. This is because it is not so much the bare fact of the birth which absorbs the narrator's interest as it is the interpretation of the birth and its circumstances that heaven now offers, and the reaction of the shepherds to the angel's interpretation (Coleridge, 1993: 138).

The shepherds "were terrified," literally "feared [with] a great

fear," a not unnatural response. For the fear engendered by the
"glory of God," see Isa 6:1-5; Lk 8:34 (Johnson, 1991: 50). Fear
is also the standard reaction to angelic appearances (Lk 1:12-
13, 29-30).

Verse 10: But the angel said to them,
            "Do not be afraid; for see –
            I am bringing you good news of great joy for all the people:

As he begins to speak, the angel makes no attempt to introduce himself, nor does he mention God as the one who has
sent him to make the proclamation: the angel himself is the
subject of "to bring good news." Again the prime mover lies
hidden, with the focus on what has happened and what it means
rather than upon either the one who has made it happen or
the messenger he now sends. In the messenger's words, there is
a complementarity between "to you" and "to all the people,"
that is, Israel. While admitting that a new reference to the
new people of God, both Jews and Gentiles, is *possible* in Lk
2:10, it is rather *unlikely* (Wilson, 1973: 35). Again, public and
private dimensions converge in the narrative, here in a way
that points to the mediating function of the shepherds (Bovon,
1991: 124).

In Greek, the statement begins with "for behold," also used
in Lk 1:44,48; 6:23; 17:21; Acts 9:11, and only once in the rest
of the New Testament (2 Cor 7:11). "I am bringing you good
news" (*euangelizesthai*), is another favorite Lukan verb (ten out
of eleven Gospel usages), already used of the birth of John the
Baptist in Lk 1:19. But Luke uses the noun *euangelion* only in
Acts 15:7; 20:24, probably under influence of the Septuagint,
which prefers the verb to the noun (Brown, 1977: 402). The
verb became a standard term in the church for Christian proclamation. It had a significant background in Isa 40:9, "Get you
up to a high mountain, O Zion, herald of good tidings; lift up
your voice with strength, O Jerusalem, herald of good tidings,
lift it up, do not fear"; Isa 52:7, "How beautiful upon the mountains
are the feet of the messenger who announces peace, who brings
good news, who announces salvation" [Note that in this last

passage several ideas and words occur that are also found in our present context]. The verb is used of the announcement of the good news of God's salvation, but Luke can also use it in a reduced sense of "preach," "teach" (Lk 3:18; 8:1; 9:6; 20:1; Acts 8:12;14:7; C.F. Evans, 1990: 151).

Every birth is greeted with joy (*chara*). The verb *chairein* and the noun *chara* occur three times in the infancy gospel, once in the beatitudes, eight times in the travel narrative (Lk 9:51–19:44), and twice in the resurrection narrative. In every case joy is related to the recognition of the present salvation process and experienced in the measure that one participates in it (Navone, 1970: 73). In Luke's Gospel joy is characteristic of faith, which establishes that saving history advances (Bovon, 1978: 423 note). The joy that has been present in Luke from the beginning is here underlined. If God is at work in the beginning and at the end – and the angels confirm this (Lk 24:4) – the people (Lohfink, 1975: 28) receive peace (cf. Lk 24:36) and great joy (cf. Lk 24:52). The literary feature of inclusion suggests the appropriation by faith of the birth of the son, and then of his new birth in the resurrection (Bovon, 1991: 123-124).

Verse 11: to you is born this day in the city of David a Savior who is the Messiah, the Lord.

Verse 11 gives the content of the proclamation and the reason for joy. The shepherds are told a number of things already known to the readers: (1) what has happened ("is born"); (2) when it has happened ("this day"); (3) who has been born ("Savior, Messiah, Lord"); (4) where it has happened ("in the city of David").

For the first time in the Lukan narrative Jesus is called "Savior," since this title's one earlier appearance referred to God (Lk 1:47). The Benedictus spoke obliquely of a "horn of salvation" (Lk 1:69; NRSV: "a mighty savior"), the one as yet unknown who would bring God's salvation. But now the identity of the shadowy figure is known – the savior himself, he who brings the salvation of God that the narrator has been careful to define from Lk 1:47 until now. The Benedictus' image of "the horn of salvation" gives way to the newborn child, to whom the image seems hardly to fit. If the redefinition of salvation as forgiveness seemed strange, then the proclamation of a new-born child as savior seems even stranger. All the more so since the angelic proclamation uses the present tense "is" rather than a future. The newborn child is already savior and the messiah, the Lord (Coleridge, 1993: 139-140). The only other Lukan usages of "savior" occur in Acts 5:31 and 13:23, both times with reference to Jesus. The use of the cognates "salvation" (*sōteria*) and "to save" (*sōzō*), together with related concepts, however, shows that salvation is a key Lukan theme (Marshall, 1970: 88-102; Strauss, 1995: 113-114). It is interesting to note that in his Pentecost speech Peter also brings two of these three titles together: "...God has made him both Lord and Messiah" (Acts 2:36).

"This day" (*sēmeron*; translated "today" in Lk 4:21; 5:26; 19:5, 9; 22:34, etc.) is a characteristic Lukan expression that is found twenty times in the Lukan narrative, capturing the Lukan sense of realized eschatology, the sense that the prophecies are *now* fulfilled, and that the last times are at hand. Some find here an echo of Ps 2:7, "He said to me, "You are my son; today I have begotten you" (Brown, 1977: 425), but this is hard to determine in view of the allusive use of Scripture throughout the Lukan narrative.

As already seen in Lk 2:4, "the city of David" is normally the designation of Jerusalem, as in 2 Sam 5:7,9. Yet David himself is known in the Old Testament as the son of "an Ephrathite of Bethlehem in Judah" (1 Sam 17:12), or as the son of "Jesse the Bethlehemite" (1 Sam 17:58). Hence the Lukan conflation found here, possibly added for extra-Palestinian readers (Fitzmyer, 1981: 406).

The title "Savior" could have a background in the Old Testament, where it was used of God (Ps 25:5, etc.) in his saving activity towards Israel; as also of those that God empowers to deliver his people from oppression (e.g., the Judges; cf. Acts

13:17-23). But it was also a familiar term in Hellenistic piety for (divine) heroes (e.g., Heracles), or great men, to mark their special position as conferring benefits on humankind, whether political (e.g., emperor Augustus), philosophical (e.g., Epicurus), or medical (e.g., Aesculapius). The expression "savior of the inhabited world" (*oikoumenē*) is for the first time applied to Julius Caesar and the expression "savior of the world (*kosmos*)" to emperor Hadrian (117-130 A.D.). But the term "savior" never becomes a technical one applied only to the emperor. It can, therefore, not be considered an "imperial title" in the strict sense of the word (Frankemölle, 1983: 91). It was also applied to cult divinities such as Mithras or Isis. It is this latter background which may be responsible for its application to Jesus, which takes place in the later strata of christology. Thus in the gospels it occurs again only in Jn 4:42 in the Hellenistic expression "the savior of the world" (C.F. Evans, 1990: 204). The title "savior" combines elements both sacral and secular. The Magnificat and Benedictus have made it clear how the title relates Jesus to God, and how it, therefore, has a sacral edge. But in another way the title "savior" resumes the contrast between the sway of Caesar and the sway of God, since this was a title used of rulers in the Hellenistic world, and applied specifically to Caesar Augustus, chiefly as the architect of the *Pax Augusta*. If Augustus was hailed throughout the empire as the source of salvation and peace, so too were God and his messiah in the Benedictus. The real question, therefore, concerns how we are to understand salvation and peace and how they come about. The *Pax Augusta* and the *Pax Christi* are not necessarily identical (Coleridge, 1993: 140-141). In fact, it can be said that the messianic peace and the *Pax Romana* are incompatible. There is only one Jesus praxis. The Sermon on the Mount (as indeed the whole Bible) is unmistakable and clear when we read it not as a mere collection of isolated sentences but as statements linked to the praxis of the people who stood behind them, namely the followers of Jesus (Schottroff, 1992: 163).

The combination "the Messiah, the Lord" (*christos kurios*;

literally, "Christ Lord") without articles occurs nowhere else in the New Testament; other possible translations are "Christ the Lord" and "the Anointed Lord." The way in which *christos* is linked with *kurios* is unusual. It is one thing to claim that Jesus is the Davidic messiah, as is done in the title *christos*, used here for the first time of Jesus; but it is another thing to associate the messiah with God in the way that is done by the juxtaposition of *christos* with *kurios* without the article, which until now has been reserved for God. On the one hand, the effect of the juxtaposition is to associate the Davidic messiah and God in an unusual way. On the other hand, the effect of titles such as "savior" and "lord," which if not exclusively Hellenistic were at least used widely to refer to the imperial power, contrasts the Davidic messiah with the Roman emperor in a way that continues and specifies the contrast between Caesar and God established in the early verses of the episode. The combination of the sacral and the secular in the titles reinforces the process of defamiliarization already at work in the episode in phenomena such as the newborn messiah in a manger and the angel appearing to shepherds. Worlds converge unexpectedly in a way that defamiliarizes and, in that sense, redefines both (Coleridge, 1993: 141-142). The phrase occurs once in the Septuagint, as a mistranslation in Lam 4:20; it occurs also in Ps Sol 17:36. Luke is the only Synoptic Gospel to use the title "the Lord" frequently of Jesus (fourteen times, compared to once each in Mark and Matthew; Brown, 1977: 402-403; for an extensive discussion of these two titles, see Fitzmyer, 1981: 197-204). It has been suggested, not without reason, that *christos* is Luke's most important christological title (Fitzmyer, 1981: 197; C.F. Evans, 1990: 73; Strauss, 1995: 114-116).

Verse 12: This will be a sign for you:
          you will find a child wrapped in bands of cloth
          and lying in a manger."

In this verse where the angel offers the shepherds a sign that they have not sought, we find an even more astonishing juxtaposition than that of *christos* and *kurios*. The angel reports to the

shepherds the surprising details that the narrator gave the readers in verse 7b: "[she] wrapped him in bands of cloth, and laid
him in a manger." As far as the *shepherds* are concerned, one
wonders what the function of the sign might be [but see what
was said above about the shepherds and their life and expecta-
tions]. There is not the bare minimum of detail to guide them
on their way: they are not told where to look, who the child's
parents are or what the child's name is; and far from serving as
a sign which might confirm the angel's proclamation, it seems
more a sign designed to overturn any expectation they may have
had of the Davidic messiah and to test the shepherds'readiness
of belief. Again that is how it seems *to us*, but we should also
refer to what was said above about the *shepherds*.

As far as the *readers* are concerned, the function of the sign
is easier to determine. Where in verse 7 the narrator made it
seem that the placing of the child in the manger was the result
of misfortune coming in the wake of the imperial decree, as the
spokesperson of heaven, the angel in verse 12 now makes it
clear that not only the birth but also its peculiar circumstances,
are as God wants it. An answer to the question, "who is in
control?," comes from heaven itself, and is an answer that shows
that the "how" of divine control is paradoxical. The angel's speech,
then, has a double function: it announces and interprets the
birth for the shepherds, and interprets the circumstances of the
birth for the readers (Coleridge, 1993: 142-143).

The formulation of the text, "This will be a sign for you:
you will find...," clearly shows that the sign is not just the child
in the manger; the shepherds' *finding* of the child in the manger
is part of the sign. If in Isa 1:3 we were told that Israel, unlike
the donkey, did not know where to look for the manger, now
the shepherds, representatives of "all the people," will find the
manger again.

Verses 13-14: (13) And suddenly there was with the angel
a multitude of the heavenly host,
praising God and saying,
(14) "Glory to God in the highest heaven,
and on earth peace among those whom he favors."

The angelic song is in effect a proclamation of the results of the birth of Jesus rather than a hymn of praise directly addressed to God (Marshall, 1978: 111). Just as the shepherds provide earthly validation of the honor ascribed to Jesus at his birth, so also do God's heavenly messengers, his angels. In this way the whole of the inhabited world, both earth and heaven, publicly recognizes the honor being claimed for Jesus (Malina-Rohrbaugh, 1992: 296). Strictly speaking, these verses interrupt the story, which continues in verse 15 with the shepherds verifying the statement of the single angel in verses 10-12. It is a very miniature canticle, now on the lips of angelic and not human beings, in the form of two parallel and chiastic lines, though of unequal length:

> *Glory* <u>in the highest</u> <u><u>to God</u></u>,
> and <u>on earth</u> *peace* <u><u>among those whom he favors</u></u>.

In this arrangement there are three elements in each line: a noun (italics), a localization phrase (underlined once), and a directional phrase (underlined twice).

The word "suddenly" (*exaiphnēs*) marks either an end-time occurrence (eschatological) or a supramundane occurrence (see Lk 9:39; Acts 9:3; 22:6; Danker, 1988: 59). "A multitude of the heavenly host" is a variant of a septuagintal expression, "the host of heaven" (1 Kgs 22:19; Jer 19:13; Hos 13:4; 2 Chron 33:3, 5). The word "host" is a military term, indicating that from the vantage point of the government of heaven, the whole story is filled with divine glory and power and splendor (Tiede, 1988: 72). To highlight his own prestige, Caesar Augustus wrote in his *Res Gestae* (10) that Rome had never seen so great a multitude as the one gathered from every part of Italy for his election. In Luke's narrative Jesus eclipses Augustus. The phrase "heavenly host" (cf. Acts 7:42) is similar to formulations used in the Old Testament both of heavenly bodies (Jer 8:2; 19:13) and of God's attendants (1 Kgs 22:19). In intertestamental times, angels are associated with stars (cf. Enoch 43; Danker, 1988: 59). The function of the heavenly host is again interpretative, as the angels proclaim the meaning and effect of the divine action as glory in heaven to God and peace on earth (Coleridge, 1993: 143).

The "glory" referred to here differs from the *doxa kuriou*, "the glory of the Lord" (Lk 2:9), which expresses the perceptible manifestation of God's presence. The formula used here is, rather, close to that in Ps Sol 18:10, "Great is our God and glorious (*endoxos*), dwelling in the highest." The phrase "in the highest" refers, not to degree, but to God's abode (cf. Job 16:19; Ps 148:1; Sir 26:16; 43:9). It is in contrast to "earth" in the next line (Fitzmyer, 1981: 410).

"Peace" is one of Luke's ways of summing up the effects of the Christ-event. Whereas in heaven the one result of the birth of the saving Messiah Lord is the intense glorification of God everywhere, on earth what corresponds to the coming of this person is peace among human beings. Two things can be noted about this correspondence. Firstly, peace is the only concept that Luke desires to make known here. This, in itself, is worth noting. Secondly, it is not altogether clear against what opposite peace is to be understood here. It is not at once clear whether Luke is talking about a personal, psychological or spiritual peace to come to each human being, or about a social peace, a peace that primarily looks to humans living together. In any event, it is clear enough that the birth of the saving Messiah Lord should result in peace. It is understanding what this person can do (for the individual and for society) that should help pinpoint in just what the peace announced by the angels consists (Kilgallen, 1989: 67). At any rate, the word means more than the cessation of strife, and is used to indicate the full sum of blessings associated with the coming of the messiah. He will bring a new situation of peace between God and humankind in which his blessings can be communicated to them; peace is thus tantamount to salvation (Marshall, 1989: 112). It is not easy to say whether the proper background of this term is the pervasive *Pax Augusta* in the contemporary Roman world or the Old Testament understanding of *shalom*.

It may be that both are at work. Certainly Luke's dating of the birth of Jesus to a census taken during the reign of the emperor Augustus implies an association, if not a contrast, with the peace of that long reign. On the other hand, the connotations of the Hebrew root *slm*, "be whole, complete," seem to be implied in the Lukan use of the term "peace." In the Old Testament, *shalom* expresses not merely an absence of war or hostilities, but much more the state of bounty or well-being that comes from God and includes concord, harmony, order, security, and prosperity (Isa 48:18; 54:10; Ez 34:25-29; Pss 29:11; 85:8-10; Jer 16:5; Num 6:24-26). In time "peace" became the mark of the awaited messianic kingdom, derived from Isa 52:7 (the heralds of peace; Fitzmyer, 1981: 224-225). Lk 2:14 is not the first time the word has appeared in the infancy narrative. It appeared in Lk 1:79 as the last word of the Benedictus, where it described the effect of the enlightened human being's recognition that God has fulfilled his promise. In Lk 2:29, "peace" will appear again to describe the effect of God's fulfillment of his promise to Simeon. Later in the Gospel, it will appear in Lk 19:38 in a context very much like that of Lk 2:14. As Jesus enters Jerusalem, "the whole multitude of the disciples," reminiscent of the "multitude of heavenly host" in Lk 2:13, will proclaim, "Peace in heaven, and glory in the highest heaven!," with both "glory" and "peace" referring to heaven, and heaven therefore acknowledged as the source of the peace that comes with the recognition that God has fulfilled his promise. Then, in Lk 19:42, the narrator will have Jesus say of Jerusalem: "If you, even you, had only recognized on this day the things that make for peace!" – and this just before Lk 19:44 where Jesus foresees the destruction of Jerusalem "because you did not recognize the time of your visitation from God." The effect of this is to link "the time of the visitation" and "things that make for peace" in the same way as in Lk 2:14, and again to tie "peace" to the recognition that God has fulfilled his promise (Coleridge, 1993: 144).

Peace is proclaimed to "those whom he favors" (*anthrōpois*

eudokias), which moves the scope of God's action and the possibility of human recognition of it beyond the bounds of Israel. Indeed, with its implied universalism, *anthrōpois eudokias* represents a step forward in the angelic proclamation of joy that is for "you" and "all the people" (verse 10). Throughout verses 11-14 the focus has expanded in three steps: from the shepherds ("you") to Israel ("all the people") and now beyond Israel to "those whom he favors." But what is the force of *eudokias*? Today the tendency among scholars is to evaluate *eudokia* as divine rather than human even though one must then supply in translation an absent reference to God (Brown, 1977: 404). An array of arguments have been offered, including parallels from Qumran texts, in favor of *eudokias* as applying to God rather than to human beings (Fitzmyer, 1981: 411-412).

But if, as most scholars now hold, it refers to divine favor rather than human good will, the question arises as to why the narrator does not have *eudokias autou*, "*his* favor," in order to remove the present ambiguity. But other questions also arise. Might the narrator have decided to omit *autou*? And if he did, then why? If the omission creates an ambiguity which serves the narrator's purpose, and thus an ambiguity he intentionally creates, it may not after all be so necessary to opt for divine favor or human good will. The bare *eudokias* does indeed serve the narrator's purpose because it captures both a sense of God's favor moving from heaven to earth and of human good will moving from earth to heaven as well as among humans. In that sense, it expresses in a single word the two-way vertical movement that marks the chorus of the angels: If the divine visitation and human recognition of it are parts of a single process, then so too are the coming of God's favor to earth and the good will that opens the human being to receive God's favor. This single process with its double movement is captured nicely by the ambiguous *eudokias* in a way that confirms the narrative's sense of the necessary link between divine visitation and human recognition (Coleridge, 1993: 145).

Verse 15: When the angels had left them and gone into heaven,
         the shepherds said to one another,
         "Let us go now to Bethlehem
         and see this thing that has taken place,
         which the Lord has made known to us."

With verse 15 we reach the section dealing with the reactions
to the annunciation and manifestation presented in Lk 2:8-14
(Brown, 1977: 410; Fitzmyer, 1981: 392). "When the angels
had left them... said," literally reads: "and it happened (*kai egeneto*),
when the angels had left them and gone into heaven, (that)
the shepherds said..." With the return of the angels to heaven,
the narrative shifts from the vertical to the horizontal, as the
narrator has the shepherds speak not to the angels but to each
other. The implication of what they say is that they freely decide to go to Bethlehem – their decision contrasting with the
obedience demanded from Joseph (and Mary) by the imperial
decree (Gueuret, 1983: 116), and the imperfect "they were saying" (*elaloun*) implying that their decision was more a process
than a flash of inspiration. They recognize that it is God himself who stands behind the revelation: "the Lord has made known
to us." That they decide to go shows that they have, in their
own way, come to faith (Coleridge, 1993: 146).

   In the second half of verse 15, it is clear that the shepherds
know where to go ("let us go now to Bethlehem"), who is behind the revelation ("which the Lord has made known to us"),
and what to look for ("this thing that has taken place"). What
is not so clear is why the narrator has them go. They themselves say, "Let us go... and see this thing that has taken place."
Here there seems to be a play on the ambiguity of *rhēma* (NRSV:
"thing"), with the shepherds going to see both what heaven has
uttered ("the word") and what heaven has enacted ("this thing";
Coleridge, 1993: 146). This is a Semitism: the Greek word *rhēma*
means "word"; but here and in Lk 2:17,19 it translates the double
connotation of the Hebrew *dabar*, "word" and "deed." This is a
deed that speaks (Brown, 1977: 405; cf. *rhema* in Acts 10:37).
It has even been proposed to divide Lk 2:15-20 into three subsec-

tions: (1) Lk 2:15-16: *dabar* as event: the seeing of the shepherds; (2) Lk 2:17-19: *dabar* as word: the proclamation of the shepherds; (3) Lk 2:20: *dabar* as doxology: the praise of the shepherds (Wolff, 1981: 29). "The Lord" here clearly refers to God, not Jesus (Klostermann, 1929: 39). God is present since he revealed his plan through his spokespersons, the angels (Bock, 1994: 221).

There is no hint in the narrative that the shepherds need to see in order to verify what the angel has said; and their words in verse 15 give no hint of puzzlement or questioning. The indications are that, like Mary in Lk. 1:39-56, they go not in order to believe, but because they believe; and they will see because they believe. The narrator has the shepherds go in order to secure the point made in earlier episodes that it is faith that stirs the action, and to make the new point that it is faith that confers sight. The shepherds, having heard the word of the angel, do not go to hear another word (as did Mary to Elizabeth). They talk once they arrive, and there is no report of anyone else saying anything. They go to see the sign and to pass on the interpretative word that they have heard to those who may have witnessed the facts, but need to hear an interpretation so that the facts may become a sign that leads to understanding; and when eventually the shepherds depart from the scene in verse 20, they will be depicted praising God "for all they had heard and seen." It is hearing and seeing that bring about praise (Coleridge, 1993: 146-147).

Verses 16-17: (16) So they went with haste
and found Mary and Joseph,
and the child lying in the manger.
(17) When they saw this,
they made known what had been told them
about this child.

The announcement sets off a chain reaction. First, the shepherds respond in faith and go to find the child (verse 16). Then they tell others what caused them to seek the child (verse 17). The shepherds' reponse in faith and testimony is similar to Mary's instant response to the word in Lk 1:39 (Marshall, 1978: 113; Schürmann, 1969: 116 n. 150; Danker, 1988: 60). Next, the shepherds' reaction causes the audience to react to their testimony (verse 18), which in turn leads to a response by Mary (verse 19; Bock, 1994: 221).

The shepherds went "with haste," literally "hurrying" (*speusantes*), which almost functions like an adverb, "hurriedly they went..." (Plummer, 1901, 59-60; Brown, 1977: 406; Fitzmyer, 1981: 412). The expression implies the ready obedience of the shepherds to the revelation, similar to that of Mary in Lk 1:39 (Brown, 1977: 331,406; but neither Mary nor the shepherds had been told to go and see).

The impression in verse 16 is that the shepherds found the child immediately, though what they find when they arrive is not exactly what the angel promised. We are told first that they find the parents, "Mary and Joseph," of whom the angel has said nothing; and then we are told that they find the child in the manger, with nothing said about the swaddling cloths mentioned by both the narrator in verse 7 and the angel in verse 12.

Verse 17 begins with the word "seeing" (*idontes*); but it is verse 16 that recounts the process of the shepherds' seeing, and so has the readers see with them. In verse 17, the narrator uses the verb "they made known" (*egnōrisan*), another form of which is used in the shepherds' speech in verse 15 (*egnōrisen*). The effect of the verbal link is to associate the shepherds with the angels. There is a second verbal link with, *lalēthentos*, "saying," in verse 17 and *lalēthenthōn*, "saying," in verse 18; and then the narrator has the shepherds return praising God, using "glorifying and praising God" in verse 20, just as earlier he had described the angelic host as "praising God and saying glory in the highest to God" in verses 13b-14a. The paradox, as the narrator has it, is that the shepherds become interpreting angels (Danker, 1988: 61) and, like the angels, they do not worship the child in the way of the Matthean magi (Mt 2:11; Coleridge, 1993: 147-148). What the shepherds see and testify to (Trémel, 1981: 603-604) is something that prophetic words and angelic testimony have addressed (Lk 1:31-35; 2:4,11,14; Schürmann, 1969: 117). The full understanding by people will come later. But for now, to the voices of the angels is added the testimony of humans. What they hear and see, they report (Tiede, 1988: 73). This is another of the narrative's ways of ensuring that the focus remains on the human response to the birth and the revelation of its meaning (Coleridge: 1993: 148). The audience of the shepherds' testimony is unspecified, though Lk 2:18 makes clear that it was more than the child's family (Marshall, 1978: 113). "They made known," not merely to Mary and Joseph, but to the inhabitants of Bethlehem generally (Plummer, 1901: 60).

Verses 18-19:   (18) and all who heard it were amazed
                       at what the shepherds told them.
                (19) But Mary treasured all these words
                       and pondered them in her heart.

In narrating the reaction to the shepherds' report, the narrator unexpectedly introduces a group that he calls "all who heard," about whom nothing is said in verses 6-7 and about whom no detail is given now. Their presence in the narrative is strictly functional: the narrator has no interest in them for their own sake. They are important rather for what they do; having seen the newborn child, they now hear the shepherds' report and marvel at what they hear (Coleridge, 1993: 148). The Greek is typically Lukan, and the same reaction occurs in Lk 1:21, 63; 2:33 (Brown, 1977: 406). *Thaumazein*, "to wonder," "to be astonished," is a normal response to description of divine actions but not necessarily indicative of faith (cf. Acts 3:12). Wonderment can even be associated with disbelief, as in Lk 24:41 (Danker, 1988: 61). Their astonishment implies incomprehension.

In turning first to "all who heard" in verse 18, the narrator points to the essentially public character of the announcement which, as the angel declared in verse 10, is a "great joy for all the people." Mary and Joseph are never addressed personally by the shepherds, as they will be later by Simeon. At this stage, they take their place among "all who heard," and are made therefore to share the astonishment of the crowd. Yet in recounting Mary's personal reaction in verse 19, the narrator implies that here, as in verse 10 where the joy was both "to you" and "to all the people," the public dimension stands in tension with the private (Coleridge, 1993: 149).

It seems strange, at first, that Mary should be in any way astonished after what she has heard from Gabriel. Some try to explain her surprise by claiming that Mary does not share the amazement or incomprehension of the crowd (Plummer, 1901: 60). One may have gone too far by stating that it is rather Mary's "non-savoir" [not knowing] that is underlined here (Gueuret, 1983: 124). But others, in disputing this claim, deal too lightly with the element of "non-savoir" in their determination to read the verse as an oblique reference to Mary as source of the Lukan narrative (Laurentin, 1982: 236 note 23), which is an ultimately unprovable claim. To presume that Mary does not share at all in the amazement presumes that she is not included among "all who heard" in verse 18; and it would seem strange that the narrator would report her response in terms so similar to those in which he has reported the reaction of "all who heard" in Lk 1:66, if he intended her response to be different. The language is not identical [the main difference is that the verbs in Lk 2:19 are more active than *ethento* (NRSV: "pondered") in Lk 1:66]. This suggests that there is something different about Mary's response, as one might expect given the revelation she has received. What emerges in verse 19 is that, because of what she knows, Mary handles her astonishment and incomprehension creatively. The question is, then, not whether faith includes incomprehension, but what faith does with incomprehension. For faith and incomprehension to cohabit creatively there is a need to do what Mary is reported as doing in verse 19: "She treasured all these words and pondered them in her heart" Coleridge, 1993: 150). The verse has parenetic force: like Mary, the reader should faithfully meditate on the events and so discover the right meaning (Schneider, 1977: 68).

The use of the imperfect "she kept" suggests that Mary's pondering was more than a temporary questioning. The verb is at times translated "treasure, cherish" to avoid the hint of incomprehension, but here it has the more neutral sense of "keep, preserve." The less neutral and more important word is the participle "pondering" (*sumballousa*), which specifies how Mary kept all these things in her heart. A study on the meaning of that word concludes that it means to interpret obscure events, hitting upon the right meaning, often with divine help (Van Unnik, 1973: 79-86).

The process implied by "kept" (*sunetērei*; NRSV: "treasured") is a process of interpretation, an attempt, as "pondered" (*sumballousa*; NRSV: "pondering") further indicates, to put the pieces together to see the pattern. After the shepherds' visit and revelation, Mary has more pieces than she had before, and she will have still more after each of the remaining episodes of the infancy narrative. What she begins in verse 19 is the process of putting the pieces together in an act of interpretation that will enable the ultimate recognition of the pattern. Not only does faith not exclude such a process, but positively demands it. In that sense, Mary's word of faith in Lk 1:38 is shown to be the beginning, not the end, of a journey that is growing more complex (Coleridge, 1993: 151). A mental process is clearly intended here, as in Lk 2:51 (Johnson, 1991: 51). In the Old Testament the pattern of keeping words in the heart occurs in Gen 37:11 (Brown, 1977: 407). In contrast to the transient wonder of others who heard the news in Lk 2:18, Mary retained the memory of what she heard and sought its meaning (Brown, 1978: 147-152; Beck, 1989: 114). Mary is here presented as an example for the readers (cf. Lk 8:15; Kremer, 1988: 38). The rhetorical function of references to "pondering in the heart" is to deter suspicious or cynical reading. Characters sometimes perform cognitive actions that are meant to be emulated by the reader (Rabinowitz, 1987: 55); they may be *performative* not just informative. When Mary (with whom the readers identify strongly) "treasures" and "ponders all these things in her heart" (Lk 2:19,

51), the reader is to respond similarly, that is, to value, remember, and reflect on the significance of what has transpired (Darr, 1992: 98).

Verse 20: The shepherds returned,
            glorifying and praising God for all they had heard and seen,
            as it had been told them.

In verse 20 the focus returns to the shepherds. As in most of the previous episodes, the theme of departure terminates this Lukan infancy narrative scene. The combination "glorifying and praising" occurs in Dan 3:26,55LXX in the "song of the three children." The combination of praise and glory was already associated with the heavenly host in Lk 2:13-14 (Brown, 1977: 407). Compare Acts 4:20, "for we cannot keep from speaking about what we have seen and heard."

The shepherds recognize the coherence between what they have heard and what they have seen. The narrator has them put fact and interpretation together. It is that vision which stirs them to praise. They believed what they had heard and, because of the revelation, have now understood what they have seen. It is that combination of faith and understanding that opens the way to both praise of God and proclamation to human beings. Their praise is prompted not only by the coherence between what they have heard and what they have seen, but also by the fact that God chooses to visit his people in the midst of poverty and powerlessness, in a manger and among shepherds (Coleridge, 1993: 152; for a list of reasons why the shepherds suit the narrator's purpose, see Ibidem, p. 153).

Verses 21: After eight days had passed,
            it was time to circumcise the child
            and he was called Jesus,
            the name given by the angel
            before he was conceived in the womb.

As mentioned above, we prefer to treat this verse separately rather than to see it as belonging to Lk 2:1-20. The child, who has not appeared since verse 16, now appears, though he remains wholly passive. The parents are not mentioned explicitly in a verse in which all but one of the verbs is passive. Only "to circumcise" is active, though even then it is not said who performs the action (Gueuret, 1983: 126-127; Laurentin, 1982: 239-241). In Lk 1:31b, Gabriel had said to Mary, "you will name him Jesus"; but now she is left out of consideration by the passive "he was called." In contrast to Lk 1:57-80, we are not told who names the child. [In Mt 1:25 it is clear that Joseph names the child]. What matters for the narrator is not who does the naming, but that the child be named in accordance with the divine will communicated by Gabriel, who appears here as an anonymous "angel" in a way that leaves him too out of consideration and focuses on the unfolding of the divine plan. The refusal to mention the parents in verse 21 works in the same direction as the decision to make not them but the shepherds the first human characters to proclaim and interpret the birth: it ensures that the initiative is seen to belong to God rather than to the parents (Coleridge, 1993: 153-154).

6. *The Presentation in the Temple (Lk 2:22-40)*

Verses 22-39 form a literary unit, while verse 21 remains an isolated verse (different: Fitzmyer, 1981: 419) and verse 40 concludes the parallel with John the Baptist (Lk 1:80). The episode takes place in Jerusalem (Lk 2:22,25,38). In the context of the previous pericope one could expect that Jerusalem would only be a stop-over on the way back from Bethlehem to Nazareth. But, on the contrary, Luke presents here the capital as the destination required by the law. Like "Jerusalem" (verses 22 and 38), the "law" forms an *inclusio*, which seals the unity of verses 22-39: the ideas of event and accomplishment of the law frame this pericope (verses 22a and 39a). Luke's art gives to the pericope its cohesion, on the one hand, and inserts it in a series of episodes to testify to the continuity of the story which he presents, on the other hand. In verse 6, the time has come for Mary to give birth; in verse 21 for the circumcision of Jesus;

and in verse 22 for his presentation to the Lord. Only after this scene does the summary of verse 40, in the imperfect tense, introduce a pause (Bovon, 1991: 133-134).

One of the leitmotifs of Lk 2:22-40 is that both the law and the prophets are fulfilled in Jesus. Some Old Testament passages from Malachi and Daniel may have contributed to the present Lukan sequence. The story of John the Baptist promised that he would go before the Lord in the spirit and power of Elijah (Lk 1:17), indeed go before the Lord to prepare his ways (Lk 1:76). There is no doubt that such descriptions reflect Mal 3:1, "See, I am sending my messenger to prepare the way before me" – a passage that a later addition to Malachi (3:23-24 = NRSV 4:5-6) interpreted as a reference to Elijah. Now the Mal 3:1-2 passage goes on to promise: "the Lord whom you seek will come suddenly to his temple... who can endure the day of his coming?" After the description of John the Baptist in Lk 1, is it accidental that in Lk 2 the child Jesus, who has been hailed as Lord (Lk 2:11), comes to the temple to be recognized by Simeon who was "looking forward to the consolation of Israel"? And Simeon predicts in Lk 2:34-35 that this coming of the Lord to the temple is the beginning of his role as a sign of discrimination so that many will fall – or, in the words of Malachi, many will not endure to the day of his coming (Brown, 1977: 445; Laurentin, 1982: 82). Thus some scholars argue that the prophecies of Malachi underlie the account of the presentation of Jesus in the temple. It is possible to read Lk 19:45–21:38 as the paradoxical fulfillment of Mal 3:1b; but it is hard to read Lk 2:22-40 as foreshadowing Lk 19:45–21:38. Moreover, if it is so that Lk 2:22-40 should be read in the sense that the Lord comes suddenly to his temple in fulfillment of the prophecy of Mal 3:1, then it is strange that only verse 34 in the whole episode refers specifically to Jesus. If the narrator were concerned to recount the climactic coming of the Lord to his temple, then surely the figure of Jesus would be accentuated in a way he is not in fact. It is a question of deciding where the narrative finds its focus and of identifying the data that justify the decision about the narrative focus. The episode seems to focus less on Jesus himself and more on the way the characters interpret God's action in Jesus (Coleridge, 1993: 157, 161). Another biblical passage that may have influenced Luke's inclusion of the scene of Jesus at the temple is Dan 9:21-24, which mentions the angel Gabriel and the seventy weeks of years. This passage forms the background of Gabriel's appearance to Zechariah in Lk 1:8-23, an appearance that marks the end of the seventy weeks of years. In Dan 9:24 we are told that when this comes, the Holy of Holies will be anointed. It is difficult to know whether in this text the Holy of Holies or Most Holy means a thing, a place, or a person. Luke may have interpreted it to be a person. The angel Gabriel told Mary that the miraculously conceived child would be "holy" (Lk 1:35). Now this child is brought to the temple because he is "designated as holy to the Lord" (Lk 2:23). Is this the anointing of the Most Holy foretold by Daniel for the end of the seventy weeks of years? (Brown, 1977:445-446).

The episode can be divided into four or five parts:

(1) The setting wherein Joseph and Mary bring the child Jesus to the temple at Jerusalem (Lk 2:22-24);

(2) The greeting of the child by Simeon and his double oracle about the child's destiny (Lk 2:25-35);

(3) The greeting of the child by the prophetess Anna (Lk 2:36-38);

(4) The conclusion involving a return to Galilee and Nazareth (Lk 2:39);

(5) The refrain on the child's growth (Lk 2:40; Brown, 1977: 446).

Verses 22-24: (22) When the time came for their purification
according to the law of Moses,
they brought him up to Jerusalem
to present him to the Lord

(23) (as it is written in the law of the Lord,
"Every firstborn male shall be designated as holy
to the Lord")

> (24) and they offered a sacrifice
>   according to what is stated in the law of the
>   Lord,
>   "a pair of turtledoves or two young pigeons."

In verse 21, the demands of the law were implied, but in verses 22-24, they are made explicit (Salo, 1991: 49-55). Three different readings exist of the beginning of verse 22: "his purification," "her purification," and "their purification," the one preferred by NRSV. All three have had their defenders. Saint Jerome was in favor of the first reading mentioned, which was also appreciated by Lagrange (Robert, 1990: 449-450). The reading "her purification" is apparently a "correction" which tries to circumvent the difficulties of the first one. One author has drawn up an inventory of the "anomalies" in the passage that have long been noted (Laurentin 1982: 95-98, 237-245). The "justifications" for a plural, "their purification," have been by and large unsatisfactory. Recently it has been suggested that Luke deliberately included Joseph who thus, be it in modest way, contributed to the contrast between rites that had lost their relevance for the third evangelist and the realization of the promises of the Spirit (Robert, 1990: 450, 454-455).

It is striking that in such a short passage, the narrator mentions the law three times: in verse 22, we have "according to the law of Moses," in verse 23, "as it is written in the law of the Lord," and in verse 24, "in the law of the Lord." Not only that, but the law is also cited twice. The citations are free-wheeling. Verse 23 combines Ex 13:2LXX, 13:12, 13:15, and perhaps Num 8:15-16, which refers to the consecration of the Levites. The citation in verse 24 is a form of Lev 12:8LXX. In the previous episode, the narration of the birth was set against the background of imperial authority. Now the narrative of the coming of Jesus to the temple is set against the background of Mosaic authority; and Mary and Joseph are as obedient to the demand of the law as they were in Lk 2:1-5 to the demand of Caesar (Coleridge, 1993: 158).

Yet the situation is more subtle than this, given that the

narrator in verse 22 refers to the law as "the law of Moses," but then in verses 23-24 refers to the law as "the law of the Lord." The shift from "Moses" to "the Lord" is related to the statement in verse 22 that the parents bring Jesus to Jerusalem "to present him to the Lord." It serves two narrative purposes.

First, it points to a difference between the authority of Caesar and the authority of Moses. Caesar may unwittingly collaborate with the divine plan, but it is nowhere said that the emperor exercises the authority of God. But now with the twofold reference to the law as "the law of the Lord," the narrator leaves no doubt that the law of Moses is of God. It bears an authority which exceeds any human authority.

Secondly, the move from "Moses" to "the Lord" shifts the emphasis from Moses to God. Moses has been absent from the narrative until this point, with the emphasis falling instead upon the figures of Abraham and David. But as soon as Moses is mentioned for the first time in the infancy narrative, he disappears again. This happens so that God, rather than Moses, appears as prime mover. Both the name of Moses and the rites specified by the Mosaic law are passed over. Again the purpose of the visit to Jerusalem will never be developed. We are told in verses 22-24 that Mary and Joseph take the child to the temple to perform the rites of purification and presentation, and in verse 39 that they leave having performed the rites; but of the actual performance of the rites nothing is said. This is similar to Lk 1:5-25, where the incense-burning was not narrated, and in both Lk 1:57-80 and 2:21 where the circumcision was never narrated. The decision not to narrate these rites casts the focus elsewhere (Coleridge, 1993: 159).

One of the peculiarities of these first verses is the apparent confusion of the two Mosaic stipulations – the purification of the mother after the birth of a male child, and the presentation of the first-born male to God. Various reasons have been given for this confusion (Brown, 1977: 447; Schürmann, 1969: 122; Fitzmyer, 1981: 421; Ernst, 1977: 115). The narrator mentions first the purification, though the mention is complicated by the use of "their" (*autōn*) rather than "her" (autē), which might have been expected, since it was only the mother who had to undergo the rite of purification. But if the narrator is more concerned with focus in the narrative than with an exact report of the Mosaic legislation, then "their" makes sense. It ensures that the focus does not fall exclusively on any of the key human characters – Mary, Joseph, or Jesus. What matters at this point is that the law, rather than any of the characters, appears as prime mover in the narrative, just as at the start of the previous episode the narrator made Caesar seem the prime mover. In the same way now he sets a context for the narration of God's intervention (Coleridge, 1993: 160).

All enduring societies provide their members with ways of making sense out of human living. Such ways of making sense out of life are systems of meaning. One traditional way of talking about such an overall system of meaning is called the purity system, the system of pure (in place) and impure (out of place) or the system of clean (in place) and unclean (out of place). Pure and impure, clean and unclean, can be predicated of persons, groups, things, times, and places. Such purity distinctions embody the core values of a society and thereby provide clarity of meaning, direction of activity, and consistency for social behavior. What accords with these values and their structural expression in a purity system is considered "pure," and what does not is viewed as "polluted" (Malina-Rohrbaugh, 1992: 318-319).

Lev 12 required that a Jewish woman who gave birth to a son should forty days after the birth go to Jerusalem and offer, for the purposes of ritual purification, two sacrifices in the temple. In the case of a firstborn son there was also a requirement that he be acknowledged as belonging to the Lord in a special way (Ex 13:2,12,15). In fact the child had to be redeemed by the payment of five shekels (Num 18:15-16). Though this payment could be made anywhere in the land, the ideal was to present the child at the temple (Neh 10:35-36). And when this was done, the purification and presentation would be done together (Nolland, 1989: 124).

Having mentioned the purification, the narrator turns to the presentation of the child for which, according to many scholars (Schürmann, 1969: 122; Ernst, 1977: 115; Brown, 1977: 450-451; Fitzmyer, 1981: 421; Bovon, 1991: 136), 1 Sam 1-2 has served as inspiration, although there are obvious differences (Laurentin, 1982: 95). For the first time God is mentioned explicitly: "they brought him up to Jerusalem to present him to the Lord." From now on, the law will no longer be referred to as "the law of Moses" as in verse 22, but three times as "the law of the Lord" (Lk 2:23,24,39). The shift of focus from Moses to God begins the more general shift from the narration of obedience to the Mosiac law, in which the law appears as prime mover, to the narration of the divine intervention, in which God will appear as prime mover. It is again a question of who or what has the initiative (Coleridge, 1993: 160-161).

Verse 24 presents the parents as people of modest means, unable to afford the lamb and bird prescribed for the purification, and offering instead the two birds prescribed as a concession to those of modest means (Lev 5:11; 12:8), although this does not reveal the socio-economic background in great detail (Ernst, 1977: 114). This serves the same purpose as the report in the previous episode, namely, to emphasize the strangeness of the circumstances into which Jesus was born (Coleridge, 1993: 161-162).

For the first time in the infancy narrative, Jerusalem is named (Gueuret, 1983: 232-240); and it occurs in the form "*Hierosoluma*," which is found four times in the Gospel of Luke. In verse 25, the city is again named, but this time as *Hierousalēm* (twenty-six times). In Acts the usage is more evenly distributed (thirty-nine times *Hierousalēm* and twenty-five times *Hierosoluma* (Brown, 1977: 437). The combination raises the question of whether or not any special significance may be attached to the different forms of the city's name (Sylva, 1983: 207-211). It is doubtful that any conclusions may be drawn from this variation as to Luke's sources. He seems to use the two forms indifferently (C.F. Evans, 1990: 212). But, accepting that the Septuagint form *Hierousalēm* has a sacral resonance where the secular form *Hierosoluma* does not, the juxtaposition of the two forms means that the sacral and secular mingle here as they did in the previous episode in the titles "savior" and "lord" (Coleridge, 1993: 162).

Verses 25-27: (25) Now there was a man in Jerusalem whose name
                    was Simeon;
                this man was righteous and devout,
                looking forward to the consolation of Israel,
                and the Holy Spirit rested on him.
            (26) It had been revealed to him by the Holy Spirit
                that he would not see death
                before he had seen the Lord's Messiah.
            (27) Guided by the Spirit, Simeon came into the temple;
                and when the parents brought in the child Jesus,
                to do for him what was customary under the law,

In a switch similar to that to the shepherds in Lk 2:8, the narrator turns unexpectedly to the figure of Simeon; and as he does he begins the narration of the interpretation of the signs of fulfillment in this episode. At first the focus is upon the man Simeon and his piety (Salo, 1991: 55), which is described in terms of his devotion to the law and cult ("righteous and devout," here best translated as "God-fearing"; Coleridge, 1993: 163, note 1), and his faith in God's promise ("looking forward to the consolation of Israel," – "consolation" echoing Second Isaiah [Isa 40:1; 49:13; 51:3] and Third Isaiah [Isa 61:2; 66:13]). At this point, Simeon is like Zechariah and Elizabeth in the first episode (Lk 1:6) and Joseph of Arimathea, "who was waiting expectantly for the kingdom of God" (Lk 23:50-51). Lk 2:25-38 constitutes a self-contained passage for which Lk 2:25, "...looking forward to the consolation of Israel," and Lk 2:38, "...looking for the redemption of Israel," act as an inclusion (Koet, 1990: 39).

The name Simeon has appeared earlier in the Torah. Strikingly enough not in Deut 33, where Jacob blesses his sons and where the name Simeon is passed over. The reason for this is that Simeon had a bad name because together with Levi he had punished the defenceless inhabitants of Shechem (Gen 34).

Moreover, Simeon played a very questionable role in the treatment of his brother Joseph. But later on in the *Targum* Simeon is gradually rehabilitated. This rehabilitation finds its climax in Lk 2 (van Ogtrop, 1991: 26; Derrett, 1993: 209-212, 216).

The presentation of Simeon becomes less conventional and more detailed at the end of verse 25 where it is stated that "the Holy Spirit rested on him." A cluster of references to the Spirit in the following verses define more precisely how the Spirit functioned in the life of Simeon. In verse 26, the Spirit is cited as the source of special revelation: "It had been revealed to him by the Holy Spirit" that he would live to see the messiah. The phrase "guided by the Spirit, Simeon came into the temple" (verse 27) refers to the state of inspiration that not only led Simeon into the temple, but that also led to his spontaneous outburst of praise. Thus in Lk 2:25-27 the Spirit functions as the Spirit of prophecy, granting special revelation, guidance, and inspiring speech. So, Simeon's words and actions possess a high degree of reliability (Menzies, 1991: 120; Shepherd, 1994: 122; Tannehill, 1986: 40-44). Not only is Simeon elaborately designated as a reliable prophetic spokesperson, but his actions and words together enact Luke's distinctive prophecy-fulfillment literary pattern (Johnson, 1991: 56).

In verse 26 the narrator discloses that Simeon has received a private revelation by the Holy Spirit. At that point, we have come a long way from the first notice that Simeon was "righteous and devout"; and we have moved a long way inwards. That does not mean that we are given any profound psychological insight into Simeon: that is not the narrator's purpose. He is not interested in Simeon himself, but in Simeon as one who, like Zechariah and Mary, had received a divine promise. It is often assumed that he was old; yet the narrator says nothing to allow the assumption of old age. Some suggest that he was a priest (Nolland, 1989: 119, 120-121, 124-125). But again the narrator gives no indication that he was a priest, with the blessing of verse 34 not necessarily priestly (Coleridge, 1993: 164 note 2). "To see the Lord's Messiah" is to discern the fulfillment of God's promises to console, redeem, and save his people (Tiede, 1988: 75).

After the introduction of Simeon in verses 25-26, the narration of the promise's fulfillment begins in verse 27. In the previous episode, the narrator stated that the shepherds came freely and in faith to the birth scene, but now, by contrast, he has Simeon come to the temple under the impulse of the Holy Spirit (compare Lk 4:1: "Jesus, full of the Holy Spirit,... was led by the Spirit in the wilderness"). Simeon comes to the temple (*hieron*), that is, the temple courts, and, since Mary was allowed there, either the court of the women or the court of the Gentiles (C.F. Evans, 1990: 215), with the same qualified freedom we have seen already in inspired characters, such as Elizabeth in the third episode and Zechariah in the fourth. The impulse of the Holy Spirit may not abolish human freedom, but it does qualify it. The difference between Simeon here and the inspired characters of earlier episodes is that the Holy Spirit – initially at least – inspires Simeon to act, that is, to come to the temple, rather than speak. This is the infancy narrative's first and only instance of action under the direct influence of the Holy Spirit, and as such it adds an important element to the narrative's understanding of the role of the Holy Spirit. In the previous episode, the shepherds heard the angelic revelation and then, of their own will, decided to act. Now, however, the Holy Spirit intervenes at the point of both revelation and action. The action of the Holy Spirit is both more inward and more comprehensive than the action of the angel (Coleridge, 1993: 165).

In verse 27b, the narrator refers to Mary and Joseph as "the parents," which some have taken to indicate an ignorance on the narrator's part of the virginal conception of Jesus, so proving that the second phase of the infancy narrative is compiled from a different source (Plummer, 1901: 67). Having made clear in Lk 1 the nature of Jesus' origin, Luke has no problem with using the word "parents" here for Mary and Joseph (Nolland, 1989: 119). In fact, there may be good reasons for a narrator who is supposed to be well aware of the virginal conception to refer to Mary and Joseph as "the parents" nonetheless. For one thing, the emphasis is here on their religious and social role rather than on them personally; and the description of them as "the parents" captures that well. Secondly, to name them in relation to Jesus (as the expression "the parents" does) allows the narrator to shift the focus for the first time from Mary and Joseph as the ones who bring Jesus to the temple to Jesus himself as the one about whom Simeon will prophesy. Once Jesus is named, the names of Mary and Joseph disappear from the infancy narrative, with the sole exception of Lk 2:34 where Mary is referred to by the narrator as "Mary his mother" at a point where Simeon focuses on her specifically. Through this and the following episode the focus moves slowly but surely from the parents to Jesus; and the shift is reflected in the way the characters are named by the narrator (Coleridge, 1993: 165-166).

"To do for him as was customary under the law" is a further grounding of the event in pious observance of the law of God. But the statement is somewhat strange, as neither purification of the child nor his presentation *in the temple* were prescribed in the law (C.F. Evans, 1990: 215). Luke's primary interest in the narrative is in the presentation rather than the purification. Verse 27 seems to reinforce this perspective, and the statement that "when they had finished everything required by the law of the Lord, they returned to Galilee" in Lk 2:39 also refers mainly to this event, though it may include the purification (Wilson, 1983: 22). The variety of Lukan material on the law and the absence of any clear signs of reflection on it in the Gospel, in marked contrast to Mark and Matthew, suggest that the question of Jesus' attitude towards the law was not a problem for Luke and his readers (Ibidem, 57).

Verses 28-32: (28) Simeon took him in his arms and praised God, saying,

                (29) "Master, now you are dismissing your servant in peace, according to your word;

                (30) for my eyes have seen your salvation,

> (31) which you have prepared in the presence of all
>   peoples
> (32) a light for revelation to the Gentiles
>   and for glory to your people Israel."

The answer to the question of whether or not Simeon will recognize the messiah comes in both action (verse 28a) and word
(verses 28b-32): under the influence of the Holy Spirit he both
recognizes and interprets "the messiah of the Lord" (verse 26).
Simeon takes the initiative as he holds the child in his arms in
a gesture symbolizing the new concreteness and immediacy of
God's action. The performance of Simeon is accomplished in
two stages in which Simeon takes the floor, one directed to
God, the other to the parents, especially the mother. The cognitive level and the somatic level are engaged in the first part
of the performance. In order to take the child into his arms
("conjonction cognitive"), Simeon must first have recognized
him ("performance cognitive"): he confirms this in his discourse.
Without repeating the name of Jesus, the recognition of Jesus
as "savior" (verse 30) is one aspect of the sanction. But this
sanction is also related to the recognition of the Lord as the
subject of the action: it is he who has prepared this salvation
(Lk 2:31), as well as to the addressees of the performance: the
Gentiles and Israel, the people of God (Lk 2:32; Gueuret, 1983:
130-131). But the Nunc Dimittis speaks not so much about
Jesus in himself as about what God is doing through Jesus
(Coleridge, 1993: 167).

The hymn is also the first time in the infancy narrative that
a character addresses God directly. Gabriel in his oracles, Elizabeth in her prophetic cry, Mary in the Magnificat, Zechariah in
the Benedictus and the angels in the Gloria, have all spoken of
God in the third person, but now Simeon speaks of God in the
second person. The effect of this is to accentuate God in a way
that makes the Nunc Dimitis more radically theocentric than
either the Magnificat or the Benedictus.

The hymn fits rather more neatly into its narrative context
than the Magnificat and the Benedictus fit into theirs. The

speaker's statement, "Now you are dismissing your servant in peace," would suit the situation of an aged Simeon but, unlike in the case of Anna, it is not explicitly said that he is old (van Bruggen, 1993: 90). Nevertheless, the hymn could be omitted without disrupting the narrative. If the Nunc Dimittis were omitted, Lk 2:33 would follow 2:28 in precisely the same manner as Lk 1:65 follows 1:64; in both cases wonder would follow an unspecified blessing of God. The narrative may originally have mentioned Simeon's praise without explicitly giving its content, just as it mentions Anna's praise without quoting it (Lk 2:38).

The *structure* of the hymn is relatively obvious: it consists of three couplets, the last of which contains synonymous parallelism. But to note the structure is not to describe the *form* of the poem adequately. Several commentators have suggested that it is a prayer (Ernst, 1977: 117; Marshall, 1978: 119). More commonly it is treated as a hymn (Schürmann, 1969: 125; Ernst, 1977: 117).While the two categories are not to be completely separated, it seems that the latter is the more accurate description of the poem. It displays the same basic structure as the Magnificat and the Benedictus: (1) Word of praise (verse 29); (2) Motive clause (verse 30); (3) Statements expanding the motive clause (verses 31-32). This is the typical structure of the kernel of the declarative psalm of praise. Although the hymn, unlike the Magnificat and the Benedictus, addresses God directly, it does not make a request to him (Farris, 1985: 143-145).

The language of the Nunc Dimittis is different from anything in the Magnificat or Benedictus. Although the use of scripture is as allusive as ever, the voice of Second Isaiah is recognizable (Brown, 1977: 458-459); and this is in service of the different christology that the Nunc Dimittis articulates – the vision of a messiah who is for all peoples (Coleridge, 1993: 169).

Verse 28 has Simeon blessing God, but the text of his praise is not given. What is given in the Nunc Dimittis is the motive for his praise: God has fulfilled his promise. But the hymn not only states the motive for praise; like the earlier hymns it also interprets God's action. Once again the narrator leaves interpretation to one of his characters, with the hymn interpreting the moment of encounter in the temple in a way that looks beyond the encounter itself to the larger meaning of God's action in Jesus. The promise made by the Holy Spirit to Simeon was that he would see the messiah; yet now by the Holy Spirit's impulse he not only sees but he interprets what he sees. Again the fulfillment of the promise draws him beyond the bare terms of the promise itself (Coleridge, 1993: 167-168).

Verse 29 as a whole is best considered a somewhat extravagant word of praise. Addressing God with the rare appellation "Master," Zechariah recognizes God's fingerprints in the activity surrounding Jesus. The coming of Jesus is the coming of salvation, in continuity with prophetic anticipation (Green, 1995: 38). Luke's introduction treats the Nunc Dimittis as if it were a hymn, "and praised God, saying." Verse 29 appears to reflect Jacob's words upon seeing Joseph alive and well (Gen 46:30). That these words were considered to be an expression of praise is shown by the expansion of the biblical account in Jubilees 45:3-4, "And Israel said unto Joseph: 'Now let me die since I have seen you, and now may the Lord of Israel be blessed... It is enough for me that I have seen your face...'." (Farris, 1985: 145).

The hymn begins with an emphatic "now." Throughout the infancy narrative there is a sense that the present moment is the time of salvation: "Surely, from now on..." (Lk 1:48); "... to you is born this day..." (Lk 2:11). The entire Third Gospel is presented as the fulfillment of messianic time. The frequency with which Luke employs the adverbs "now" (*nun*) and "today" (*sēmeron*) underscores the fact that the time of salvation has begun with Jesus (Navone, 1970: 183).

Although the expression "let depart in peace" (NRSV: "dismissing in peace") can refer to a simple earthly parting (see Acts 15:33), as from the court of a great ruler (Tiede, 1988:

76), in this case the verb is clearly a euphemism for death (see Gen 15:2; Num 20:29; Tob 3:6,13; 2 Mac 7:9; Farris, 1985: 146). Simeon speaks of himself as a "servant" who has been performing the lengthy task of a watchman; the release from the task will come in death. The word "servant" (*doulos*) is the same as the one Mary applied to herself in Lk 1:38. It stands in contrast to "Master" (*despotēs*), used in the vocative of God in the same verse (Brown, 1977: 428).

For "in peace," see Gen 15:15, "you shall go to your ancestors in peace." In the Greek, "in peace" appears at the end of the couplet in an emphatic position. It doubtless corresponds to the Hebrew *shalom*. Peace is an essential characteristic of the messianic kingdom (Ps 72:7; Zech 8:12; Isa 9:6). It is "into the way of peace" that "the dawn" will guide his people (Lk 1:78-79), and peace is promised by the angels to those on whom God's favor rests (Lk 2:14). Simeon is among that number (Farris, 1985: 147). It is a death in peace that Simeon says can now be his. A peaceful death is perhaps at first glance nothing of importance. Yet, even here, now in the circumstance of death, the "peace" of which Simeon speaks is to be understood as a quality of death owed to the coming of the saving Messiah Lord. Death can be peaceful because the salvation promised (verse 30) is now at hand. Whatever was lacking in the Jewish experience up to the time of Jesus and was to be overcome by the fulfillment of hopes – it is this that is replaced by peace. Once again, then, peace is owed to divine intervention, in the form of salvation.

This salvation, Simeon's words indicate, is summed up in the one whom he holds in his arms. In particular, this saving person will be a glory for Israel, so long humiliated, and a light to non-Jews, so long in the darkness of ignorance. From his words, then, we can conclude that peace is not only the result of the fulfillment of promises that replace a time of sorrow, but it is a peace that encompasses glory for Israel and enlightenment for the Gentiles. Given the role of Jesus vis-à-vis human beings, peace is all the more visibly a gift from God, as glory

and enlightenment that follow from the peace is a gift of fulfillment of hopes (Kilgallen, 1989: 68-69).

In the present context, "according to your word" refers back
to the promise to Simeon that he would not die before seeing
the Lord's messiah. In a wider sense, however, the phrase corresponds to the thought expressed in Lk 1:55,73: the present
salvation is the fulfillment of God's past promise.

Verse 30 explains why Simeon can accept his death and
indicates the motive of his thanksgiving: he has seen salvation.
Certainly, one cannot see God, but one can contemplate his
works in history. Hebrew faith praises God in hymns (Ps 97[98]:2-
9) for victories obtained, while Jewish hope confidently expects
new ones. Verse 30 is formulated in terms inspired by Old Testament language (Jones, 1968: 41). It alludes clearly to Isa
40:5LXX: "all people shall see it [salvation]," which will be used
again in Lk 3:6. The text shows clearly that for Luke christology
is, in the first place, soteriology. God's eschatological intervention is "salvation," salvation as deliverance and well-being (Bovon,
1978: 255-284).

God has prepared his salvation "in the presence of all peoples."
This phrase is inspired by Isa 52:10, "before the eyes of all the
nations." The universalism that sounded still indistinctly in the
Magnificat (Lk 1:50) is heard now in full voice; and God's action is seen to move beyond the nationalistic bounds set by the
Benedictus. Indeed, in its interpretation of the divine action,
the Nunc Dimittis mentions first the Gentiles and then Israel.
Nevertheless, one has spoken of a "subordinated universalism"
in the sense that, although the Gentiles are mentioned first and
twice in the hymn, its climax is the "glory" that the messiah's
coming means for Israel (Brown, 1977: 459). Notwithstanding
claims to the contrary (Kilpatrick, 1965: 127), it seems clear
that "peoples" in verse 31 refers to the two groups mentioned
in verse 32, the Gentiles and Israel (Plummer, 1901: 69; Brown,
1977: 440). Such a reading of "peoples" also fits better with the
infancy narrative's expanding focus from the individual to the
nation to the world (Coleridge, 1993: 168, note 2). Salvation

had not been prepared in the secret of Israel's own life but in the presence of all peoples. In Jesus it now shone as a light that would extend revelation to Gentiles and Israel alike (LaVerdiere, 1982: 36).

"A light for revelation to the Gentiles" is an allusion to the Servant Song in Isa 49:6, "I will give you as a light to the nations, that my salvation may reach to the end of the earth." The noun "light," which is in apposition to "salvation," is the object of the verb "have prepared." It is more difficult to determine the relations of the nouns "light" and "revelation" to the noun "glory" in the next line. "Glory" could stand in apposition to "light" (the terms are parallel in Isa 60:1, the type of Isaian passage echoed in the Nunc Dimittis), and thus serve as another object of "have prepared." However, it is more likely that "glory" is in apposition to "revelation"; thus, a light both for revelation and for glory. Revelation for the Gentiles and glory for Israel are two equal aspects of the one salvation and light that God has prepared. Neither is subordinate to the other (Brown, 1977: 440).

Thus a new aspect is here added to the fulfillment theme of the infancy narrative. The salvation that God has prepared is described as "a light for revelation to the Gentiles and for the glory of your people Israel." Up to this point in the narrative the benefits of salvation have been spoken of only for Israel. Now it is revealed that the salvation that the messiah will bring is not only for the glory of Israel, but will also shine the revelatory light of salvation on the Gentiles (Strauss, 1995: 117-118).

Verse 33: And the child's father and mother were amazed at what was being said about him.

At the end of Zechariah's inspired interpretation Mary and Joseph are astonished, like the neighbors and relatives in Lk 1:63 and "all who heard" in Lk 2:18. In the two previous instances, astonishment signalled incomprehension, and there is no reason to think that it does not carry the same nuance here. It may be difficult for the parents to connect Zechariah's words with their child (Danker, 1988: 67; Cousin, 1993: 43). Or it may be simply a normal reaction to the experience of a divine revelation (Brown, 1977: 440; Marshall, 1978: 121; Stein, 1992: 116). From a narrative point of view, the parents' astonishment serves to underline the mysterious character of a divine visitation that makes Simeon suddenly proclaim, in a way hitherto unheard of in the scope of salvation, that God is working in Jesus. It should be noted that Joseph and Mary are referred to, respectively, as "the child's father" and "the child's mother." They are again named not in their own right, but in a way that relates them to Jesus; and the effect of this is to underscore again that they are important not in themselves, but only in relation to Jesus (Coleridge, 1993: 171-172).

Verses 34-35: (34)   Then Simeon blessed them
                     and said to his mother Mary,
                     "This child is destined for the falling and the
                        rising of many in Israel,
                     and to be a sign that will be opposed
             (35)   so that the inner thoughts of many will be revealed—
                     and a sword will pierce your own soul too."

In verse 34, Simeon, who in verse 28 blessed God, now blesses the parents. The narrator therefore has him offer a blessing that moves in two directions; and just as in verse 28 his blessing was a recogition of God's role in the unfolding drama, so now in verse 34 it is a recognition of the role of the parents in the same drama. The role of the parents is clearly different from that of God, but the repetition of "to bless" establishes the link between the two, stressing the part the parents play as collaborators with God. Unexpectedly he then turns to Mary, with Joseph vanishing from the narrative once more because, in what follows, the narrator is keen to dramatize more of what faith involves, and in that dramatization throughout the infancy narrative Mary is the key figure and Joseph plays no part at all (Coleridge, 1993: 172).

Throughout the oracle the emphasis is not so much on Jesus himself as on the reactions to him and the consequences of

these reactions. Therefore in verse 34 he is referred to in relation to "his mother Mary," and in verse 35 he is not mentioned
at all. It is also significant that Simeon blesses not the child but
the parents, which contrasts with the apocryphal accounts where
Simeon not only blesses the child but actually worships him
(*Gospel of Pseudo-Matthew* 15:2). Rather than to focus upon
the newborn child in himself, the narrative focuses upon the
reactions to him in the future and the consequences of these
reactions for both Jesus (rejection as "a sign that will be opposed") and "the many"; the rise of some, the fall of others, the
disclosure of hidden thoughts for all (Ibidem).

The language of the oracle is again Isaian, though more
obliquely so than in the Nunc Dimittis. Special attention has
been paid to Isa 51:17-23 as background to verses 34-35, and
many scholars (Brown, Schürmann, Bovon, Danker, Marshall,
Nolland) see Isa 8:14 and/or 28:16 underlying the announcement that Jesus is set "for the falling and the rising of many."
The allusion to Isa 52:10 in Lk 2:30-31 exemplifies the influence of Isa 51–52 on Simeon's hymn and prophecy. If in the
Nunc Dimittis the Isaian language allowed the narrator to shape
a vision of a messiah for all peoples, now in the oracle of
verses 34-35 it allows the narrator to add a second element to
the revelation which comes through the Holy Spirit and Simeon
– the vision of a messiah who is rejected (Bock, 1987: 85-88).
This is in contrast to the royal language of the oracle of Gabriel
in Lk 1:30-35, of Zechariah in the Benedictus and the angels
in Lk 2:11-14. There the note was triumphant but now it is
not. The presentation and purification of Jesus recall the story
of Samuel's dedication to the Lord (1 Sam 1–2) and the rules
for the purification of a Nazirite (Num 6). Thus Jesus is prepared for his future task as a light of revelation to the Gentiles (see Acts 10; Miyoshi, 1978: 96-100).

The oracle is the first hint in the infancy narrative of trouble
of any kind, let alone rejection. The rejection of Jesus in Nazareth
(4:28-30) is already hinted at in 2:34b (Prior, 1995: 198). For
both characters and readers, then, this announcement is news.

With the characters, readers must grapple with the novelty and obscurity of what Simeon prophesies (Coleridge, 1993: 173). The narrator now reveals that the decision to believe is not based upon possession of all the facts. Once the decision is made, as in Mary's case, there is much to be discovered; and some of that may prove daunting.

Simeon foretells that Jesus will be "a sign that will be opposed," though he does not specify what kind of sign he will be. The image is that of the stone of stumbling in Isa 8:14-15, which is appropriated by Lk 20:17-18. The spatial movement of falling and rising is the same as in the Magnificat (Lk 1:51-53). The prophetic image suggested by "a sign that will be opposed" is this: Jesus is within the people a stone of stumbling, a sign to create opposition, and in response to him the people will be divided, some falling and some rising (Johnson, 1991: 55-56). The Nunc Dimittis says *what* the messiah will signify, indeed what he signifies *already*: peace and salvation (light, glory). But it does not say *how* this is so in the present or *how* it will be so in the future. The key question, therefore, concerns the right interpretation of the ambivalent sign. Simeon appears as a paragon of right interpretation; and the fall of some and the rise of others in Israel looks to the narrative of Luke-Acts in which some will accept Jesus (interpret the sign rightly) and others reject him (interpret the sign wrongly). Those who interpret rightly will rise, and those who interpret wrongly will fall – and all this as part of the divine plan, as is implied by the divine passive "is destined." God sends a messiah who is "glory for your people Israel," but whose coming brings not only peace and salvation to the world, but also division and judgment. His rejection, far from falling outside the scope of God's plan or even thwarting it, is part of God's plan (Coleridge, 1993: 174-175). There is a double significance to Jesus' ministry. For the humble and the poor it is positive, salvation; for the haughty and the rich it is negative, judgment (Stein, 1992: 117).

Having prophesied that by God's decision Jesus is "a sign

that will be opposed," Simeon switches suddenly to Mary in verse 35a (NRSV: 35b): "and a sword will pierce your own soul too." The verse is obscure, and it has been the subject of extensive patristic and modern mariological reflection. Much of this reflection is poor methodologically, for it seeks to interpret Luke through non-Lukan material – material of which Luke and his community may have been totally ignorant. Mary is the addressee of the entire oracle, since she is the character who throughout the infancy narrative embodies the process of recognition and who, as part of that process, is faced with the need to deal with a new and daunting revelation. But now Simeon speaks not only *to* Mary but also *about* her (Coleridge, 1993: 176). He turns to Mary immediately after he has prophesied that Jesus will be "a sign that will be opposed" – which might be taken to indicate that the sword of which Simeon speaks is a metaphor for the pain Mary will experience as a result of her son's rejection; and there has been no shortage of commentators to read verse 35a in such terms (see Brown, 1977: 462-463). By this reckoning, the sword is an image of shared pain (Tiede, 1988: 78; Bovon, 1991: 145).

Yet a survey of the image's biblical background suggests other possibilities. The most illuminating of these in the context is the sword as metaphor of divine judgment (Brown, 1977: 463-464). One has noted a range of texts from Ezekiel in which the sword is an image not just of destruction, but of discrimination (Ez 5:1-2; 6:8-9; 12:14-16; 14:17).

Closest to Lk 2:35 stands Ez 14:17, "Or if I bring a sword upon that land and say, 'Let a sword pass through the land,' and I cut off human beings and animals from it." To this point, the perspective of the oracle has been a perspective of divine judgment – a judgment that will bring about division within Israel. This favors an interpretation of the sword as a metaphor of judgment rather than pain. To understand the sword in this way would mean that in turning from Israel to Mary, Simeon, turning also from nation to individual, prophesies that the divine judgment that comes in Jesus will have dimensions both public and personal (Coleridge, 1993: 176-177).

To understand the sword as a metaphor of pain links Mary more to the sign to be interpreted: she stands *with* Jesus sharing the pain of his rejection. But to read the sword as a metaphor of judgment understands Mary more as interpreter, as one who stands before the sign of Jesus and indeed all the signs of God's action in the process of interpretation. This also accords with the narrative's emphasis on the human response to God's action, in the narration of which Mary has played a prominent role from the second episode until now. In verse 35 Mary appears as the believer who, faced with the supreme sign of her own son and in the process of struggling with the puzzlement he will provoke, will herself be subject of the divine judgment proclaimed by Simeon in verses 34-35. Faith does not confer exemption from that.

An interpretation such as this suggests that Mary appears in verse 35 not so much as the embodiment of Israel (against Legrand, 1981: 226; Johnson, 1991: 57), but more as a paradigm of the believer (see Lk 8:21; 11:27-28). There is a kind of parallel between the experience of Israel and the experience of Mary, but this does not mean that she is an embodiment of the nation. Nor is it that Mary shares the fate of Jesus (against Winandy, 1965: 349), but she shares the fate of all believers who in the process of interpretation demanded by faith must struggle with the puzzling sign of Jesus and run the risk of wrong interpretation (Coleridge, 1993: 177-178). At the level of human drama, the revelatory significance of Jesus will not be obvious to all, nor accepted by all (Johnson, 1991: 57).

Recently a "new" interpretation of Lk 2:34-35 has been proposed based on the fact that for "sword" Luke chose the uncommon word *romphaia* instead of *xiphos*, the equivalent of the latin *gladius* (Derrett, 1993: 207-218). The congratulations of Gabriel to Mary informed her that she would bear a son who would be the Lord Messiah. The angel tells the shepherds of the birth of a savior, while a priestly prophet had sung of the coming of salvation (Lk 1:69,71; 2:11), which was merely redemption for the Jews (Lk 1:68; see verses 71,74). Simeon now recognizes Jesus as the bringer of salvation to Jews and Gentiles, passing over all questions of formal proselytism (Luke denies circumcision is requisite at Acts 15:1,5,28-29). Jesus will have global significance irrespective of race. Simeon and Anna look forward to the second redemption (Lk 2:25,38) from the second "Egypt" which is the Jewish and Gentile world as they know it. Lk 2:35a, "and a sword will pierce your own soul too," should not be taken as a parenthesis, which is inconsistent with biblical style. Yet it could be an editorial addition (Marshall, 1978: 122). It is now the third member of a prophecy, and the "so that" clause explains the purpose of all three above-stated phenomena. The three come in ascending order of significance at Mary personally, as well as in the logical sequence of causality.

First, despite what was said in favor of Jesus' royal destiny above (Lk 1:32-33), Mary must accept that Jesus "lies" (like a stone) for the fall (stumbling) of many in Israel (i.e., Jews at large, not least Mary herself: Amos 5:2) and the getting up again (Jer 8:4-5) of many (*polloi* does not necessarily mean all). This dilemma does not face Gentile converts. In other words, Jesus is an occasion for sin amongst Jews, as he himself fears (Lk 7:23). This fall due to stumbling is different from the fall that results from the divine retribution (Ez 32:10-12); and recovery after such a fall, i.e., repentance, is a cause of salvation.

Second, against the background of that sombre challenge there is the special challenge of Jesus' being a "sign" (Isa 55:13LXX), which is "disputed," and at least temporarily rejected. Although Jesus is a miraculous "sign," he will be denied as such by those who "stumble at" him. As we know from Luke-Acts, openness to Gentiles was denied by observant Jews at the time, and Paul's contests with Judaizers confirm the continuance of this problem.

Third, the process of saving and enlightening Israel cannot be accomplished without controversy and slander (Lk 5:22; 6:8; 9:46-47; 11:17, etc.). Mary herself, so heartily congratulated (Lk 2:34a), suffers contradiction together with her son (Winandy). According to this interpretation, the over-dramatic word *romphaia* is not the Word of God, nor Mary's anxiety or doubt as depicted at Mt 26:31 (Basil, *Letters*, 260,113-114), nor the sight of the crucifixion itself (Jn 19:25; Klostermann, 1975: 43-44), nor God's vengeance against Israel represented by Mary, which is rejected by scholars as an unexpected idea (C.F. Evans, 1990: 219), but slander, reproach (Ps 42:11 [10]), which to Jews and Gentiles, is depicted as a sharp weapon, like a sword or dagger (Ps 55:21; 57:4; 64:3; Lagrange, 1922: 88). Note in Prov 12:18LXX: "Rash words are like sword thrusts."

Fourth, the stumbling-block is notoriously negative in character (Lev 19:14; Isa 8:14, 15, 18; 28:16; 57:14; Mt 21:44; 24:10; 26:33; Rom 9:32, 33; 11:19; 14:21, etc.). A mother believes in her son, yet her faith is "spoken against" (Lk 8:21; cf. Gen 33:9). Some have thought (no doubt rightly) that Mary must have been pained to see how the new religion repudiated natural ties, even with biblical authority. Famliar with "signs" (Lk 1:20; 2:12), will she repudiate *this* sign?

But all three consequences of Jesus' life have been foreseen "so that the inner thoughts of many may be revealed/disclosed." "Disclosed" because such revelations unmask something discreditable (Prov 11:13; 27:5; Marshal, 1978: 123). An exposing of intentions is forced upon minds (*kardia* is a Hebraism for "mind") by the need to choose between Jesus' programme and the dominant vogues of Jewry, not to speak of Gentile cultures (Derrett, 1993: 212-215).

In verse 32a, the effect of the messiah's coming was described as "a light for revelation to the Gentiles"; and now the purpose of the sword of judgment that will pass through both Israel and Mary is described: "so that the inner thoughts of many may be revealed." In both cases we are dealing with revelation, but revelations of a quite different kind. On the one hand, the effect of the messiah's coming is described horizontally in terms of geographical spread, reaching out to the Gentiles. On the other hand, it is described vertically in terms of an inner penetration, reaching the depths of the hidden "thoughts" (*dialogismoi*; Coleridge, 1993: 177-178). With the exception of Lk 1:29 and 3:15, the term *dialogismos* and its verbal equivalent define the mental process of those actively opposed to Jesus (Lk 5:21-22; 6:8; 9:46-47; 12:17; 20:14; in 24:38 it is usually translated as "doubts"). That a prophet can read people's hearts is axiomatic, as we learn from Lk 7:39-40 (Johnson, 1991:56). The verb for "revealed" (*apokalyptō*) makes an ironic contrast to the noun "revelation" in verse 32. Outsiders will benefit from the light; insiders will be exposed by the light.

Simeon began with a vision of large vistas for Israel (verses 29-32). He closes with a compelling demand for a decision that no one can evade. The high spiritual moment, the crescendo of full-throated choirs – all this may give a feeling of walking in the presence of God. But the critical hour is the moment when one encounters the needs of the poor, the outcast, the forgotten ones; when the course lies to the right or to the left, to the safe and easy haven or to the dangerous, the creative, and the imagined possibility. Then the integrity of the heart's devotion will be known. The sword that has gone through the land (see Lk 12:51, "Do you think that I have come to bring peace to the earth? No, I tell you, but rather *division*"; Mt 10:34, "Do you think...; I have not come to bring peace, but a *sword*"); the chasms in the social structure – these have also at the beginning of the twenty-first century laid bare the emptiness of much that lays claim to God and have annulled much of the vision of what might have been (Danker, 1988: 69-70).

Verses 36-38: (36) There was also a prophet,
             Anna the daughter of Phanuel,
             of the tribe of Asher.
             She was of great age,
             having lived with her husband seven years after
               her marriage,

> (37) then as a widow to the age of eighty-four.
>   She never left the temple
>   but worshiped there with fasting and prayer night
>   and day.
> (38) At that moment she came,
>   and began to praise God
>   and to speak about the child
>   to all who were looking for the redemption of
>   Jerusalem.

The narrator decides to report nothing of the parents' reaction to Simeon's oracle. At a point where they might be expected to be even more astonished and perplexed than in verse 33, the narrator turns instead to the figure of Anna. The removal of the parents from our attention is reinforced by the fact that Anna never mentions them or pays any attention to them [Compare the *Arabic Infancy Gospel* 6:2 which has Anna congratulate Mary]; and this is because she, like the narrator, is less interested in the parents and their reaction than in the meaning of God's action in Jesus (Coleridge, 1993: 178).

The second witness in the temple precincts is Anna. In Greek her name is spelled the same as Hannah's in 1 Samuel. It is unfortunate that the NRSV, like so many other translations, obscured Luke's evident effort to signal the intimate connection of his total infancy narrative with the early chapters of 1 Samuel. Anna is one of a number of female prophets who appear in the Bible: Miriam (Ex 15:20), Deborah (Judg 4:4), Hulda (2 Kgs 22:14), Noadiah (Neh 6:14), the wife of Isaiah (Isa 8:3), and Jezebel (Rev 2:20). To a large extent, prophesying found continuance in the proclamation of the later regularized public ministry. Like Simeon, this aged woman is a model of the type of person who is open to the vision of the new age: "In the last days it will be, God declares, that I will pour out my Spirit upon all flesh, and your sons and your daughters shall prophesy... even upon my slaves, both men and women, in those days I will pour out my Spirit; and they shall prophesy" (Acts 2:17-18). Until ecclesiastical regulations foreclosed on the right of women to use such gifts as hers within the perimeters of the sanctuary, the people of God found enrichment through the preaching of such as Hannah (Danker, 1988: 70).

Verses 36-38 furnish a reprise to the crucial revelations of the Simeon story. Luke often has stories in pairs, and women figure prominently in the narrative. Details are given with respect to her age, practice of worship, and tribal heritage. Anna is "of the tribe of Asher," a tribe in northern Palestine which is mentioned last in the list of Jacob's sons (Gen 49:20). Anna represents Asher with her longevity and vigor. The privilege of Asher was not his wealth (Gen 49:20), but his ability to retain (Deut 33:25b) in old age the qualities of youth (Deut 33:25) – the ability manifested in Caleb, the ideal servant of Yahweh (Num 14:24; Josh 14:6-11; Derrett, 1993: 209, 216). When Simeon and Anna, representatives of two tribes that had receded into the background, come suddenly to the fore, it is to be considered a first step in the restoration of the unity among the twelve tribes of Israel (van Ogtrop, 1991: 27).

The patriarchal culture of Israel is evident in the way Anna is identified with reference to her father Phanuel, and her dead husband (Tiede, 1988: 78). Having lost her principal means of support, she spent her time continually in the temple precincts. There she worshiped God with "fasting and prayer night and day." This appraisal bears the marks of what is called a hyperbole, or literary exaggeration, designed to accent her profound piety.

Luke's description on the whole bears a remarkable resemblance to an earlier portrayal of Judith, a heroine of Jewish history. Judith was also a widow, and she fasted all the days of her widowhood, except on festivals (Judith 8:4-8). She refused offers of a second marriage and died at the age of 105 (Judith 16:22-23). The high age attributed by Luke to Anna parallels that of Judith. Given fourteen years as the age of the marriage, seven additional years plus eighty-four would add up to 105 years. Luke's ambivalent syntax not only permits this view of a very advanced age but even seems to demand it (Danker, 1988: 71).

The issue of why people fasted in New Testament times is

rarely raised by interpreters and, when it is, it is generally answered with highly subjective, untestable reasons or with present-day ideas. But as a rule, the culturally specific meaning of fasting is ignored. What then is the social meaning of fasting? Why did first-century Mediterraneans practice the willful non-consumption of food and drink? How did such behavior fit into some larger frame of understanding of how the world works that would legitimate such non-consumptive behavior? The existence of such non-consumption in various human groups can be explained variously. As conclusion of a social science and symbolic approach to fasting, it may be concluded that fasting is a form of communicative non-consumption, a refusal to participate in the reciprocities that constitute social interaction. This refusal encodes a message of request for status reversal. Insofar as persons capable of status reversal stand vertically above or horizontally on par with the one fasting, the message may have either a vertical or horizontal dimension. In a strong group, vertical direction seeks power to effect change, and horizontal dimension seeks commitment or solidarity to effect change. The rejection of fasting in a social script that values such behavior points either to acquiescence in the status quo (hence recriminations of "sinner, glutton, drunkard" to shame the non-faster, as in Lk 7:31-35) or to a perception that the requested status reversal has already been realized in some way, hence the rejection of fasting since it would be communicating the wrong communication (Malina: 1986: 185-204).

Anna is said to have been devoted to prayer, and it was this prayer that oriented her towards awaiting, and thus seeing, the messiah when he came. Anna's thanksgiving is especially significant because it expresses the awareness that the hope that has formed her prayers has now been answered. Therefore, "she praised God" (anthōmologeito tōi theōi). The anti- in this form of the verb underlines the fact that Anna's praise is an answer to God's gracious action, which is itself an answer to her prayers (see Ps 79:13). Anna's thanksgiving, which is the only other place in Luke-Acts where an -omologeō word is used to refer to praise, provides a particularly clear parallel to the opening line of Jesus' prayer: "I thank you, Father" (*exomologoumai soi, pater*; Lk 10:21; Crump, 1992: 65).

A number of differences between the presentation of Simeon and Anna can be pointed out which suggest that we are dealing not with a repetition, but with a reprise that implies complementarity – and a complementarity that anticipates much of what will follow in the Lukan narrative. The key Old Testament text that Peter will use to interpret the moment of Pentecost in Acts 2:17-21 will be Joel 2:28-32 (see above), in which the promise is that the Holy Spirit will be poured out on all flesh and that all will therefore prophesy – male and female, young and old (Coleridge, 1993: 179-180).

Although the text of Anna's prophecy is not given, we are informed that, like the Nunc Dimittis, it is theocentric. Anna "began to praise (*anthōmologeito*) God"; and in what follows, Jesus is referred to simply as "him" (*autou*) in a situation that creates ambiguity, which leads some scholars to ask whether *autou* here refers to Jesus or to God (Laurentin, 1983: 252). This is an ambiguity that in most other instances the Lukan narrator would resolve by using the character's name (Aletti, 1988: 40). The decision not to name Jesus is governed by the desire to control the focus at this point. The phrase "she began to praise God" implies an address of God. The verb *anthōmologeō* is used only this once in the New Testament and suggests the ideas of recognition, obedience and proclamation that occur in praise rendered publicly to God in return for his grace (Marshall, 1978: 124).

Anna's credentials as a "prophet" help the reader be sure that Simeon was also a prophet (Tiede, 1988: 78). But in two important ways Anna's prophecy is different from Simeon's hymn and oracle; and these differences show further why the narrator decides to introduce the figure of Anna.

Firstly, in verse 38b, she turns from God to others, as did Simeon in verses 34-35; but Anna turns to a wider circle. She speaks not to the parents, but "to all who were looking for the redemption of Jerusalem." This again clearly refers to Second Isaiah (Isa 40:2; 52:9). In that sense, her role is to spread the news of the messiah's coming and its effect beyond the bounds of the family (Fitzmyer, 1981: 423). It is difficult to establish to whom exactly she is supposed to speak. The phrase "to all" here seems as much an exaggeration as "the whole assembly of the people" in Lk 1:10, since it is hardly likely that Anna managed to contact all who were awaiting the redemption of Jerusalem. But the use of "all" emphasizes the range of Anna's prophecy and makes her word resound beyond the physical confines of the temple precincts. The imperfect "she began to speak" (*elalei*) suggests that Anna's proclamation was more than a brief and isolated event (Fitzmyer, 1981: 431).

Secondly, in having Anna focus on the fulfillment of the promise of a redeemed Jerusalem as the meaning of what God is doing in Jesus, the narrator places the threatening oracle of verses 34-35 between two jubilant proclamations of salvation. This implies that, although there are dark nuances to the divine visitation, its ultimate meaning is light. This again refers to the wider radius of the Lukan narrative in which rejection and persecution will appear as the very things that give new impetus to the divine plan in its trajectory through time (Coleridge, 1993: 182-183).

The expression "all who were looking for the redemption of Israel" is synonymous with "the consolation of Israel" Lk 2:25) and echoes Isa 52:9, "he has redeemed Jerusalem." At the time of the second revolt of Palestinian Jews against Rome (A.D. 132-135) documents were sometimes dated to the years of "the redemption of Israel" or of "the freedom of Jerusalem." These phrases are not identical with the Lukan phrases, but they show that the latter reflect actual aspirations of Palestinian Jews of the time (Fitzmyer, 1981: 432).

Verses 39-40: (39) When they had finished everything
                    required by the law of the Lord,
                    they returned to Galilee,
                    to their own town of Nazareth.

> (40) The child grew and became strong.
>   filled with wisdom;
>   and the favor of God was upon him.

Luke terminates with a twofold conclusion: verse 39 terminates the immediate scene; verse 40 terminates the infancy narrative. Even if one does not accept the thesis that at the first stage of Lukan composition the infancy narrative ended at Lk 2:40 and that Lk 2:41-52 was added by Luke later, one must agree that the story of Jesus *as an infant* terminates at Lk 2:40. He will be a boy of twelve in the next scene. So Lk 2:39-40 provides a transition out of the infancy material proper (Bock, 1994: 253). It is true that verse 39a, "When they had finished everything required by the law of the Lord," is part of the framework of the presentation scene, related by way of inclusion to Lk 2:22-24. But when this is woven together with verse 39b, "they returned to Galilee, to their town of Nazareth," we have the same combination of motifs as in 1 Sam 2:20. There we are told that after Elkanah and Hannah came up to the sanctuary to offer sacrifice and were blessed by the aged Eli for having dedicated Samuel to the Lord, "they would return to their home" (Brown, 1977: 468).

Just as there was no report of the parents' reaction after Simeon's oracle in verses 34-35, neither is there now after Anna's prophecy. The narrator makes a point of underlining that, for all the surprises in the temple, Mary and Joseph fulfilled the prescriptions of the law – which is called here not simply "the law" or "the law of Moses" but "the law of the Lord." The link with God is explicitly stated; and it emerges at the end as at the beginning of the episode that the law and prophecy of the kind narrated are in no way opposed. Both are of God (Coleridge, 1993: 183).

Verse 39 completes a narrative arc that began in Lk 2:4 with Mary and Joseph leaving for Bethlehem. The narrative has moved from Nazareth to Nazareth, with the narrator in Lk 2:4 reporting that Joseph and Mary "went from the town of Nazareth in Galilee to Judea...," and in verse 39 that parents and child "returned to Galilee, to their town of Nazareth." The inclusion seals the narrative arc and, with repeated mention of Galilee and Nazareth serves to emphasize the *secular space* after the consistent emphasis on the *sacral space* through the episode. Jerusalem and the temple have dominated the narration to the point where in shifting from sacral to secular space there is a need to stress the secular, lest it be obscured and the effect of the narrative's tactic of moving between worlds be correspondingly diminished (Coleridge, 1993: 183-184). The family returned to Galilee only after performing everything (*panta*) according to the law. It seems as if Luke deliberately uses every opportunity to stress the faithfulness of Jesus' parents (and apparently also Jesus himself) to the law (Salo, 1991: 456).

Although Jesus was brought up in Galilee and in a village despised by religious circles, he shared in the traditions of his ancestors. And he had familial roots. This factor would be important for Greco-Roman readers, but it forms a contrast to the apparent rootlessness of Jesus' adult life. John had gone into the wilderness (Lk 1:80). Jesus remains with his parents. [But he will have his days in the desert (Lk 4:1-13)] (Danker, 1988: 72). It is not clear whether Luke makes a deliberate distinction between John's desert discipline in the prophetic spirit till the time of his mission and Jesus' domestic growth in wisdom, i.e., the knowledge of God and divine things, to be demonstrated in the next episode (C.F. Evans, 1990: 221). The fact that Galilee is the home of Jesus, Mary, and Joseph is emphasized several times (Lk 2:4,39,51). This region is clearly one of the major arenas of divine activity (Darr, 1992: 135).

The narration becomes more elliptical than ever in verse 40, as the single verse narrates the twelve years lying between this and the following episode. We are told that the child grew in wisdom and grace. The report of Jesus' growth here is fuller and more specific than the report of John's growth in Lk 1:80. There it was reported simply that John "grew and became strong in spirit." In verse 40, however, the action of God is more explicit, as is the wisdom theme that recalls Isa 11:2, "The spirit of the Lord shall rest on him, the spirit of wisdom and understanding." "Filled with wisdom," which is not said of John, prepares for the next episode, Jesus sitting among the teachers in the temple (see Lk 2:47; cf. 2:52; Fitzmyer, 1981: 432). At this stage we are not told what the signs of this wisdom and grace might have been. That will come in the following episode. Verse 39 has shown that the divine plan unfolds not only in dramatic moments such as the encounters filling the last two episodes, but also in the ordinariness, indeed the hiddennes of Nazareth. Now verse 40 makes it plain that the divine plan also unfolds in the slow, undramatic rhythms of a child's growth (Coleridge, 1993: 184).

A number of Old Testament passages serve as background for the stereotyped statement of verse 40. The first part, "the child grew," is said of Isaac (Gen 21:8); the second part, "the child... became strong," resembles what is said of Samson (Judg 13:24LXX). The relation of the second and third parts in the case of Jesus is like a combination of 1 Sam 2:21, "and the boy Samuel grew up in the presence of the Lord," and 2:26, "Now the boy Samuel continued to grow both in stature and in favor with the Lord and with the people." Thus, the Samuel motif runs through the two verses of the Lukan conclusion. This conclusion prepares the reader both geographically and biographically for the appearance of Jesus of Nazareth, coming from Galilee and preaching a message full of wisdom and exemplifying God's gracious favor (Brown, 1977: 469). The description also parallels that of Moses in Acts 7:22 (Harrington, 1991: 56).

7. The Finding of Jesus in the Temple (Lk 2:41-52)

Is this scene the most important of the infancy narrative [and a foretaste of the resurrection (Laurentin, 1966: 8)] or the onset of an apocryphal weakening, the first sign of a collapse? (Bovon, 1991: 153). Certainly it is an episode that is judged in many different ways. It has been described as "a supplement" (Plummer, 1901: 6), and as a secondary addition unbalancing the original diptych of the infancy narrative (Brown, 1977: 251-

252). It has been claimed that in order to understand it the reader need not be acquainted with the preceding parts of the infancy narrative (Van Iersel, 1960: 154). Even more emphatic is the judgment that holds that it is an independent unit that does not depend on anything that precedes in the infancy narrative and that could be dropped without any great loss to the narrative (Fitzmyer, 1981: 435). Not all would agree, however (Laurentin, 1966: 93; Schürmann, 1969: 133). At any rate, properly speaking, the story is not part of the *infancy* narrative since it occurs many years after the events of Lk 1:5–2:39 (Brown, 1977: 479-480; Fitzmyer, 1981: 434-435; Strauss, 1995: 120-121). But an episode from the in-between years of Jesus' life is a fitting transition to the main Gospel account that will begin in Luke 3. Here Jesus as a pre-adolescent for the first time takes an active part, and the unique relatedness to God that marks his adult life comes into clear focus (Nolland, 1989: 128). It has also been claimed that from a narrative point of view Lk 2:41-52 is not an independent unit, and that it could not be dropped without substantial loss to the infancy narrative (Coleridge, 1993: 187-188).

From a *narrative point of view*, the episode may not be an independent unit, but still there are things that distinguish it from the previous episodes. For the first time in the narrative, Jesus acts and speaks as a free agent; there is no hint of either angels or the Holy Spirit, and it has been remarked that the story is a natural one, and does not include any supernatural features (Marshall, 1978: 126). The Old Testament citations and echoes dwindle to almost nothing (Nolland, 1989: 128). The language of this episode is also less semitized than that of the previous episodes (Laurentin, 1957: 142; Brown, 1977: 480; Fitzmyer, 1981: 435). These are interrelated phenomena which call not just for observation but also for explanation.

From an *anthropological point of view*, it should be observed that in all myths concerning initiation the hero has to leave his mother (and father), usually at the age of twelve or thirteen, in search of a father figure different from that of his own father, and that in the process he is helped by teachers he meets on his journey. This is a must if the hero is to grow up and to discover his true self. Afterwards he returns to his home. Isn't that what we have here in Lk 2:41-52? Jesus leaves his father and mother because he must be in the things of his father. His parents find him listening to the teachers in the temple [Luke has "beautified" the story by having Jesus also ask questions by which he astonishes the bystanders and his parents]. Then he goes home with his parents to Nazareth.

Commentators have been slow to agree on the focus of the episode. Bultmann favors a double focus which includes (1) the exceptional wisdom of the child Jesus (Bultmann, 1972: 300; Lk 11:31, "something greater than Solomon is here"?), and (2) his decision to stay in the temple as revelation of his destiny. Others point to the christological revelation of verse 49 as the episode's center of gravity (Schürmann, 1969: 133; Brown, 1977: 490; Fitzmyer, 1981: 437; Bovon, 1991: 150; Stein, 1992: 124). The range of opinion suggests that the episode, though brief, is not straightforward, and that it may be worth testing the contending claims by posing the questions of narrative criticism.

Some proponents of narrative criticism consider Lk 2:41-52 the climax of the infancy narrative and, therefore, the most important episode of the infancy narrative – at least in narrative terms. This is because it recounts the moment when Jesus appears for the first time as *interpreter of himself*. Indeed, in this final episode of the infancy gospel, for the first time Jesus, the central hero of Luke's story, plays an active role (Nolland, 1989: 127). In earlier episodes, other characters have interpreted Jesus, his identity and role. Now he interprets himself and his action; and at that point leadership in the interpretative task passes to Jesus, with whom it will remain throughout the Third Gospel (Coleridge, 1993: 188-189).

The form of this account is that of a *pronouncement story* in that its goal and culmination come in the concluding statement or pronouncement by Jesus in Lk 2:49. This is the first such story in the Gospel (Stein, 1992: 120). In this instance, the pronouncement is integrally related to the narrative setting. It puts on the lips of Jesus an implied statement about who he is, making manifest to his parents the way in which he is related to God – as an obedient Son of his heavenly Father. This manifestation stands in contrast – in the overall Lukan setting – to the revelations that have been made about him by others (by Gabriel, by the shepherds, by Simeon, by Anna; Fitzmyer, 1981: 436).

Verses 41-42: (41) Now every year his parents went to Jerusalem
for the festival of the passover.
(42) And when he was twelve years old,
they went up as usual for the festival.

The narrator begins by evoking a conventional world; he does so in ways that establish in the episode two related contexts.

First, he stresses that the Passover pilgrimage to Jerusalem is made in conformity to custom. In verse 41 we have "every year," and in verse 42 "as usual" (more literally: "according to custom"), both of which evoke the regular recurrence of religious practice, though without mentioning the element of obligation. [It is clear from Deut 16:16 that adult males were supposed to go to Jerusalem for the Passover, though it is difficult to know how widely the practice was observed in the first century]. Jesus will not enter Jerusalem again in Luke's Gospel until the Passover season of his royal entry into the city, cleansing of the temple, teaching in it (Lk 19:28-48; Tiede, 1988: 79-80). The temple-piety that marked Mary and Joseph in the previous episode is shown to be an enduring part of their life. The first context evoked in the episode, then, is *religious*.

Secondly, the language is strongly familial. Mary and Joseph are referred to as "his parents," which again defines them not in themselves but in relation to Jesus, and so stresses the bond of family. It is the parents who take the initiative, with the sole mention of Jesus being the mention of his age in verse 42. It is suggested that Luke, by choosing to have Jesus at the age of twelve, presents him as still immature, not fully developed either spiritually or rationally, in order to make his wisdom appear all the more clearly (De Jonge, 1977-1978: 317-324, especially 322). But this age appears frequently in the ancient world as that of adolescense, and it may be too conventional to argue that, since thirteen years and one month was the time when the Jewish boy undertook the obligations of the law, this journey was a preliminary visit to accustom the boy Jesus to the future (C.F. Evans, 1990: 224). The child is backgrounded in a way that underscores the bond of family. The second context evoked is therefore *familial* (Coleridge, 1993: 189-190).

The festival of the Passover was one of the three annual festivals Jewish men were required to celebrate in Jerusalem (Deut 16:16). Passover itself was the opening feast of the seven-day (or eight-day by another reckoning) festival called the Feast of the Unleavened Bread, and was celebrated on the fifteenth of Nisan. The entire feast, however, was popularly called Feast of Passover (cf. Lk 22:1). Passover commemorates God's deliverance of exodus of his people out of Egypt and the death angel's passing over Israel's firstborn (Stein, 1992: 121).

Verses 43: When the festival was ended and they started to return,
          the boy Jesus stayed behind in Jerusalem,
          but his parents did not know it.

As in earlier episodes the fulfillment of the prescriptions – in this case the celebration of the Passover – is never narrated. Preferring to leave the Passover festival buried in silence between verses 42 and 43, the narrator moves immediately to its aftermath. The interest focuses on the action of the principal verb: "the boy Jesus stayed behind in Jerusalem" (Nolland, 1989: 129). The reader is told that Jesus remained in Jerusalem, but the narrator says nothing of why, – which was anyway ultimately irrelevant for his purpose (Stein, 1992: 121) – and none of the reasons that have been suggested by scholars find any warrant in the narrative itself (Coleridge, 1993: 191, note 1). From verse 43 onwards, the question for the readers is, "why has Jesus stayed in Jerusalem?"; but for the parents the question will become in verse 45, "where is Jesus?" (Coleridge, 1993: 190-191).

Verses 44-45: (44) Assuming that he was in the group of travelers,
                       they went a day's journey.
                       Then they started to look for him among their
                       relatives and friends.
                (45) When they did not find him,
                       they returned to Jerusalem to search for him.

In verse 44, the narrator begins the narration of interpretation,
and he does so by turning to the parents. The verse explains
how it was possible for the parents not to know that Jesus had
stayed behind (Nolland, 1989: 129). They are faced with a fact
– the absence of Jesus – and therefore with a question which
comes only slowly: where is he? Their first interpretation of the
fact and answer to the question is that Jesus is "in the group of
travelers" – which the well-informed readers know to be wrong.
On the basis of this first interpretation, they proceed a day's
journey before eventually seeking Jesus among the company.
"A day's journey" would normally be a rough unit for measur-
ing distance (Num 11:31; 1 Kgs 19:4), probably between thirty
and forty kilometers [from Nazareth to Jerusalem was a distance of about one-hundred and twenty kilometers], but here
in verse 44 the thought is probably that only after striking camp
at the end of the first day's travel could Mary and Joseph be
sure that Jesus was not in the traveling-party (Nolland, 1989:
130). They are then faced with a second fact – that Jesus is not
"in the group of travelers," a term that suggests a pilgrimage
party made up of relatives and neighbors from the same village
(Johnson, 1991: 59). At that point they realize that their first
interpretation was wrong; and with that realization, their question, "where is Jesus?" grows more urgent. As it does, the effect
of suspense gains momentum (Coleridge, 1993: 191-192). Verse
44 prepares for the "three days" in verse 46.

In verse 45, the narrator has the parents return to Jerusalem, a second action that presumes a second interpretation –
that Jesus, if not among "the group of travelers," must have
remained in Jerusalem. In the Greek text the participles and
the verb present an interesting picture. Both the participle "[not]
finding" and the verb "they returned" are aorist. They did not

find him in the caravan and made a decision to go back to Jerusalem, their failure to locate him being expressed in summary tenses. In contrast, "searching" is a present participle. When they got to Jerusalem, they began the process of searching for him – language reflecting the passage of time as they anxiously sought for the missing child (Bock, 1994: 266). At this point, the parents move towards the knowledge given to the readers in verse 43. Yet without the aid of an omniscient narrator they can only suppose what the readers know with certainty. They again "assume" as they did at the start of verse 44. Still, the fact that they move towards the readers' knowledge means that the narrator is building a *rapprochement* between parents and readers (Coleridge, 1993: 192),

Verses 46-47: (46) After three days they found him in the temple,
sitting among the teachers,
listening to them and asking them questions.
(47) And all who heard him were amazed
at his understanding and his answers.

Between verses 45 and 46 the narrator decides for another silence, with nothing said of what happened to either Jesus or the parents in the three days mentioned early in verse 46. Our knowledge of the circumstances is too limited to say how far the scene is idealized (C.F. Evans, 1990: 225). The phrase "after three days" has suggested to some interpreters Luke's use of "the third day" in reference to the resurrection of Jesus (e.g., Johnson, 1991: 59), but the references in the Gospel (Lk 9:22; 18:33; 24:7, 46) specifically note "on the third day," and the phrase "after three days" is used in other contexts in Acts 25:1; 28:17 (Danker, 1988: 75). The three day period is so conventional that a prefiguration of the resurrection is unlikely (Marshall, 1978: 127). Some scholars (e.g. Laurentin, 1966: 101-102) claim that the three days anticipate the three days between Jesus' death and resurrection. But convincing counterarguments have been advanced by scholars who insist upon the formulaic character of the phrase and favor a general translation such as "after several days" (De Jonge, 1977-1978: 324-327).

The omissions in verses 46-47 are substantial. First, nothing is said of how the parents react when they find Jesus – the effect of which is to leave the parents in the background for the moment, with Jesus in the foreground. Secondly and more importantly, there is no report of the exchange between the teachers and Jesus such as we find in the apocryphal accounts, e.g., in the *Infancy Gospel of Thomas* 19:2, where they are reduced to silence (C.F. Evans, 1990: 225). The effect of the silence is to focus upon Jesus rather than upon the content of his replies to the teachers or upon the teachers themselves. The narrator's decision not to report any exchange between Jesus and the teachers also suggests that this is not where the episode's center of gravity is to be found (Coleridge, 1993: 193-194). Verses 46-47 may be meant to foreshadow the interests of the man Jesus, who will often be engaged in debates over the law. However, here there appears none of the hostility to the teachers of the law that will mark Jesus' attitude in his public ministry towards the scribes and lawyers, for in the present scene "temple piety" prevails (Brown, 1977: 488).

The backgrounding of the teachers continues in the phrase "all who heard," which includes the teachers but does not focus upon them. At the same time, it is hard to know who exactly is included in the group of "all who heard." As in Lk 2:18, it would seem to include the parents among those who are amazed at Jesus' display of intelligence; and the omission of the subject in verse 48 seems to support this (Coleridge, 1993: 194).

The phrase "all who heard" is reminiscent of Lk 1:66 (referring to those in the Judean hills who hear the news of John's birth and its circumstances) and Lk 2:18 (referring to those at the birth scene who hear the shepherds' tale). Yet we are dealing with the Lukan technique of reprise (and not just repetition), since the two instances, though similar, are not identical. Now in verse 47 it is Jesus who is heard rather than Zechariah and the neighbors or the angel and the shepherds (Lk 1:66; 2:18). Where in the previous two instances there was a source (Zechariah and the angel) and a mediation (the neighbors and the shepherds), now source and mediation converge in Jesus. This means that the focus in verses 46-47 is less on the process and content of the communication and more on the communicator himself: Jesus (Coleridge, 1993: 194-195).

The reaction, "they were amazed" occurs eleven times in Luke-Acts. Luke will use the verb *existanai* again either intransitively or in the middle voice in Lk 8:52; 24:22, and often in Acts (2:7, 12; 8:13, etc.) to express a reaction of wonder or surprise at something in the life of Jesus or the sequel of it (Fitzmyer, 1981: 442). The reaction of the onlookers indicates that Jesus is gaining honor. In each case Jesus shows himself to be more than people expected, given the stereotyped honor status ascribed to him by virtue of his background (Malina-Rohrbaugh, 1992: 299).

The parents' question, "where," is now answered; and both their first supposition (that Jesus, if he is not in the traveling party, must be in Jerusalem) and their later supposition implied if not expressed in the narrative (that Jesus must or might be in the temple) are shown to be right. But the answer to one question brings about another. The question "where?" now becomes the question "why here?", as will appear when Mary speaks in verse 48. For the readers, the question "why?" persists, though now in different terms. Since verse 43 the readers' question has been, "why has Jesus remained in Jerusalem?"; but now, learning that Jesus is not just in Jerusalem but also in the temple among the teachers, the question becomes, "why there?" With the parents, the readers ask if Jesus left his family simply to engage the teachers in discussion? The understanding of the parents and that of the readers begins to converge as the episode builds up to the moment of revelation in verse 49 (Coleridge, 1993: 195).

The heightening of attention on Jesus and his authority in verses 46-47 moves in three steps – from "hearing" to "questioning" to "answering." One has rightly cautioned against making too much of Jesus sitting in the midst of the teachers as if he had become the teacher of the teachers. In this connection it has been noted that the seated position could equally be the position of the disciple (e.g., Acts 22:3; Brown, 1977: 474). He who begins by listening becomes more active in the act of questioning, and more active still as he answers questions put to him – and answers in a way that causes amazement. Yet there is no indication that the understanding (*sunesis*) displayed by Jesus is the result of a divine inspiration or revelation of any kind. The emphasis of the word is on insight rather than knowledge. Luke sees this *sunesis* as an example of the *sophia*, "wisdom," which he stresses in Lk 2:40, 52 (Brown, 1977: 475). The display is exceptional enough to evoke amazement but it is not unique, since similar displays of human precocity, if uncommon, are not unknown now nor were they in the ancient world. The motif of a hero who shows unusual intelligence even as a child is common in Greek and Hellenistic biography and occurs in Hellenistic-Jewish writers like Philo and Josephus (Bultmann, 1963: 300-301; Creed, 1957: 44; Brown, 1977: 481-482; de Jonge, 1977-1978: 339-342). At this point, Jesus might be judged yet another precociously intelligent child giving signs of future greatness. One may even wonder whether we are not dealing here with an "anticipation" of the statement attributed to Jesus in Lk 11:31, "...something greater than Solomon is here." The readers and the parents know him to be much more, as he himself will declare in verse 49. In verses 46-47, Jesus engages the teachers in an astonishing way as one indication of what his identity enables. But this is not an end in itself, since it prepares for verse 49 where, in turning to interpret himself, Jesus' interpretative word will appear more stark and enigmatic, evoking not astonishmernt but perplexity, and will appear as a word that casts his future greatness in a quite different light (Coleridge, 1993: 196). This depiction identifies Jesus for the knowing reader, long before the gospel story proper begins. The picture fits with the way the *Wisdom of Solomon* has stated the identity of the righteous one, "He professes to have knowledge of God and calls himself a child of the Lord... Let us see if his words are true, and let us test what will happen at the end of his life"

(Wisd 2:13, 17; Tiede, 1988: 80). It is interesting to note that instead of Mark's and Matthew's version of the confession of the centurion, "Truly this man was God's Son!" (Mk 15:39; Mt 27:54), Luke reads "Certainly this man was innocent" (Lk 23:47; *dikaios*, literally "righteous").

> Verse 48: When his parents saw him they were astonished;
> and his mother said to him,
> "Child, why have you treated us like this?
> Look, your father and I have been searching for you in
> great anxiety."

Between verses 47 and 48 the narrator sets another of the silences that punctuate the episode. Nothing is said of what happens to the teachers and others of "all who heard," who simply disappear from the scene. As he moves to what will be the climactic moment of both interpretation and revelation, the narrator retires from the public to the private arena, narrowing the focus from "all who heard" to the parents alone. Verse 48 offers an inside view of the parents (*exeplagēsan*, "they were astonished"), and also it makes clear that it is not only hearing Jesus that provokes their astonishment, but also seeing him. The vocabulary suggests that they are even more astonished by *where he is* (*exeplagēsan*) than by *what he says* (*existanto*; Laurentin, 1956: 33-34), although this has been queried by some (Brown, 1977: 475). It can be safely stated that the change of verb suggests that there is something different about this reaction, whether or not it be in this case a difference of intensity (Coleridge, 1993: 197, note 2).

Puzzled by his disappearance, the parents are astonished by where they find him. More than ever, the strange action of Jesus demands interpretation; and it is Mary's question that voices the demand. The narrator refers to her as "his mother" in a way that underlines again the family bond. To the same end, the narrator also depicts Mary as referring to Jesus as "child," thus emphasizing his relationship to his parents, and to Joseph as "your father." Joseph is silent throughout, but he is given pride of place in Mary's expression, "your father and I" (*ho patēr sou kagō*), which is considered an unusual word order (De Jonge, 1977-1978: 330-331). The effect of the word order is to stress the phrase "your father."

Mediterranean families are patriarchal. A father's authority is the foundation on which the family discipline rests. Authority links everything together: man and wife, fathers and children, teacher and student, master and disciple, subject and governor, humankind and God. The honor of the father depends very much on his being able to impose discipline on every family member (see Sir 3:6-7; Prov 3:11-12; Heb 12:7-11; 1 Tim 3:4; Malina-Rohrbaugh, 1992: 300).

The expression "your father" used in reference to Joseph, the play on the word "father" and the stress on the family bond in what Mary says prepare for what Jesus will say in verse 49, where the question of belonging will be cast in a quite different light. Joseph's paternity is emphasized in verse 48 in order to prepare for its transcendance in verse 49 (Coleridge, 1993: 198). Quite apart from the doctrinal problems associated with calling Joseph "your father," the phrase "your father and I" is an appeal to authority, to filial bonds and responsibilities (Tiede, 1988: 81-82). The expression "in great anxiety" (*odunōmenoi*) implies mental and spiritual pain or sadness. The verb *odunasthai* occurs four times in Luke-Acts and nowhere else in the New Testament (Brown, 1977: 475). Luke uses it for both mental and physical suffering (Lk 16:24-25; Acts 20:38; Johnson, 1991: 59). It is possible that for Luke, this is the beginning of Mary's experience of the sword (Lk 2:35; C.F. Evans, 1990: 225).

The inner reaction of the parents to the disppearance is twofold: there is both bafflement ("Why have you treated us like this?") and anguish ("in great anxiety"). There is nothing surprising in such a reaction: it is completely conventional. What matters more from a narrative point of view is that the narrator allows the character to articulate the reaction that he himself has not reported earlier. Faced with the fact of Jesus in the temple among the teachers, Mary cannot find her way to right interpretation. How can *who he is* and *what he has done* be reconciled? For the parents and the readers to answer that question, Jesus himself must speak for the first time in the Lukan narrative. In the previous two episodes, the human characters have needed divine intervention to come to right interpretation. Now they need the intervention of Jesus (Coleridge, 1993: 199).

Verse 49: He said to them,
    "Why were you searching for me?
    Did you not know that I must be in my Father's house?"

Jesus meets his mother's question with two questions of his own, which are at best an oblique reply. But is seems to be too strong to interpret Jesus' response as a counter-accusation. The answer to his first question ("Why were you searching for me?") is obvious – at least on the level with which Mary asks her question. What emerges, however, is that Jesus is speaking on another level, that he and his parents are at cross-purposes. This was not true of Jesus and the teachers. He met the teachers on their own ground and on their own terms; but he does not meet his parents on the grounds and the terms expressed in Mary's question. His words in verse 49 disrupt the logic of convention that has held sway to this point and to which Mary's question gave voice. In order to answer her own question or to understand the answer Jesus gives, Mary must again move ground on her journey of discovery (Coleridge, 1993: 199-200).

Jesus' answer is sometimes read as a counter-accusation, as if Jesus' own question has something of a repraoch in it too (Fitzmyer, 1981: 443). But it is important to note that while after the incident the parents are left with much food for thought (verses 50-51), it is Jesus whose behavior is modified: he goes back with his parents after all and is obedient to them (Nolland, 1989: 131).

The narrator has Jesus offer an interpretation of both his absence from the company and his presence in the temple – the interpretation that neither his parents nor the readers, left to their own devices, have been able to supply. In verse 43 the narrator said nothing of why Jesus remained in Jerusalem, preferring to leave the revelation of motive until now when he can place it on the lips of Jesus himself. Now Jesus reveals that he has left his parents and installed himself in the temple not simply because of an irresistible urge for theological discussion, but because he is the Son of God (Coleridge, 1993: 200). This is an instance of the indirect christology of the Lukan narrative, in which the narrator will have Jesus point the way but leave it to the characters and readers to follow (Aletti, 1988: 42 and 203). Although Luke-Acts contains twenty explicit references to God the Father, these references are unevenly divided. The Gospel contains seventeen references, with the first reference occurring in Lk 2:49 and the last referrence occurring in a resurrection narrative (Lk 24:49). In contrast, Acts contains only three references to the Father, and all three are in the first two chapters of the book (Mowery, 1990: 124).

What is difficult for Mary and the readers is to discover the coherence between Jesus' identity and his action. Yet the form of his question ("Did you not know that I must be in my Father's house?") implies that a grasp of this coherence is the knowledge that enables right interpretation and that both parents and readers are expected to share (Coleridge, 1993: 201).

If it is now clear that Jesus has remained in the temple among the teachers because he is the Son of God, it remains unclear what exactly he means by the oblique and enigmatic statement that he must be "in the things of my Father" (*en tois tou patros mou*; Laurentin, 1966: 38-72). The ambiguity of this sentence results from Luke's use of the plural article *tois* without an immediately corresponding noun (Weinert, 1983: 19). Commentators have sought to show that the enigmatic phrase must mean either "in the affairs of my Father" (i.e. action) or "in the house of my Father" (i.e. place; Sylva, 1987: 133-134; Tiede, 1988: 82; the issue is at what *place* he could be expected to be found), with the weight of opinion favoring the second translation. Certainly the phrase can have that meaning; but that is not to say that it can have *only* that meaning.

Moreover, it has been noted that if Luke had only wanted to say "I must be in my Father's house," he expressed himself in an unnatural and even extraordinary manner (De Jonge, 1977-1978: 332). Given that elsewhere he refers to the house of God as *oikos* (Lk 6:4; 11:51; 19:46; Acts 7:47), Luke might simply have written *ho oikos tou patros mou*, as he does in Lk 16:27. Furthermore, the expression *ta tou* with the genitive of a noun is never found in the New Testament in the sense of "the house of." Yet this is not to say that it cannot have this sense in Lk 2:49, since evidence from outside the New Testament suggests that it can (Job 18:19LXX; Tob 6:2; Esth 7:8; Laurentin, 1966: 58-61). Still, that does not answer the question of why, if he wanted to say no more than that, did Luke choose so odd an expression? (Coleridge, 1993: 201-202). The crucial issue seems to be the phrase "I must" (Tiede, 1988: 82; Nolland, 1989: 130-131).

Four reasons have been offered in support of the claim that the phrase cannot mean only "in my Father's house":

(1) The *dei* ("must") looks comprehensively to all that will be involved in the unfolding of God's plan. Its range is too broad to allow so restrictive an understanding.

(2) Having just said that he must be *en tois tou patros mou*, Jesus leaves the temple in Lk 2:51 and retires to Nazareth, which implies that he is as much *en tois tou patros mou* in Nazareth as he was in the temple. Location is not decisive.

(3) The incomprehension of the parents is the result not just of the play on the word "father" (against Laurentin, 1966: 78), but of the enigmatic character of Jesus' entire pronouncement. That the narrator has the parents perplexed immediately after the pronouncement suggests that he wants to underscore the ambiguity of what Jesus has said. Their perplexity would be hard to explain if the narrator had meant for Jesus simply to say that he must be "in the house of my father."

(4) Jesus' question presumes a positive answer from the parents. Yet they cannot have been expected to know that Jesus

was in the temple. What they might have been expected to know, however, is that Jesus, as God's son, must take his unique place in the unfolding divine plan.

Taken together, these four points are persuasive enough to suggest that "in the house of my father" is one of several meanings that the narrator gathers together in the ambiguity of *en tois tou patros mou* – an ambiguity best captured in a literal and unspecific translation such as "the things of my father." The effect of the ambiguity is to leave the readers sharing the parents' perplexity and asking what it might mean to be "in the things of my father" (De Jonge, 1977-1978: 331-337), which question will be answered in the course of the entire Lukan narrative. Those who defend the translation "in the house of my father" (Laurentin, 1966: 56-68) call, e.g., on the parallels in Lk 6:4 and 19:46 where the temple is referred to as God's house (Stein, 192: 123; cf. Nolland, 1989: 131-132).

At this point of the narrative, what matters is not that the question be answered, but that it be made clear to both characters and readers that, however perplexing his actions may be, Jesus always acts as Son of God and therefore in obedience to the will of God he calls "my father" (Cullmann, 1959: 270).

As Jesus comes to the point of revelation in verse 49, there emerges a distinctively Lukan christology that has Jesus as prime interpreter of himself. He assumes the leadership in the interpretative task as the one who reveals the coherence between his identity and his action; and this is a role that he will retain throughout the Third Gospel. A christology, such as this has its roots in the Old Testament christology, which has dominated the infancy narrative to this point (Bock, 1987: 55-90), but which has its own originality – particularly in the way it focuses upon Jesus as interpreter. Such christology will take a crucial step forward in Lk 4:16-30 (Aletti, 1988: 39-61) and come to full flower finally in Lk 24:13-49 (Aletti, 1988: 177-198). In both episodes, Jesus appears as he does already in Lk 2:41-52 in the role of "the unique hermeneute" (Aletti, 1988: 42). Where in the earlier episodes the narrator introduced both heavenly agents and human characters, now in this episode Jesus appears as both heavenly agent and human character, as the point at which divine visitation and human recognition converge (Coleridge, 1993: 203-204).

The absence of any heavenly prompting suggests that Jesus has acted freely and independently in a way true of neither the shepherds nor Simeon and Anna. Similarly, the phrases "he remained" in verse 43 and "have you treated" in verse 48, both with Jesus as subject, suggest that it is Jesus who has taken the initiative; and at the age of twelve puts him at the age of discretion at which he is capable of independent action (Brown, 1977: 473). It appears, then, that the narrator is keen to underscore that Jesus has acted in free obedience to what he has come to recognize as God's will.

At the same time, the *dei* ("it is necessay"; NRSV: "must") of verse 49 reintroduces into the narrative's presentation of the divine plan the dynamic of necessity that appeared first in Lk 1:5-25. This is the first of the many appearances of the Lukan *dei* which occurs eighteen times in the Gospel and twenty-four times in Acts, enough to make it a distinctively Lukan expression when compared to its frequency in other New Testament writings (Matthew: 8; Mark: 6; John: 10; Pauline Letters: 16; Pastorals: 9; Revelation: 8 (Cosgrove, 1984: 168-190). The verb *dei* refers in the first place to the necessity with which God's intention, once revealed, must be fulfilled; and only in the second place does it refer to the duty that God laid upon Jesus, and which Jesus took upon himself (De Jonge, 1978-1979: 350-351). In Lk 2:49, as often throughout the Lukan narrative, it implies subjection to an already declared divine plan that seeks human collaboration but is not thwarted by human rejection. Luke's verb of divine necessity, *dei*, can be used to outline and call for proper response to God (Green, 1995: 35).

Jesus has come to a knowledge of what God asks of him and of the necessity that imposes on him – a knowledge that enables right interpretation and that is the fruit of neither heavenly revelation nor precocious human intelligence. It comes instead from the peculiar relationship with God that Jesus proclaims in verse 49. He describes his relationship with God as father-son relationship; and it is this that is implied as the source of the knowledge that enables his interpretation.

Verse 49 is the first indication of a break with biological family and the emergence of a new "fictive" kin group for Jesus. Later he distances himself from Mary and her Mediterranean maternal claims on him (Lk 11:28). This is an especially important theme for Luke. In antiquity, the extended family meant everything. It not only was the source of one's honor status in the community, but also functioned as the primary economic, religious, educational, and social network. Loss of connection to the family meant the loss of these vital networks as well as loss of connection to the land. But a surrogate family, what anthropologists call a fictive kin group, could serve many of the same functions as a biological family. The Christian group acting as a surrogate family is for Luke the locus of the good news. It transcends the normal categories of birth, class, race, gender, education, wealth, and power – hence it is inclusive in a startling new way. For those already detached from their biological families (e.g., non-inheriting sons who go to the city), the surrogate family becomes a place of refuge. For the well-connected, particularly the city elite, however, giving up one's biological family for the surrogate Christian family, as Luke portrays Jesus demanding, was a decision that could cost one dearly (see Lk 9:57-62; 12:51-53; 14:26; 18:28-30). It meant an irrevocable break with the networks on which the elite life-style depended. And it seems that Luke is concerned largely with problems of such elite persons (Malina-Rohrbaugh, 1992: 335-336).

The interpretation that Jesus offers in verse 49 is so enigmatic that it prompts at least as many questions as answers. The ambiguity of verse 49 leaves both readers and characters asking what the phrase "in the things of my father" might mean. The question will become more perplexing with Jesus' return to Nazareth in obedience to Mary and Joseph; and it is the question that the entire Lukan narrative will set itself to answer.

What the programmatic statement of verse 49 implies is that he is always speaking and acting as Son of God and therefore in obedience to the God whom he calls "my father." Throughout the Third Gospel, therefore, it is Jesus himself who in word and action will answer the question that his own words and actions in the episode have stirred (Coleridge, 1993: 212).

Verse 50: But they did not understand what he said to them.

The parents prove unable to come to the right interpretation that Jesus has come to and that he has passed on. It has been denied that the reference is to any lack of understanding of Jesus' divine filiation (Laurentin, 1966: 184), but this claim has been rejected (Brown, 1977: 484, note 19). In the past attempts have been made to preserve Mary from this lack of understanding. Some relate the ignorance only to Joseph, but the reference to "they" is against this limited connection. Others relate the ignorance to bystanders, but the dialogue before our present verse involves the parents, as does the reference to Mary following the remark. Still others allude to an unmentioned saying of Jesus being the source of the ignorance, but such an appeal is special pleading and cannot honor the literary flow of the passage (Bock, 1994: 272). All such attempts do violence to the text and lose sight of the contrast between Jesus' wisdom and understanding as God's Son (Lk 2:40,47,52) and his parents' lack of understanding. Similar misunderstandings occurred throughout his ministry (Lk 4:22; 9:45; 18:34; 24:5-7, 25-26, 45) and would only be remedied by the resurrection (Stein, 1992: 123). The literary function of verse 50 is to mark the christological depth of Jesus' statement, a depth to which Mary and Joseph are not at once able to penetrate (Schürmann, 1969: 137; Nolland, 1989: 133).

The parents are reduced to a silence that contrasts with the proclamation he has made as fruit of his own recognition. With the parents reduced to silence by their incomprehension, the narrator infringes his rule of external narration and offers an inside view of the characters, speaking for them since they cannot speak for themselves. What is puzzling is that for Jesus to be "in the things of my father" should mean the kind of thing he has done. Throughout the Third Gospel, Jesus will be shown as consistently "in the things of my father," but often in enigmatic ways, most especially in the passion narrative. But here for the first time, and in ways proleptic of the whole, a gap is set between the "what" and the "how" of Jesus' being "in the things of my father" (Coleridge, 1993: 206-207).

It is idle to speculate what it was that the parents failed to understand. Luke here assimilates the event to the later gospel story. As with the disciples, so here, Jesus speaks on a different plane, and is met with human incomprehension (see Lk Lk 9:45; 18:34; C.F. Evans, 1990: 226).

The initiative in the interpretative task passes at this point from angels and inspired human characters to Jesus. This is another way of saying that it passes from God to Jesus, since though he has chosen to work through angels and the Holy Spirit it has been God who held the initiative. But now, with no mention of either angels or the Holy Spirit, the initiative passes to Jesus. From now on, to interpret rightly the signs of God's action both characters and readers will need to listen to Jesus. This will be said explicitly by the voice from heaven in Lk 9:35, "This is my Son, my Chosen; listen to him" (Coleridge, 1993: 207-208).

Verse 51a: Then he went down with them and came to Nazareth, and was obedient to them.

The "exit" in verse 51a corresponds to the "entry" in verses 41-42 (Nolland, 1989: 133).

At first it seems strange that Jesus, having just announced that he must be "in the things of my father," should return to Nazareth with Joseph and Mary. Having proclaimed his allegiance to his heavenly father, Jesus returns to the town of the man who appears to be his father. This immediately expands the sense of what it means for him to be "in the things of my father." It means not only that he stay unexpectedly in Jerusalem or in the temple, but also that he return with Joseph and

Mary to Nazareth. Clearly, then, it is not location that decides what it might mean for Jesus to be "in the things of my father" (Coleridge, 1993: 208).

Jesus continues to be the subject, the parents now accompanying him rather than he them, but it is emphasized that the divine filial consciousness expressed in verse 49 was not incompatible with continuing obedience to his parents (C.F. Evans, 1993: 227). Jesus' continuing submission to his parents may be stressed because of the way in which he has seemed to have been insubordinate in Jerusalem (Nolland, 1989: 133).

What is decisive is that, wherever he is, Jesus be obedient to the will of his heavenly father; and it appears that the will of his heavenly father now is that he be obedient to the will of his parents, as is suggested by "and was obedient to them." To return with them does not mean a return to the logic of convention voiced in Mary's question nor an immediate revision of the different logic implied in Jesus' reply. If he returns to Nazareth with his parents, it is within the context established in verse 49. His obedience to the will of God may entail a transcendence of parental authority, but this does not mean a rejection of parental authority. This is as we have seen it with both imperial and Mosaic authority in the previous two episodes (Coleridge, 1993: 209).

Luke seems to be interested, first, in the contrast that although Jesus was God's Son, he allowed himself to obey human parents; and, second, in explaining how, although Jesus had already revealed his divine sonship, he did not publicly begin his mission till after his baptism (Brown, 1977: 478). Indeed, no sooner has Jesus come enigmatically to center stage than he is again removed from it until he reappears years later in Lk 3:21, with only the second growth-report in verse 52 between now and then. Jesus may disappear from center stage and John may reappear in Lk 3:2, but the the plan of God will remain at center stage. Indeed what emerges is that the comings and goings of the key characters are part of God's unfolding plan (Coleridge, 1993: 209). The literary function of verse 50 is to mark the christological depth of Jesus' statement in verse 49, a depth to which Mary and Joseph are not at once able to penetrate (Schürmann, 1969: 137; Nolland, 1989: 133).

Verse 51b: His mother treasured all these things in her heart.

Verse 51 looks back to both Lk 1:66 and 2:19. The reference to "treasuring" or "keeping" has to do with careful recall, keeping a close eye to something (Gen 37:11 [Jabob of Joseph's dream]; Bock, 1994: 273). In Lk 1:66 and 2:19 the report implied three things. First, words are heard that are not understood. Secondly, the words have mysterious and portentous implications for the future of the one spoken about. Thirdly, the act of storing in the heart implies not only incomprehension, but also an openness to clarification in the future, a preparedness to live with unclarity in the belief that clarity will come in time.

The same three things are also implied in this third instance, though as in Lk 2:19 it is not only the words spoken that are puzzling, but also the events witnessed, *ta rhēmata* being the equivalent of the Hebrew *dabar*. In the three instances the words spoken and the speaker are different, but the pattern is the same, as is the purpose of remembering. In Lk 2:19, it was *what the shepherds said of Jesus* that was puzzling and portentous, but here it is *what Jesus says of himself*. By placing this reference to Mary's remembering after the report of her incomprehension, the narrator makes it clear that her remembering relates to the way in which she deals with incomprehension. The same is true of Lk 2:19, where we saw that the question was not whether faith and incomprehension were compatible, but how faith handles incomprehension (Coleridge, 1993: 209). Mary may not have understood what Jesus did or what he said of himself, but she is not unresponsive to the mystery that surrounds him. Her lack of understanding is not permanent; for the fact that she keeps with concern such events in her heart is by way of preparation for a future understanding as a member of the believing community (Brown, 1977: 494).

The narrator has Mary ponder not only what she hears from

Jesus, but also the odd juxtaposition of his statement in the temple that he must be "in the things of my father" and his return to Nazareth in subjection to his parents. The fact that the narrator reports Mary's incomprehension after the report of Jesus' return to Nazareth, and not immediately after Jesus' statement in verse 49 implies that it is not only Jesus' enigmatic words that call for pondering, but also his return to Nazareth and his subjection to his parents. Like the readers, Mary must ponder what it might mean for Jesus to be "in the things of my father," given that it can mean both his puzzling stay in Jerusalem and his less puzzling return to Nazareth. In her remembering, Mary begins to traverse the gap between the "what" and the "how" of Jesus being "in the things of my father." She grapples with the enigma of what it means for Jesus to be the Son (Coleridge, 1993: 209-210).

The episode is concluded by the emphatic statement that Jesus' parents did not understand the meaning of his words, but his mother kept all these words in her heart. Remarks such as this open the way for Mary's continued, but changed, role, determined by the word rather than by her rights as mother. Mary is the only person from the infancy narrative, apart from Jesus and John, who reappears in the following story and also in Acts. But it means that Mary becomes a receiver rather than a giver (Seim, 1994b: 733).

Verse 52: And Jesus increased in wisdom and in years,
and in divine and human favor.

Verses 51-52 conclude both the pericope, verses 41-50, and the infancy narrative as a whole (Nolland, 1989: 133). The word *hēlikia* is well attested in both the sense "age" and the sense "stature." The latter meaning, "stature," is certain in Lk 19:3; the former, "age" (NRSV: "years") may be prefereable in Lk 12:25. Here, in Lk 2:52, the order of terms favors the latter (Nolland, 1989: 133; the RSV has "stature"). The term here translated "years" suggests more than just advancing age. Reputation, maturity, and stature are involved – all critical to the place of a Mediterranean male in society. This description, borrowed from 1 Sam 2:26, presents an almost programmatic statement in Luke's assessment of Jesus. The one of lowly birth, whose ascribed honor status warranted no such statement in the eyes of the culture, is attested to by both God and human beings (Malina-Rohrbaugh, 1992: 299).

The two growth-reports of verses 40 and 52 are similar but not identical. Some differences are worth noting. First, in verse 52 the narrator names Jesus *absolutely* for the first time in the infancy narrative. Earlier in this episode, he has been "the boy Jesus" (Lk 2:43) and "child" (Lk 2:48); and in the previous episodes he was "this child" (Lk 2:17), "the child Jesus" (Lk 2:27), and "the child" (Lk 2:40). But now, as he becomes for the first time an independent agent in the narrative, he becomes simply "Jesus."

Secondly, the addition of "in human favor" depicts Jesus as one who has entered the public arena and who is becoming increasingly the object of human attention, as the episode has indeed shown. Where in verse 40 there was the sense that things were between Jesus and God, in verse 52 there is more the sense that things are between Jesus, God and human beings, as they have been in the last episode.

Thirdly, the phrase "the favor of God was upon him" in verse 40 conveys a more passive sense than does "he increased in divine and human favor" in verse 52. The movement in verse 40 is from God to Jesus, whereas the movement in verse 52 is more from Jesus to God and human beings. This is again appropriate at a point where Jesus has become for the first time an independent agent in the narrative (Coleridge, 1993: 210-211). No matter how *charis* is to be understood here, "favor" (NRSV) or "grace," it is clear that the latter is not to be burdened with the late medieval and Renaissance debate about what kind of grace he enjoyed (Fitzmyer, 1981: 446).

The growth in favor may be related to the obedience that Jesus shows his parents at Nazareth. The son who is obedient and keeps the commandments is assured in Prov 3:4: "you will find favor and good repute in the sight of God and of people"

(Brown, 1977: 495). For a similar statement concerning the development of Jesus' character, see Heb 5:8-9; 2:14-18. It has correctly been pointed out that one must desist from using the present scene to establish a historical development (or lack of development) in Jesus' self-awareness (Stein, 1992: 123). In the final episode of the infancy narrative divine visitation and human recognition converge to produce a distinctively Lukan christology that will remain decisive through the whole of the Third Gospel (Coleridge, 1993: 211-212).

Concluding, we may say that the main purpose of the infancy narrative as a whole is not so much to establish a relationship between Jesus and John the Baptist, nor to identify Jesus as a Palestinian Jew born in Bethlehem and raised in Nazareth, as it is to make christological affirmations about him from the begining of his earthly ministry (Fitzmyer, 1981, 446). As Raymond Brown and others have argued, Luke pushes back the affirma- tions as to who Jesus was from the period when he was clearly acknowledged as Messiah, Lord, Savior, Son of God, etc., – that is, with titles born of the *post-resurrection* experience of the early Christians – to the period of Jesus' birth (Brown, 1977: 29-32).

BIBLIOGRAPHY

Aletti, Jean-Noël. *L'art de raconter Jésus Christ. L'écriture narrative de l'Evangile de Luc.* Parole de Dieu. Paris: Editions du Seuil, 1988.

Alexander, Loveday. "Luke's Preface in the Context of Greek Preface-Writing," *Novum Testamentum* 28 (1986), 48-74.

_____. *The Preface to Luke's Gospel: Literary Convention and Social Context in Luke 1:1-4 and Acts 1:1.* Cambridge: Cambridge University Press, 1993.

Anderson, Janice Capel. "Mary's Difference: Gender and Patriarchy in the Birth Narratives," *Journal of Religion* 67 (1987), 183-202.

Applebaum, S. "Economic Life in Palestine," in Safrai, S. and M. Stern. eds. *Jewish People in the First Century* . Vol 2. Assen: Van Gorcum, 1976.

Baily, M. "The Crib and Exegesis of Luke 2:1-20," *Irish Ecclesiastical Record* 100 (1963), 359-376.

_____. "The Shepherds and the Sign of a Child in a Manger," *Irish Theological Quarterly* 31 (1964), 1-23.

Batey, Richard A. *Jesus and the Forgotten City: New Light on Sepphoris and the Urban World of Jesus.* Grand Rapids, MI: Baker Bookhouse, 1991.

Baum, Armin Daniel. *Lukas als Historiker der letzten Jesusreise.* Wuppertal: R. Brockhaus Verlag, 1993.

Beare, Francis Wright. *The Earliest Records of Jesus.* Nashville: Abingdon, 1972.

Beasley-Murray, George R. *Jesus and the Kingdom of God.* Grand Rapids: Eerdmans, 1986.

Beavis, Mary Ann. "Expecting Nothing in Return: Luke's Picture of the Marginalized," *Interpretation* 48 (1994), 357-368.

Beck, Brian B. *Christian Character in the Gospel of Luke.* London: Epworth Press, 1989.

Bemile, Paul. *The Magnificat within the Context and Framework of Lukan Theology. An Exegetical Theological Study of Lk 1:46-55.* Frankfurt am Main-Bern-New York: Verlag Peter Lang, 1986.

Benoit, Pierre. "L'enfance de Jean Baptiste selon Luc 1," *New Testament Studies* 3 (1956-1957), 169-194.

Berger, Klaus. "Die königlichen Messiastraditionen des Neuen Testaments," *New Testament Studies* 20 (1973-1974), 1-44.

Bock, Darrell L. *Proclamation from Prophecy and Pattern. Lucan Old Testament Christology.* Sheffield: JSOT Press, 1987.

_____. *Luke. Volume I: 1:1-9:50.* Baker Exegetical Commentary on the New Testament. Grand Rapids: Baker Books, 1994.

Bovon, François. *L'Evangile selon Saint Luc (1,1-9,50).* Commentaire du Nouveau Testament IIIa. Geneva: Labor et Fides, 1991.

_____. *Luc le Théologien. Vingt-cinq ans de recherches (1950-1975).* Neuchâtel-Paris: Delachaux & Niestle, 1978.

_____. *Luke the Theologian: Thirty-Three Years of Research (1950-1983).* Allison Park: Pickwick, 1987.

_____. "Die Geburt und die Kindheit Jesu: Kanonische und apokryphe Evangelien," *Bibel und Kirche* 42 (1987), 162-170.

Brenner, Athalya. "Female Social Behavior: Two Descriptive Patterns Within the 'Birth of the Hero' Paradigm," *Vetus Testamentum* 36 (1986), 257-273.

Brindle, Wayne. "The Census and Quirinius: Luke 2:2," *Journal of the Evangelical Theological Society* 27 (1984), 43-52.

Brodie, Thomas Louis. "Towards Unravelling Luke's Use of the Old Testament: Luke 7:11-17 as an *Imitatio* of 1 Kings 17:17-24," *New Testament Studies* 32 (1986), 247-267.

Brown, Raymond E. *The Birth of the Messiah. A Commentary on the Infancy Narratives in Matthew and Luke.* Garden City, New York: Doubleday & Company, 1977.

_____. "Luke's Description of the Virginal Conception," *Theological Studies* 35 (1974), 360-362.

_____. *The Virginal Conception and Bodily Resurrection of Jesus.* New York: Paulist Press, 1973.

Brown, Raymond E. and others. *Mary in the New Testament.* Philadelphia: Fortress Press, 1978.

Bultmann, Rudolf. *The History of the Synoptic Tradition.* Oxford: Basil Blackwell, 1972.

Burger, C. *Jesus als Davidssohn: Eine traditionsgeschichtliche Untersuchung.* FRLANT 98. Göttingen: Vandenhoeck & Ruprecht, 1970.

Cadbury, Henry J. *The Style and Literary Method of Luke.* Cambridge: Harvard University Press, 1920.

_____. *The Making of Luke-Acts*. London: SPCK, 1958.

Carroll, John T. *Response to the End of History: Eschatology and Salvation in Luke-Acts*. Atlanta, Georgia: Scholars Press, 1988.

Carter, Warren. "Zechariah and the Benedictus (Luke 1:68-79): Practicing What He Preaches," *Biblica* 69 (1988), 239-247.

Chathanatt, John. "The Magnificat: a Hymn of Liberation," *Vidyajyoti* 56 (1992), 653-658.

Coleridge, Mark. *The Birth of the Lukan Narrative. Narrative as Christology in Luke 1-2*. JSNT Supplement Series 88. Sheffield: JSOT Press, 1993.

_____. "In Defence of the Other: Deconstruction and the Bible," *Pacifica* 5 (1992), 123-144.

Conrad, Edgar W. "The Annunciation of Birth and the Birth of the Messiah," *Catholic Biblical Quarterly* 47 (1985), 656-663.

Cosgrove, C.H. "The Divine *DEI* in Luke-Acts: Investigations into the Understanding of God's Providence," *Novum Testamentum* 26 (1984), 168-190.

Cousin, Hugues. *L'Evangile de Luc*. Commentaire Pastoral. Paris: Editions du Centurion, 1993.

Craddock, Fred B. *Luke*. Interpretation: A Bible Commentary for Teaching and Preaching. Louisville, KY: John Knox Press, 1990.

Creed, John Martin. *The Gospel According to St. Luke*. London: Macmillan & Co, 1957.

Crump, David. *Jesus the Intercessor: Prayer and Christology in Luke-Acts*. Tübingen: J.C.B. Mohr (Paul Siebeck), 1992).

Cullmann, Oscar. *The Christology of the New Testament*. Philadelphia: The Westminster Press, 1959).

D'Angelo, Mary Rose. "Women in Luke-Acts: A Redactional View," *Journal of Biblical Literature* 109 (1990), 441-461.

D'Sa, T. "Mary the Contrary. A Reflection on the Annunciation and Visitation as Models of Commitment and Evangelization," *Vidyajyoti* 58 (1994), 623-635.

Danker, Frederick W. *Jesus and the New Age. A Commentary on Luke's Gospel*. Second Edition. Philadelphia: Fortress Press, 1988.

Dahl, Nils A. "The Story of Abraham in Luke-Acts," in Keck, Leander E. and J. Louis Martyn. eds. *Studies in Luke-Acts*. Nashville: Abingdon Press, 1966. 139-158.

Darr, John A. *On Character Building. The Reader and the Rhetoric of*

Characterization in Luke-Acts. Louisville, KY: Westminster/John Knox Press, 1992.

Daube, D. "Shame Culture in Luke," in Hooker, Moira D. and S.G. Wilson, eds. *Paul and Paulinism*. Essays in Honour of Charles K. Barrett. London: SPCK, 1982. 355-372.

Davis III, C.T. "The Literary Structure of Luke 1-2," in Clines, David J.A. and others. eds. *Art and Meaning, Rhetoric in Biblical Literature*. Sheffield: JSOT Press, 1982. 215-229.

Dawsey, James M. "The Form and Function of the Nativity Stories in Luke," *Melita Theologica* 36 (1985), 41-48.

_____. *The Lukan Voice: Confusion and Irony in the Gospel of Luke*. Macon: Mercer University Press, 1986.

_____. "What is in a Name? Characterization in Luke," *Biblical Theology Bulletin* 16 (1986), 143-147.

_____. "The Origin of Luke"s Positive Perception of the Temple," *Perspectives in Religious Studies* 18 (1991), 5,22.

De Boer, Martinus C. "God-Fearers in Luke-Acts," in Tuckett, C.M. ed. *Luke's Literary Achievement*. Sheffield: JSOT Press, 1995. 50-71.

de Cantanzero, "Fear, Knowledge, and Love: A Study in Old Testament Piety," *Canadian Journal of Theology* 9 (1963), 166-173.

Decock, P.D. "Inculturation and 'Communism' in Luke-Acts," *Grace and Truth* [Hilton, South Africa], 2 (1989), 54-64.

De Jonge, Henk J. "Sonship, Wisdom, Infancy: Lk II,41-51a," *New Testament Studies* 24 (1977-1978), 317-354.

Delorme, Jean. "Le monde, la logique et le sens du Magnificat," *Sémiotique et Bible* n. 53 (1989), 1-17.

Derrett, J. Duncan M. "'Antilegomenon, romphaia, dialogismoi (Lk 2:34-35): The Hidden Context," *Filologia Neotestamentaria* 6 (12, 1993), 207-218.

Dillon, Richard J. "Previewing Luke's Project from His Prologue (Luke 1:1-4)," *Catholic Biblical Quarterly* 43 (1981), 205-227.

Dinkler, Erich. "*Eirēnē* – The Early Christian Concept of Peace," in Yoder, Perry B. and Willard M. Swartley. eds. *The Meaning of Peace: Biblical Studies*. Louisville, KY: Westminster/John Knox Press, 1992. 164-207.

Douglas, Mary. *Purity and Danger: An Analysis of the Concepts of Polution and Taboo*. London: Routledge & Kegan Paul, 1966.

Downing, F. Gerald. "A Bas les Aristos: The Relevance of Higher Literature for the Understanding of the Earliest Christian Writings," *Novum Testamentum* 30 (1988), 212-230.

_____. "Theophilus' First Reading of Luke-Acts," in Tuckett, C.M. *Luke's Literary Achievement*. Sheffield: JSOT Press, 1995. 91-109.

Drury, John. *Tradition and Design in Luke's Gospel*. Atlanta: John Knox Press, 1977.

Dupont, Jacques, "Le Magnificat comme discours de Dieu," *Nouvelle Revue Théologique* 102 (1980), 321-343.

Ellis, E. Earl. *The Gospel of Luke*. The Century Bible. London: Nelson, 1966.

_____. "The Role of Christian Prophets in Acts," in Gasque, W.W. and Ralph P.Martin. eds. *Apostolic History and the Gospels*. Grand Rapids: Eerdmans, 1970. 5-67.

Ernst, Josef. *Das Evangelium nach Lukas*. Regensburger Neues Testament. Regensburg: Verlag Friedrich Pustet, 1977.

Evans, Christopher F. *Saint Luke*. TPI New Testament Commentaries. Philadelphia: Trinity Press, 1990.

Evans, Craig A. *Luke*. New International Biblical Commentary 3. Peabody, MA: Hendrickson Publishers, 1990.

Farris, Stephen. *The Hymns of Luke's Infancy Narratives. Their Origin, Meaning and Significance.* Sheffield: JSOT Press, 1985.

Fitzmyer, Joseph A. *The Gospel According to Luke I-IX*. The Anchor Bible 28. Garden City, New York: Doubleday & Company, 1981.

Flender, Helmut. *St. Luke: Theologian of Redemptive History*. Philadelphia: Fortress Press, 1967.

Ford, Massynbaerde J. *My Enemy is My Guest. Jesus and Violence in Luke*. Maryknoll, NY: Orbis Books, 1984.

Fabricius, C. "Zu *parachrēma* bei Lukas," *Eranos* 83 (1985), 62-66.

Frankemölle, Hubert. "Kaiserliche und/oder Christlicher Friede nach Lukas: Zur Struktur der lukanischen Geburtsgeschichte (2:1-20)," in *Friede und Schwert: Frieden schaffen nach dem Neuen Testament*. Mainz: Matthias-Grünewald Verlag, 1983. 85-97.

Franklin, Eric. *Luke: Interpreter of Paul, Critic of Matthew*. JSNT Supplement Series 92. Sheffield: Academic Press, 1994.

Freyne, Sean. "Herodian Economics in Galilee. Searching for a Suitable Model," in Esler, Philip F. ed, *Modelling Early Christianity. Social-Scientific Studies of the New Testament and Its Context*. New York: Routledge, 1995. 23-46.

Gallares, Judette A. *Images of Courage. Spirituality of Women in the Gospels from an Asian and Third World Perspective*. Quezon City: Claretian Publications, 1995.

Gaston, Loyd. "Anti-Judaism and the Passion Narrative in Luke-Acts," in Richardson, P. and D. Granskou. eds. *Anti-Judaism in Early Christianity* . I: *Paul and the Gospels*. Waterloo (Ontario); Laurier, 1986. 127-153.

Gault, Jo Ann. "The Discourse Function of KAI EGENETO in Luke and Acts," OPTAT – *Occasional Papers in Translation and Textlinguitics* 4 (1994), 388-399.

George, Augustin. "Jésus, 'Seigneur'," in *Etudes sur l'oeuvre de Luc*. Paris: Gabalda, 1978. 236-255.

Giblin, Charles H. "Reflections on the Sign of the Manger," *Catholic Biblical Quarterly* 29 (1967), 87-101.

_____. *The Destruction of Jerusalem According to Luke's Gospel*. Analecta Biblica 107. Rome: Biblical Institute Press, 1985.

Glöckner, Richard. *Die Verkündigung des Heils beim Evangelisten Lukas*. Mainz: Matthias-Grünewald Verlag, 1975.

Gloer, W.H. "Homologies and Hymns in the New Testament: Form, Content and Criteria for Identification," *Perspectives in Religious Studies* 11 (1984), 115-132.

Godet, Frederic Louis. *Commentary on Luke*. Kregel Reprint Library. Grand Rapids, Michigan: Kregel Publications, 1981.

Goulder, Michael D. *Luke: A New Paradigm* I. Sheffield: JSOT Press, 1989.

Geertz, Clifford. "Centers, Kings, and Charism: Reflections on the Symbolics of Power," in *Local Knowledge: Further Essays in Interpretive Anthropology*. New York: Basic, 1983. 121-146.

Green, Joel B. "The Death of Jesus and the Rending of the Temple Veil (Luke 23:44-49): A Window into Luke's Understanding of Jesus and the Temple," in Lovering, E.H. ed. *Society of Biblical Literature 1991 Seminar Papers*. Atlanta, GA: Scholars Press, 1991. 543-557.

_____. "The Social Status of Mary in Luke 1:5-2:52: A Plea for Methodological Integration," *Biblica* 73 (1992), 457-472.

_____. "Good News to Whom? Jesus and the 'Poor' in the Gospel of Luke," in Green, Joel B. and Max Turner eds. *Jesus of Nazareth: Lord and Christ. Essays on the Historical Jesus and New Testament Christology*. Grand Rapids: Eerdmans, 1994. 59-74.

_____. *The Theology of the Gospel of Luke.* Cambridge: Cambridge University Press, 1995.

Grigsby, Bruce. "Compositional Hypotheses for the Lucan 'Magnificat' – Tensions for the Evangelical," *Evangelical Quarterly* 56 (1984), 159-172.

Gryglewicz, F. "Die Herkunft der Hymnen des Kindheitsevangeliums des Lukas," *New Testament Studies* 21 (1974-1975), 265-273.

Gueuret, Agnes. *L'engendrement d'un recit. L'evangile de l'enfance selon saint Luc.* Paris: Editions du Cerf, 1983.

Hauck, Friedrich. *Das Evangelium des Lukas.* Theologischer Handkommentar zum Neuen Testament. Leipzig: Deichertsche Verlagsbuchhandlung, 1934.

Hendrickx, Herman. *The Infancy Narratives.* London: Geoffrey Chapman, 1984. (a)

_____. *The Resurrection Narratives of the Synoptic Gospels.* London: Geoffrey Chapman, 1984. (b)

_____. "From Luke to Theophilus," *East Asian Pastoral Review* 30 (1993), 82-101. [published in 1995].

Hengel, Martin. *Property and Riches in the Early Church.* Philadelphia: Fortress Press, 1974.

Hennesy, Anne. *The Galilee of Jesus.* Rome: Pontifical Gregorian University, 1994.

Hermans, L. "De herders in het kindsheidevangelie van Lucas," in Menken, M. et al. eds. *Goede Herders.* HTP Studies 5. Averbode: Altiora, 1983. 62-87.

Hock, Ronald F. *The Social Context of Paul's Ministry: Tentmaking and Apostleship.* Philadelphia: Fortess Press, 1980.

Horn, Friedrich Wilhelm. *Glaube und Handeln in der Theologie des Lukas.* Göttingen: Vandenhoeck & Ruprecht, 1983.

Horsley, Richard H. *Jesus and the Spiral of Violence.* San Francisco: Harper & Row, 1987.

_____. *The Liberation of Christmas. The Infancy Narratives in Social Context.* New York: Crossroad, 1989.

Horton, Fred L. "Reflections on the Semitisms in Luke-Acts," in Talbert, Charles H. ed. *Perspectives on Luke-Acts.* Edinburgh: T. & T. Clark, 1978. 1-23.

Hubbard, Benjamin J. "Commissioning Stories in Luke-Acts: A Study of Their Antecedents, Form and Content," *Semeia* 8 (1977), 103-126.

Jankowski, Gerhard. "In jenen Tagen. Der politische Kontext zu Lukas 1-2," *Texte und Kontexte* 12 (1981), 5-17.

Jegen, Carol Frances. "Lucan Reflections on Aging," *The Bible Today* 30 (1992), 335-340.

Jeremias, Joachim. *Die Sprache des Lukasevangeliums. Redaktion und Tradition im Nicht-Markusstoff des dritten Evangeliums.* Göttingen: Vandenhoeck & Ruprecht, 1980.

Jervell, Jacob. "The Church of Jews and Godfearers," in Tyson, Joseph B. ed. *Luke-Acts and the Jewish People.* Minneapolis: Augsburg Publishing House, 1988. 11-20.

Johnson, Luke Timothy. *The Literary Function of Possessions in Luke-Acts.* Missoula, Montana: Scholars Press, 1977.

_____. *The Gospel of Luke.* Sacra Pagina. Collegeville, Minnesota: The Liturgical Press, 1991.

Jones, D.R., "The Background and Character of the Lukan Psalms," *Journal of Theological Studies* 19 (1968), 19-50.

Kam, Rose Sallberg. *Their Stories, Our Stories: Women in the Bible.* New York: Continuum, 1995.

Kamphaus, Franz. *The Gospels for Preachers and Teachers.* London: Sheeds and Ward, 1974.

Kaut, Thomas. *Befreier und befreites Volk. Traditions- und redaktionsgeschichtliche Untersuchung zu Magnifikat und Benediktus im Kontext der vorlukanischen Kindheitsgeschichte.* Frankfurt am Main: Anton Hain, 1990.

Kearney, R. *Dialogues with Contemporary Continental Thinkers: The Phenomenological Heritage.* Manchester: Manchester University Press, 1984.

Keck, Leander E. and J. Louis Martyn. eds. *Studies in Luke-Acts.* Nashville: Abingdon Press, 1966.

Kilgallen, John J. "'Peace' in the Gospel of Luke and Acts of the Apostles," *Studia Missionalia* 38 (1989), 55-79.

Kilpatrick, G.D. "LAOI at Luke II.31 and Acts IV.25,27," *Journal of Theological Studies* 16 (1965), 127.

_____. "Luke 2:4-5 and Leviticus 25:10," *Zeitschrift für die neutestamentliche Wissenschaft* 80 (1989), 264-265.

Kinman, B. "Luke's Exoneration of John the Baptist," *Journal of Theological Studies* N.S. 44 (1993), 595-598.

Kingsbury, Jack Dean. *Conflict in Luke: Jesus, Authorities, Disciples.* Minneapolis: Fortess Press, 1991.

Koet, Bart. "Simeons loflied. Lk 2:29-32 als sleutel bij het evangelie volgens Lucas en de Handelingen van de apostelen," *JOTA* 5 (1990), 35-44.

Klostermann, Erich. *Das Lukasevangelium*. Handbuch zum Neuen Testament 5. Tübingen: J.C.B. Mohr (Paul Siebeck), 1929. Reprinted in 1975.

Kozar, Joseph Vicek. "The Function of the Character of Elizabeth as the Omniscient Narrator's Reliable Vehicle in the First Chapter of the Gospel of Luke," *Proceedings Eastern Great Lakes and Midwest Biblical Societies* 10 (1990), 214-222.

Kraabel, A. Thomas. "The Disappearance of the 'God-fearers'," *Numen* 28 (1981), 113-126.

Kremer, Jacob. *Lukasevangelium*. Die neue Echter Bibel. Würzburg: Echter Verlag, 1988.

Kuist, H.T. "Sources of Power in the Nativity Hymns: An Exposition of Luke 1 and 2," *Interpretation* 2 (1948), 288-298.

Kurz, William S. *Reading Luke-Acts: Dynamics of Biblical Narrative*. Louisville, KY: Westminster/John Knox Press, 1993.

Kuschel, Karl-Josef. *Abraham: Symbol of Hope for Jews, Christians and Muslims*. London: SCM Press, 1994. 97-103.

Lake, Kirsop. "Proselytes and God-Fearers," in Foakes Jackson, F.J. and Kirsop Lake. eds. *The Beginnings of Christianity*. Grand Rapids: Baker Bookhouse, 1979. 74-95.

Landry, David L. "Narrative Logic in the Annunciation to Mary (Luke 1:26-38)," *Journal of Biblical Literature* 114 (1995), 65-79.

Laurentin, René. *Les Evangiles de l'Enfance du Christ. Vérité de Noël au-delà des mythes*. Paris: Desclée, 1982.

_____. *Jésus au Temple. Mystère de Pâques et Foi de Marie en Luc 2,48-50*. Etudes Bibliques. Paris: Gasbalda, 1966.

_____. "Ce que le recouvrement (Lc 2:41-52) enseigne sur Marie," *Ephemerides Mariologicae* 43 (1993), 213-226.

LaVerdiere, Eugene. *Luke*. New Testament Message 5. Wilmington, DE: Michael Glazier, 1980.

Lawrence, J. "Publius Sulpicius Quirinius and the Syrian Census," *Restoration Quarterly* 34 (1992), 193-205.

Legrand, Lucien. *L'Annonce à Marie*. Lectio Divina 106. Paris: Editions du Cerf, 1981.

_____. "The Christmas Story in Lk 2:1-7," *Indian Theological Studies* 19 (1982), 289-317.

_____. "The Angel Gabriel and Politics. Messianism and Christology," *Indian Theological Studies* 26 (1989), 1-21.

Lentzen-Deis, Fritzleo. "Arm und reich aus der Sicht des Evangelisten Lukas," in Kamphaus, Franz et al. eds. *...und machen einander reich. Beiträge zur Arm/Reich Problematik reflektiert am Lukas-Evangelium*. Annweiler: Plöger, 1989. 17-68

Lockwood, G.J. "The Reference to Order in Luke's Preface," *Concordia Theological Quarterly* 59 (1995), 101-104.

Lohfink, Gerhard. *Die Sammlung Israels. Eine Untersuchung zu lukanischen Ekklesiologie*. Munich: Kösel-Verlag, 1975.

Maddox, Robert. *The Purpose of Luke-Acts*. Göttingen: Vandenhoeck & Ruprecht, 1982.

Mainville, Odette. "Jésus et l'Esprit dans l'oeuvre de Luc," *Science et Esprit* 42 (1990), 193-208.

Malherbe, Abraham J. *Social Aspects of Early Christianity*. Second Edition. Philadelphia: Fortress Press, 1983.

Malina, Bruce J. *The New Testament World: Insights from Cultural Anthropology*. Atlanta: John Knox Press, 1981.

_____. "The Social Sciences and Biblical Interpretation," *Interpretation* 36 (1982), 329-342.

_____. *Christian Origins and Cultural Anthropology: Practical Models for Biblical Interpretation*. Atlanta: John Knox Press, 1986.

Malina, Bruce J. and Jerome H. Neyrey. "Honor and Shame in Luke-Acts: Pivotal Values of the Mediterranean World," in Neyrey, Jerome H. ed. *The Social World of Luke-Acts: Models for Interpretation* (Peabody, MA: Hendrickson, 1991). 25-65.

_____. "First-Century Personality: Dyadic, Not Individualistic," in Neyrey, Jerome H. ed. *The Social World of Luke-Acts: Models for Interpretation*. Peabody, MA: Hendrickson, 1991. 67-96.

Malina, Bruce J. and Richard L. Rohrbaugh. *Social-Science Commentary on the Synoptic Gospels*. Minneapolis: Fortress Press, 1992.

Manns, Fréderic. "Une prière juive reprise en Luc 1:68-69," *Ephemerides Liturgicae* 106 (1992), 162-166.

Marshall, I. Howard. *Luke: Historian and Theologian*. Contemporary Evangelical Perspectives. Grand Rapids, Michigan: Zondervan Publishing House, 1970.

_____. *The Gospel of Luke. A Commentary on the Greek Text*. The New International Greek Testament Commentary. Grand Rapids, Michigan: William B. Eerdmans, 1978.

_____. "Luke and His 'Gospel'," in Stuhlmacher, Peter. ed. *The Gospel and the Gospels*. Grand Rapids: Eerdmans, 1991. 273-292.

Martin, Dale B. *Slavery as Salvation: The Metaphor of Slavery in Pauline Christianity*. New Haven, CT: Yale University Press, 1990.

_____. "Slavery and the Jewish Family," in Cohen, Shaye J.C. ed. *The Jewish Family in Antiquity*. Atlanta: Scholars Press, 1993. pp. 113-129.

Mealand, Robert. *Poverty and Expectation in the Gospels*. London: SPCK, 1980.

Meier, John P. *A Marginal Jew: Rethinking the Historical Jesus*. New York: Doubleday, 1991.

Menken, M.J.J. "The Position of *splagchna* and *splagchizesthai* in the Gospel of Luke," *Novum Testamentum* 30 (1988), 107-114.

Menzies, Robert P. *The Development of Early Christian Pneumatology With Special Reference to Luke-Acts*. Sheffield: Sheffield Academic Press, 1991.

Meynet, Roland. *Avez-vous lu saint Luc? Guide pour la rencontre*. Lire la Bible 88. Paris: Editions du Cerf, 1990.

_____. "Dieu donne son nom a Jesus: Analyse rhetorique de Lc 1,26-56 et de 1 Sam 2,1-10," *Biblica* 66 (1985), 39-72.

_____. *Quelle est donc cette parole? Lecture "rhetorique"de l'evangile de Luc (1-9 et 22-24)*. Lectio Divina 99A et B. Paris: Editions du Cerf, 1979.

_____. *L'Evangile selon Saint Luc. Analyse rhetorique*. Two Volumes: 1. Planches; 2. Commentaire. Paris: Editions du Cerf, 1988.

Minear, Paul S. "Luke's Use of the Birth Stories," in Keck, Leander E. and J. Louis Martyn eds. *Studies in Luke-Acts*. Nashville: Abingdon Press, 1980. 111-130.

Miyoshi, Michi. "Jesu Darstellung oder Reinigung im Tempel unter Berucksichtigung von 'Nunc Dimittis'," *Annual of the Japanese Biblical Institute* 4 (1978), 85-115

Moessner, David P. "The Meaning of *kathexes* in the Lukan Prologue as a Key to the Distinctive Contribution of Luke's Narrative among the 'Many'," in Van Segbroeck et al. eds. *The Four Gospels 1992. Festschrift Frans Neirynck*. Louvain: Leuven University Press, 1992. 1513-1528.

Morris, R.L.B. "Why *Augoustos*? A Note on Luke 2:1," *New Testament Studies* 38 (1992), 142-144.

Most, Wiliam G. "Did St. Luke Imitate the Septuagint?" in Evans,

Craig A. and Stanley E. Porter. eds. *The Synoptic Gospels: A Sheffield Reader*. Sheffield: Academic Press, 1995. 30-41.

Mowery, Robert L. "God the Father in Luke-Acts," in Richard, Earl. ed. *News Views on Luke and Acts*. Collegevile: The Liturgical Press, 1990. 124-132.

Moxnes, Halvor. "Patron-Client Relations and the New Community in Luke-Acts," in Neyrey, Jerome. ed. *The Social World of Luke-Acts: Models for Interpretation*. Peabody, MA: Hendrickson, 1991. 241-268.

Navone, John. *Themes of St. Luke*. Rome: Gregorian University Press, 1970.

Neirynck, Frans. *L'Evangile de Noël*. Brussels: La Pensée Catholique, 1960.

_____. ed. *L'Evangile de Luc. The Gospel of Luke*. Leuven: University Press, 1989.

Neff, Robert. "The Annunciation in the Birth Narrative of Ishmael," *Biblical Research* 17 (1972), 51-60.

Nolland, John. *Luke 1:1-9:20*. Word Biblical Commentary 35a. Dallas, Texas: Word Publishers, 1989.

Norris, Frederick W. "The Social Status of Early Christianity," *Gospel in Context* 2 (1979), 4-14. [with dialogue/comments, 14-29].

Oakman, Douglas E. "The Countryside in Luke-Acts," in Neyrey, Jerome. ed. *The Social World of Luke-Acts: Models for Interpretation*. Peabody, MA: Hendrickson, 1991. 151-179.

O'Fearghail, Fearghus. "The Imitation of the Septuagint in Luke's Infancy Narrative," *Proceedings of the Irish Biblical Association* 12 (1989), 58-78.

_____. *The Introduction to Luke-Acts. A Study of the Role of Lk 1:1–4:44 in the Composition of Luke's Two-Volume Work*. Analecta Biblica 126. Rome: Pontifical Biblical Institute, 1991.

_____. "Announcement or Call? Literary Form and Purpose in Luke 1:26-38," *Proceedings of the Irish Biblical Association* 16 (1993), 20-35.

Overman, J. Andrew. "Who Were the First Urban Christians?" in Lull, David J. ed. *Society of Biblical Literature 1988 Seminar Papers*. Atlanta: Scholars Press, 1988. 160-168.

Owen, Kris J.N. "The Magificat and the Empowerment of the Poor," *Vidyajyoti* 59 (1995), 647-662.

Parsons, Mikeal C. *The Departure of Jesus in Luke-Acts: The Ascension Narratives in Context*. Sheffield: JSOT Press, 1987.

Pervo, Richard I. "Must Luke and Acts Belong to the Same Genre?," in Lull, David J. ed. *SBL 1989 Seminar Papers.* Atlanta: Scholars Press, 1989. 309-316.

Petzke, Gerd. *Das Sondergut des Evangelium nach Lukas.* Zürcher Werkkommentare zur Bibel. Zürich: Theologischer Verlag, 1990.

Philipose, J. "*Kyrios* in Luke: A Diagnosis," *Bible Translator* 43 (1992), 325-333.

Pilch, John J. *The Cultural World of Jesus.* Collegeville: The Liturgical Press, 1995.

Plummer, Alfred. *The Gospel According to St. Luke.* The International Critical Commentary Edinburgh: T. & T. Clark, 1901. [Latest reprint in 1977].

Prior, Michael. *Jesus the Liberator: Nazareth Liberation Theology (Luke 4:16-30).* Sheffield: Academic Press, 1995.

Punayar, Sebastian. "Salvation in the Gospel of Luke," *Jeevadhara* 24 (1994), 360-372.

Rabinowitz, P.J. *Before Reading: Narrative Conventions and the Politics of Interpretation.* Ithaca – London: Cornell University, 1987.

Reid, Barbara E. "Luke: The Gospel for Women?" *Currents in Theology and Mission* 21 (1994), 405-414.

_____. "Reading Luke With the Poor," *The Bible Today* 32 (1994), 283-289.

Reiterer, Friedrich Vinzenz. "Die Funktion des alttestamentlichen Hintergrundes für das Verständnis der Theologie des Magnifikat." *Heiliger Dienst* 41 (1987), 129-142.

Resseguie, J.L. "Defamiliarization and the Gospels," *Biblical Theology Bulletin* 20 (1990), 147-150.

Richard, Earl. ed. *New Views on Luke and Acts.* Collegeville: The Liturgical Press, 1990.

Robbins, Vernon K. "Luke-Acts: A Mixed Population Seeks a House in the Roman Empire," in Alexander, Loveday. ed. *Images of Empire.* Sheffield: JSOT Press, 1991. 202-221.

_____. "Socio-Rhetorical Criticism: Mary, Elizabeth and the Magnificat as a Test Case," in McKnight, Edgar V. and Elizabeth Struthers Malbon. eds. *The New Literary Criticism and the New Testament.* Valley Forge, PA: Trinity Press International, 1994. 164-209.

Robert, René. "Comment comprendre 'leur purification' en Lc II,22?," *Revue Thomiste* 90 (1990) 449-455.

Rohrbaugh, Richard L. "The City in the Second Testament," *Biblical Theology Bulletin* 21 (1991), 67-75.

Salo, Kalervo. *Luke's Treatment of the Law: A Redaction-Critical Investigation.* Helsinki: Suomalainen Tiedeakademia, 1991.

Schaberg, Jane. The Illegitimacy of Jesus: A Feminist Theological Interpretation of the *Infancy Narratives.* San Franciso: Harper & Row, 1987.

REVIEWS on Schaberg, *The Illegitimacy of Jesus.*

Anderson, Janice Capel. *Journal of Religion* 69 (1989), 238-239.

Dietrich, Richard S. *Interpretation* 43 (1989), 208.

Malina, Bruce J. *Biblical Theology Bulletin* 18 (1988), 118-119.

Reid, Barbara E. *Catholic Biblical Quarterly* 52 (1990), 364-365.

Scheffler, Eben. *Suffering in Luke's Gospel.* Zürich: Theologischer Verlag, 1993.

Schmid, Josef. *Das Evangelium nach Lukas.* Regensburger Neues Testament 3. Regensburg: Verlag Friedrich Pustet, 1960.

Schneider, Gerhard. *Das Evangelium nach Lukas.* Ökumenischer Taschenbuch Kommentar zum Neuen Testament 3/1. Gütersloh/Würzburg: Gütersloher Verlag Mohn/ Echter Verlag, 1977.

Schottroff, Luise. "Das Magnificat und die älteste Tradition über Jesus van Nazareth," *Evangelische Theologie* 38 (1978), 298-313.

_____. "The Dual Concept of Peace," in Yoder, Perry B. and Williard M. Swartley. eds. *The Meaning of Peace: Biblical Studies.* Louisville, KY: Westminster/John Knox Press, 1992. 156-163.

_____. *Lydia's Impatient Sisters: A Feminist Social History of Early Christianity.* Westminster: John Knox Press, 1995.

Schürmann, Heinz. *Das Lukasevangelium.* Herders theologischer Kommentar zum Neuen Testament. Freiburg – Basel – Wien: Herder, 1969.

Schüssler-Fiorenza, Elizabeth. *In Memory of Her.* New York: Crossroad, 1983.

Schweizer, Eduard. *The Good News According to Luke.* Atlanta: John Knox Press, 1984.

Seccombe, David Peter. *Possessions and the Poor in Luke-Acts.* Linz: Studien zum Neuen Testament und seiner Umwelt, 1982.

Seim, Turid Karlsen. *The Double Message: Patterns of Gender in Luke-Acts.* Edinburgh: T. & T. Clark, 1994. (a)

_____. "The Gospel of Luke," in Schüssler Fiorenza, Elisabeth.

ed. *Searching the Scriptures: A Feminist Commentary*. New York: Crossroad, 1994. 728-762. (b)

Sheely, Steven. *Narrative Asides in Luke-Acts*. Sheffield: JSOT Press, 1992.

Silbermann, L.H. "A Model for the Lukan Infancy Narratives?," *Journal of Biblical Literature* 113 (1994), 491-493.

Soards, Marion L. "The Historical and Cultural Setting of Luke-Acts," in Richard, Earl. ed. *New Views on Luke and Acts*. Collegeville: The Liturgical Press, 1990. 33-47

Soares-Prabhu, George M. "Class in the Bible: The Biblical Poor a Social Class?" in Sugirtharajah, R.S. ed. *Voices From the Margin: Interpreting the Bible in the Third World*. Maryknoll, N.Y.: Orbis Books, 1991. 147-171.

Stein, Robert. *Gospels and Tradition. Studies on Redaction Criticism of the Synoptic Gospels*. Grand Rapids: Baker Book House, 1991.

_____. *Luke*. The New American Commentary. Nashville: Broadman Press, 1992.

Sterling, G.E. *Historiography and Self-definition: Josephus, Luke-Acts and Apologetic Historiography*. Leiden: Brill, 1992.

Stott, John R.W. and Robert Coote. eds. *Down to Earth: Studies in Christianity and Culture*. The Papers of the Lausanne Consultation on Gospel and Culture. London: Hodder & Stoughton, 1980. [= Gospel & Culture. Pasadena: William Carey Library, 1979].

Strack, Hermann L. and Paul Billerbeck. *Kommentar zum Neuen Testament aus Talmud und Midrash* I. Munich: C.H. Beck, 1965.

Strauss, Mark L. *The Davidic Messiah in Luke-Acts: The Promise and Its Fulfillment in Lukan Christology*. Sheffield: Sheffield Academic Press, 1995.

Strickert, F. "The Presentation of Jesus: The Gospel of Inclusion: Luke 2:22-40," *Currents in Theology and Mission* 22 (1995), 33-37.

Sylva, D.D. "*Ierousalem* and *Hierosoluma* in Luke-Acts," *Zeitschrift für die neutestamentliche Wissenschaft* 74 (1983), 207-221.

_____. "The Cryptic Clause *en tois patros mou dei einai me* in Lk 2:49b," *Zeitschrift für die neutestamentliche Wissenschaft* 78 (1987), 132-140.

Talbert, Charles H. "Jesus' Birth in Luke and the Nature of Religious Language," *Heythrop Journal* 35 (1994), 391-400.

Tannehill, Robert C. "The Magnificat as Poem," *Journal of Biblical Literature* 93 (1974), 263-275.

_____. *The Narrative Unity of Luke-Acts: A Literary Interpretation.* Vol.1 *The Gospel According to Luke.* Philadelphia: Fortress Press, 1986.

Theissen, Gerd. *Sociology of Early Palestinian Christianity.* Philadelphia: Fortress Press, 1985.

Tidball, Derek. *The Social Context of the New Testament: A Sociological Analysis.* Grand Rapids: Zondervan, 1984.

Tiede, David L. *Luke.* Augsburg Commentary on the New Testament. Minneapolis, Minnesota: Augsburg Publishing House, 1988.

_____. *Prophecy and History in Luke-Acts.* Philadelphia: Fortress Press, 1980.

Trémel, B. "Le Signe du Nouveau-Né dans la Mangeoire. A propos de Lc 2,1-20," in Casetti, P. et al. eds. *Mélanges Dominique Barthelémy.* OBO 38. Göttingen: Vandenhoeck & Ruprecht, 1981. 593-612.

Trible, Phyllis. *God and the Rhetoric of Sexuality.* Overtures to Biblical Theology. Philadelphia: Fortress Press, 1978.

Tuckett, C.M. ed. *Luke's Literary Achievement: Collected Essays.* Sheffield: Sheffield Academic Press, 1995.

Turner, Max. "The Spirit and the Power of Jesus' Miracles in the Lucan Conception," *Novum Testamentum* 33 (1991), 124-152.

_____. "The Spirit of Prophecy and of Authoritative Preaching in Luke-Acts: A Question of Origins," *New Testament Studies* 38 (1992), 66-88.

_____. "'Empowerment for Mission?' The Pneumatology of Luke-Acts: An Appreciation and Critique of James B. Shelton's Mighty in Word and Deed," *Vox Evangelica* 24 (1994), 103-122.

Tyson, Joseph B. *Images of Judaism in Luke-Acts.* Columbia: University of South Carolina Press, 1992.

_____. "The Implied Reader in Luke-Acts," in *Images of Judaism in Luke-Acts.* Columbia: University of South Carolina Press, 1992. 17-42.

_____. "Jews and Judaism in Luke-Acts: Reading as a Godfearer," *New Testament Studies* 41 (1995), 19-38.

van Bruggen, Jakob. *Lucas.* Commentaar op het Nieuwe Testament. Kampen: Kok, 1993.

Van Iersel, Bas. "The Finding of Jesus in the Temple: Some Observations on the Original Form of Lk II, 40-52," *Novum Terstamentum* 4 (1960), 161-173.

van Staden, P. *Compassion – The Essence of Life. A Social-Scientific Study of the Religious Symbolic Universe Reflected in the Ideology/ Theology of Luke.* Hervormde Teologiese Studies: Supplementum 4. Pretoria: Periodical Section of the Nederduitsch Hervormde Kerk, 1991.

Van Unnik, W.C. "Die rechte Bedeutung des Wortes 'treffen,' Lukas II.19," in *Sparsa Collecta: The Collected Essays of W.C. Van Unnik.* Leiden: Brill, 1973. 72-91.

Vogels, Walter. "Le Magnificat, Marie et Israel," *Eglise et Théologie* 6 (1975), 279-296.

Walaskay, Paul W. *"And So We Came to Rome." The Political Perspective of St. Luke.* Cambridge: Cambridge University Press, 1983.

Wengst, Klaus. *Pax Romana and the Peace of Jesus Christ.* London: SCM Press, 1987.

White, L. Michael and O. Larry Yarbrough. eds. *The Social World of the First Christians.* Minneapolis: Fortress Press, 1995.

Wibb, C.W. "The Characterization of God in the Opening Scenes of Luke and Acts," *Proceedings Eastern Great Lakes and Midwest Biblical Societies* 13 (1993), 275-292.

Wilson, S.G. *The Gentiles and the Gentile Mission in Luke-Acts.* Cambridge: Cambridge University Press, 1973.

_____. *Luke and the Law.* Cambridge: Cambridge University Press, 1983.

Winandy, J. "La prophétie de Syméon (Lc II,34-35)," *Revue Biblique* 72 (1965), 321-351.

Winter, Paul. "Magnificat and Benedictus – Maccabaean Psalms?," *Bulletin of John Rylands Library* 37 (1954-1955), 328-347.

_____. "The Cultural Background of the Narrative in Luke I and II," *Jewish Quarterly Review* 45 (1954), 160-167, 230-242.

Wiseman, T.P. "There went out a Decree from Caesar Augustus," *New Testament Studies* 33 (1987), 479-480.

Wolf, Eric. *Peasants.* Englewood Cliffs, N.J.: Prentice Hall, 1966.

Wolff, Anke Marina. "Der Kaiser und das Kind: Eine Auslegung von Luk. 2,1-20," *Texte & Kontexte* 12 (1981), 18-31.

Yoder, Perry B. and Willard M. Swartley. eds. *The Meaning of Peace: Biblical Studies.* Studies in Peace and Scripture, Institute of Mennonite Studies. Louisville, KY: Westminster/John Knox Press, 1992.

York, John O. *The Last Shall Be First. The Rhetoric of Reversal in Luke.* Sheffield: JSOT Press, 1993.

Zijlstra, C. "Anthropological Considerations for the Book of Luke," *Notes on Translation* 5 (1991), 1-13.